RAILROADS

OF

RHODE ISLAND

RAILROADS

OF

RHODE ISLAND

SHAPING THE OCEAN STATE'S RAILWAYS

Frank Heppner

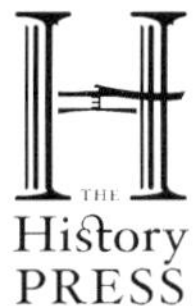

Published by The History Press
Charleston, SC 29403
www.historypress.net

Copyright © 2012 by Frank Heppner
All rights reserved

Front cover, photo courtesy of Rhode Island Railroad Museum; map courtesy of USGS.
Back cover, top, collection of Edward J. Ozog; bottom, by Frank Heppner.

First published 2012
Second printing 2014

Manufactured in the United States

ISBN 978.1.60949.333.2

Library of Congress Cataloging-in-Publication Data
Heppner, Frank H.
Railroads of Rhode Island : shaping the Ocean State's railways / Frank Heppner.
p. cm.
Includes bibliographical references and index.
ISBN 978-1-60949-333-2
1. Railroads--Rhode Island--History. 2. Rhode Island--History. I. Title.
TF24.R4H47 2012
385.09745--dc23
2011052642

CONTENTS

PREFACE

In 1969, I left my native West Coast to take a faculty job at the University of Rhode Island in Kingston. A lifelong rail enthusiast, naturally I came cross-country by train. Alas, in this next-to-last pre-Amtrak year, transcontinental rail travel was a dismal experience. After what seemed to be an eternity, the decrepit Penn Central train wheezed and screeched into Kingston. I got off and knew I had entered a new and strange world.

The little station at Kingston had beautiful architectural lines but clearly had one foot in the grave. Most of the paint had flaked off to bare wood, and the wood showed dry rot. My new department chair picked me up at the station, and as we drove up Kingston Hill to the university, I got the first of what was to be an endless series of culture shocks over the next few weeks and months.

I was a fourth-generation Californian, and aside from a dreadful year spent as a college freshman in Troy, New York, I had spent my entire life on the Left Coast. There were faculty shortages in those days, and I was offered the job in Rhode Island without an interview, so I came to Kingston sight unseen. I had heard of the "BosWash Corridor" and somehow got it into my head that the University of Rhode Island was in an urban area. Having been born in one of the most sophisticated cities in the world, San Francisco, I was looking forward to a life spent lounging in the sophisticated cafés and elegant restaurants to which I had been accustomed.

The first thing I saw as we climbed Kingston Hill was cows. Then sheep and pigs. Southern Rhode Island in those days still had a strong agricultural presence, and until only a few years before, the university had been an aggie school. The closest restaurant to campus was Iggy's Spaghetti House and Bar, and it served two kinds of wine—red and white—both delivered ice-cold like beer. So much for elegant dining.

The real shocks started the first time I tried to talk to a native Rhode Islander. Some explanation will be needed here. Tiny as it is, Rhode Island is a confederation of smaller, tightly knit and often highly competitive communities, a bit like Florence in the time of the Medicis. For example, the population of Rhode Island is less than San Diego, but there are thirty-six completely separate school districts. There are even regional accents.

A native of southern Rhode Island, where Kingston is located, lives in a vaguely defined geographic area called South County. South County is not an actual county—it's more a state of mind. The natives of South County are called Swamp Yankees, or Swampers for short. Swamper is pronounced *swampah*. Overall, the accent sounds strongly like "Downeast" Maine.

The central part of the state, centered on the suburb of Cranston (pronounced "*Craaaanston*," with a strong nasal inflection) has an entirely different accent and, in some ways, a more colorful set of words and expressions. A water fountain is a "*bubblah*," a milkshake is a "cabinet." "Don't even think of it," comes out as "*Fuggeddaboudit*." "Not without reason" is "*notfernuttin'*."

As I discovered, another defining characteristic of many native Rhode Islanders, especially Swampers, is a strong disinclination to go very far away from home. Ever. Swampers figure they need a passport to go to Providence. There is also often a singular lack of curiosity about anything outside South County.

While I was researching this book, I needed some information about the Newport and Wickford Railroad, which was located about fifteen miles north of the university. Now, to understand what follows you need to know that there is a fire tower ("*towah*") located on top of a prominent nearby hill that to some reckonings marks the border between South County and the rest of the world to the north.

I sought out an old Swamper acquaintance of mine at his place of business and asked if he knew anything about the Newport and Wickford Railroad. He allowed as how he didn't but suggested I talk to his dad, whom I remembered from previous experience knew everything there was to know about another little southern Rhode Island railroad, the Narragansett Pier Railroad, which ran only a few hundred yards from the business. Dad was chatting with one of his Swamper friends across the room.

"Russ," I asked the dad, "do you know anything about the Newport and Wickford Railroad?"

He gave me a fisheye. "That's nawth of the towah, ain't it?"

"Unh, yes."

Dismissively, he replied, "Don't know a thang 'bout it."

Over the course of time, I became increasingly captivated by the charm and distinctiveness of Little Rhody residents and, as a railfan, fascinated by its railroad history, which is complex far beyond what the size of the state would suggest. The history of individual railroads in Rhode Island has been well documented by a surprising number of excellent books, which are listed in the back of this volume. To date, however, there has not been a comprehensive general study of Rhode Island's railroads. To make it more interesting to me, and hopefully to readers, I decided to tie things together through Kingston Railroad Station as an integrating focus. I have been involved in the restoration and preservation of this wonderful old building for over thirty-five years.

ACKNOWLEDGEMENTS

I'd like to thank many people who were of enormous assistance. The Friends of the Kingston Station, as a group, provided invaluable help. Martha McCabe, who wrote an outstanding history of Kingston Station a decade ago, assembled much of the information on that wonderful old building that made my job easier. Local rail experts Steve Boothroyd, Tim Cranston, Mike Leckie, Don O'Hanley, Edward J. Ozog, Ben Perry, Everett Stuart and Robert Suppicich were invaluable sources of information and ideas. Frank Golet helped me out with early days forest cover. Scott Malloy and Maury Klein offered their experience with previous railroad books. Steve Devine, Marjorie Heppner, Mike Heppner, Gaby Kass-Simon, the Loewenstein family, Jack McCabe and Ray Wolf read draft versions of all or parts of the manuscript and offered many helpful suggestions, although any mistakes are mine alone. Ed Ozog was more than generous in giving permission to use many images from his wonderful historical collection of Rhode Island railroad photographs and ephemera. Jeff Saraceno, editor at The History Press, was an endless source of help and encouragement. Sarina Wyant, Special Collections librarian of the University of Rhode Island, assisted me with document and photo location.

Chapter 1

BEFORE THE COMING OF THE RAILS

There is an old saying in real estate: "Three things determine the value of a property; location, location and location." That has been true of Rhode Island for the last 350 years. Rhode Island is what it is today because of where it is. Since its earliest days, Rhode Island's position at the intersection of trade routes and between major population centers has determined both its economy and its character and later came to shape the nature and routing of its railroads.

A Most Peculiar Little Place

At 1,500 square miles of area (of which 500 square miles are under water), Rhode Island is the smallest state in the United States, but it has the longest name: "The State of Rhode Island and Providence Plantations." More about the name a bit later. Although it is physically smaller than San Antonio, Texas, it provides a unit of measurement for hugeness of Antarctic icebergs ("Bigger than the state of Rhode Island"). It abounds in contradictions. Rhode Island has produced some of the most distinguished and honorable national politicians of recent times, including the late Senator John Chafee and Senator Claiborne Pell, who was largely responsible for creating the Northeast Corridor rail system. However, during one recent ten-year period, an ex-governor, the ex-mayor of the largest city, the ex-mayor of the third-largest city and a superior court judge were all serving time in the slammer on various corruption charges. It is a blue-collar and public union state that has one of the largest concentrations of "old money" in the country. It was the first colony to declare independence from England but the last to ratify the Constitution. The state bird is a chicken and the state mollusc is a clam, but in an apparent lapse by the legislature, there is no state amphibian.

Many place names, like Usquepaugh, Weekapaug, Misquamicut, Quanochontaug and Saugatucket, are essentially unpronounceable to outsiders. It is fun to listen to a speaking GPS try to handle Usquepaugh. Pawcatuck and Pawtucket are at opposite ends of the state, but Pawtuxet is in the middle.

The origin of the name of the state is surrounded by mostly good-natured controversy. The current legal name, "The State of Rhode Island and Providence Plantations," refers to the fact that there were originally two colonies at the time of the granting of an English colonial charter. The first was Providence Plantations, which included the mainland portion of the state that today comprises the city of Providence, its suburbs and the southern part of the mainland. The second was Aquidneck Island, the original Wampanoag Indian name, on which is sited the present-day city of Newport. How did Aquidneck Island become "Rhode" Island? There are several hypotheses, none of which has any hard evidence.

The most common arises from the observation that Giovanni da Verrazano (sometimes spelled Verrazzano) sailed up Long Island Sound and into Block Island Sound in 1524 on a voyage of exploration for the French king Francis I. Verrazano described finding a triangular island that he named Luisa, after the king's mother, presumably off the present coast of Rhode Island. This island was "about the size of the Isle of Rhodes." He then supposedly sailed into Narragansett Bay, landing on Aquidneck Island, which over time became known as *Rhode* Island. It is not clear how "Rhode" got transferred from Block to Aquidneck Island. It is usually assumed that the island Verrazano described was today's Block Island, but the Isle of Rhodes is at least ten times larger than Block Island, and the explorer noted that it was thirty miles offshore, whereas Block Island is only about ten miles away from the mainland. Perhaps he actually landed on Martha's Vineyard, which is also triangular and much larger than Block Island. He also said that the mainland harbor he found after leaving Luisa was forty-five miles from the island, which would have more likely put him in Buzzard's Bay than Narragansett Bay. In any event, it should be noted that Verrazano was not a terribly good observer. On his East Coast voyage, having missed both Chesapeake and Delaware Bays on his way up the coast from his landfall at Cape Fear, he proposed that Pamlico Sound in North Carolina offered a route to the Pacific. After his (possible) visit to Rhode Island, Verrazano was reportedly consumed by cannibals on a later trip to the Caribbean.

The other main suggestion, which in light of Rhode Island's later history is at least plausible, is that Rhode Island was originally called derisively "Rogue's" Island by the Puritans of Massachusetts, referring to the religious dissidents who had fled Puritan rule into the new, breakaway colony. It is also possible that as Narragansett Bay was blessed with many small ports from the earliest days, "Rogue" may also have referred to the seamier kinds of characters who tend to frequent dockside areas.

A far less interesting idea is that the Dutch explorer Adriaen Block, who passed by Aquidneck Island in 1627, noted that it was "een rodlich Eylande," or a reddish island. Rodlich eventually may have morphed into Rhode.

Whatever the origin, in 2010, there was a referendum on the state ballot to officially change the name of the state to simply "Rhode Island." Proponents argued that the word "Plantations" brought back memories of slaveholding days, in which Rhode Island undoubtedly played a role. Opponents noted that the word "Plantation" simply meant a large agricultural operation, slaves or no, and to change the name would be removing a link to a colorful past. The measure was defeated 77 percent to 23 percent, so "The State of Rhode Island and Providence Plantations" it remains.

SETTING THE STAGE FOR INDUSTRY

The vast majority of early English settlers came to Rhode Island not by sea but by land from the colony of Massachusetts. The early Puritans settled first at Plimouth Plantations near Boston and, later, in the Massachusetts Bay Colony. In the 1620s, they were a rigid, religiously dogmatic group who had separated from the Church of England because they felt it had become decadent and corrupt. They therefore called themselves "Puritans." Those Puritans who strayed even slightly from the narrow path defined by this breakaway church met with unpleasant fates; recall the Salem witch trials. Not all the early settlers were comfortable with this rigidity. One such renegade was a preacher named Roger Williams, who seems to have feuded with almost everyone in the English religious establishment at one time or another, having been at various times an Anglican, a Separatist, a Congregationalist, a Baptist, an antipedobaptist and a Calvinist, finally disaffiliating himself from any organized church.

A KEY into the

LANGUAGE

OF

AMERICA:

OR,

An help to the *Language* of the *Natives*
in that part of AMERICA, called
NEW-ENGLAND.

Together, with briefe *Observations* of the Cu-
ſtomes, Manners and Worſhips, *&c.* of the
aforeſaid *Natives,* in Peace and Warre,
in Life and Death.

On all which are added Spirituall *Observations,*
Generall and Particular by the *Authour,* of
chiefe and ſpeciall uſe(upon all occaſions,)to
all the *Engliſh* Inhabiting thoſe parts;
yet pleaſant and profitable to
the view of all men :

BY ROGER WILLIAMS
of *Providence* in *New-England.*

LONDON,
Printed by *Gregory Dexter,* 1643.

Roger Williams was one of the few early English settlers in North America who took a favorable view of the natives and actually invested some time and effort in learning about them. This 1643 book outlines what he discovered about the Narragansett and Wampanoag languages. *Beinecke Rare Book Library.*

In 1636, Williams was banished from Massachusetts for promoting the then-revolutionary idea that there should be a separation between church and state. Also very unusual for colonists of the time, he had studied the language and customs of the native populations—the Wampanoag tribe on Aquidneck Island and the Narragansetts in Providence and south to the coast—and had established friendships with their leaders.

Seeking a refuge from Puritan harassment, Williams and his friends bought a large tract of land from Massasoit, the chief of the Narragansetts. It was to the east of the Providence River and west of the Seekonk River—today's East Side. However, almost immediately officials from Plymouth (the later spelling) disallowed Williams's purchase, claiming it was on land that was part of the Massachusetts royal charter. Williams and his group responded by moving farther west and establishing a new settlement at the location of today's Providence. He extended the settlement's influence by establishing a trading post in the town of North Kingstown to the south in 1637. A Massachusetts trader named Richard Smith also built a nearby trading post in the same year. One of the buildings on those grounds (called Smith's Castle) exists today and is a tourist attraction. Williams's original settlement was called Providence Plantations.

Meanwhile, another group of religious dissidents was experiencing difficulties with authorities in Massachusetts. Anne Hutchinson, a pioneer religious feminist, was preaching religious views that were heretical to the Puritans and, after a trial, was banished from Massachusetts. Her followers met with William Coddington, a Boston businessman, and, on the advice of Roger Williams, bought Aquidneck Island ("Rhode Island") from the Narragansetts. They soon established a colony at Pocasset, now called Portsmouth. After great opposition from neighboring Connecticut and Massachusetts, Roger Williams obtained a royal charter in 1647 for all the lands included in "Providence Plantations" and "Rhode Island" to be administered by a single colonial government, distinct from the other colonies in its tolerance for the presence of religious minorities who were persecuted elsewhere. Rhode Island was thus founded by people who were no great respecters of established authority, an attitude that one sometimes finds today. The eleven-foot gilt figure standing atop the statehouse dome in Providence today is not without reason called "The Independent Man."

These early settlers soon discovered an unpleasant truth: Rhode Island was simply too small to have the resources for a self-sustaining economy. The forests (and the game they contained) disappeared quickly due to an insatiable appetite for timber, firewood and agricultural land. In 1630, 97 percent of the land area of Rhode Island was covered by forest. By 1767, this had dropped to 28 percent. Once having cleared a forest, an early farmer quickly discovered that most of the soils were thin and poor, most suitable for the harvesting of rocks, which popped up fresh every year. Much of southern Providence Plantations was swampland, and unlike the situation in the American South, there was no easy or economical way to drain it for agricultural purposes.

Mineral resources were also scanty. There was essentially no mining activity in the sixteenth, seventeenth and eighteenth centuries. In the nineteenth century, granite quarries were developed in and around the coastal town of Westerly, and there was a small graphite and coal mine on the present location of the Garden City shopping center, a small coal mine in Valley Falls and an anthracite coal mine in Portsmouth that was big enough to have rail service. Today, the largest mineral industry in Rhode Island is sand, gravel and crushed stone extraction, but this was of little importance to the colonists.

Despite these formidable disadvantages, early Rhode Islanders soon discovered that they had a superb asset, one that established the success of the colony and later shaped the pattern and distribution of industry and the railroads. That asset is Narragansett Bay.

The bay is the site of the last large, all-year, warm-water protected harbor on the East Coast north of New York Harbor. It is approximately 150 sea miles closer to Europe than New York Harbor. It is deep and capacious and can accommodate the largest of ships. When the 1,132-foot-long RMS *Queen Mary 2* visited Newport in 2007, it was able to maneuver comfortably without the aid of tugs. Aircraft carriers regularly docked at Quonset Point Naval Air Station, halfway up the bay.

Narragansett Bay was (and is) a rich fishery. This abundance of marine resources makes up in part for the relative lack of suitable agricultural land for livestock in Rhode Island. More importantly, its location between two major population centers, New York and Boston, practically guaranteed that trade, especially intercontinental trade, would become a key element in Rhode Island's economic development.

Unfortunately, the very factors that guaranteed that international trade in goods and raw materials would become vital to the colony's interests also predisposed it to a type of trade that today is viewed as shameful—the slave trade. Much of the capital generated in the early colony was generated by this trade, and it provided the funds that were later used to develop industry and its accompanying railroads.

The first law making slavery legal in any of the North American British colonies was passed in 1641 by the Massachusetts Bay Colony, and similar laws were quickly passed in Plymouth and Connecticut. Although Roger Williams opposed slavery for Providence Plantations, his sentiments were not supported on Aquidneck Island ("Rhode Island"), where Newport was located, and slavery was actively supported by Newport business interests. The first slaves arrived in 1652. In 1654, Providence passed a law banning slavery, but it was not supported by Rhode Island. By 1750, Bristol and Newport were the major slave ports in the American colonies and brought enormous sums of money (for the time) to Rhode Island and Providence Plantations.

After the American Revolution in the 1770s, antislavery sentiment began to rise, and there was a nascent abolitionist movement developing in other parts of New England. However, at about that time, a new kind of financial instrument was discovered that had as much of an effect in its day as the derivatives market has had in ours. It was called the triangular trade.

The triangular trade "sanitized" the slave trade—no slaves were actually brought directly into the United States. Ships sailed from Newport eastward bearing cargos of rum and barter goods. These were traded to slave traders in Africa for boatloads of slaves, who were shipped to agricultural operations in the Caribbean that produced sugar, which in turn was made into molasses. The molasses was shipped to Newport and made into rum, and the wheel turned once again. At one time, there were over twenty rum distilleries in Newport. Until Rhode Island essentially deforested itself in the 1700s, there was also a reverse trade bringing firewood from Rhode Island to the Caribbean, where it was used in the molasses-making process.

There were multiple reasons for the decline of the triangular trade in New England. Some of the factors contributing to the gradual disappearance of the triangular trade included overproduction of sugar by the Caribbean plantations, with a resultant lowering of prices; competition from the East Indies in sugar growing; and a reduction in the population of available slaves in Africa. Perhaps the most important reason was the gradual abolition of slavery by European colonizers in their tropical colonies. Despite this, a vestigial triangular trade survived into the nineteenth century.

Rhode Island's connection with the slave trade provides yet another example of its fascinating yet vexing contradictions. Rhode Island was the first colony to proclaim separation of church and state. It provided a haven for persecuted religious minorities. It made friendship alliances with the native Indians, who were viewed as savages and even candidates for slavery by the other colonies. Yet the African slave trade and its ancillary businesses lasted far longer in Rhode Island than elsewhere, and much of its business establishment was vigorous in promoting it.

The triangular trade left a complex legacy. Certainly, it is not a history to be proud of. But it firmly established the concept that Rhode Island's very existence depended on trade, rather than agriculture or extractive industries, and established Rhode Island's central coastal location as being advantageous for trade routes. It also created large stocks of capital and capitalists, priming the state for its next, and far more respectable, economic stage: industrialization.

Mr. Slater's Experiment

The Industrial Revolution began in England in the 1700s with the development of the cotton textile industry. Prior to this time, the primary fiber made into cloth was wool, which could be domestically produced and made into thread and cloth as a cottage industry. As England developed its tropical colonies, raw cotton began to be imported, but it could not be made into cloth with simple home implements as easily as wool.

Several key inventions developed in the mid-1700s not only made the production of inexpensive cotton cloth practical but also led to a completely new and different means of manufacture for all products that would forever change the world: the factory.

The first of these inventions was the spinning jenny, invented in 1764 by James Hargreaves to make cotton yarn. The jenny was a modification of the standard treadle-operated, human-powered spinning wheel. Hargreaves's improvement was that he realized a series of wheels could be mounted side by side on a common shaft, thereby greatly increasing the amount of yarn that could be produced by a single person. Originally, the wheel assembly would be turned by the spinner, but it was quickly realized that the same system of belts and shaft used in grain-grinding mills that were powered by horses could be used for the spinning jenny, increasing production even more.

A significant improvement in spinning machinery was developed by Richard Arkwright. In 1769, he took out a patent for the water-frame yarn-making device, and in 1771, he and Jedediah Strutt built the first water-powered textile mill in the world at Cromford, England. Perhaps even more significant than Arkwright's machines was the fact that he integrated the several steps required to produce a product into a central location that we would today call a factory.

England had a well-developed patent system while these inventions were being developed, but patents were honored in the breach more often than the observance, and infringement lawsuits were as common as they are today with digital media. England was also aware that a cotton agriculture was building in the southern American colonies (cotton seeds were first planted in the Jamestown colony in Virginia in the early 1600s), and there was a strong desire that raw cotton be shipped to England for value-added processing, rather than have a colonial processing industry develop. British law thus forbade the exportation of both processing machines and their designs to the American colonies.

Into this atmosphere, a ten-year-old English boy named Samuel Slater began work in Strutt and Arkwright's first water-

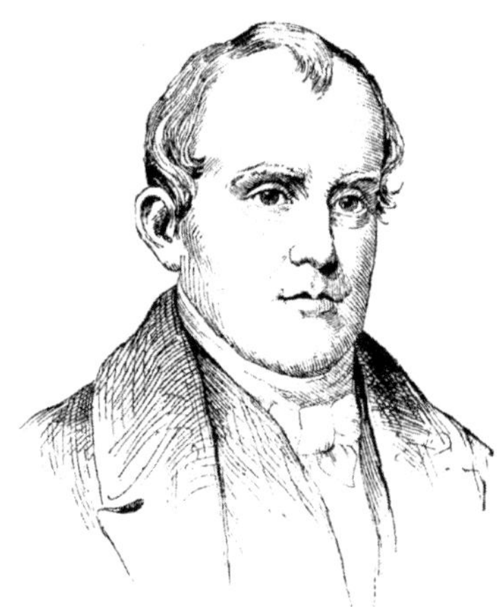

Once again demonstrating how things are relative. To the English, Samuel Slater was a patent thief who stole valuable information without payment to its inventors. To the Americans, Samuel Slater was a pioneer who, at risk to himself, established American industry. You be the judge.

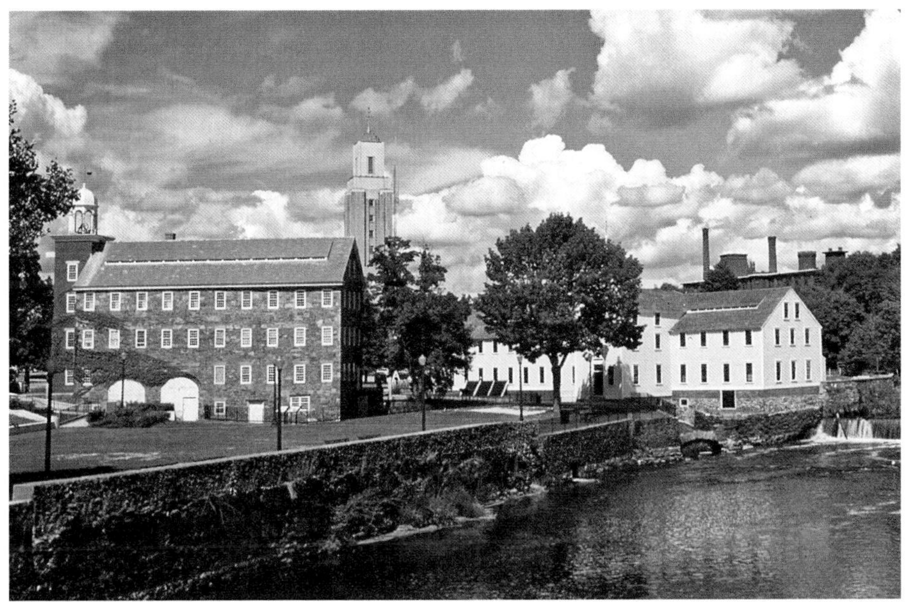

Slater's mill is today a small but excellent museum in Pawtucket. *Photo by Dawn Bowen.*

powered cotton mill in 1778. Having skill, ambition and an excellent mind, he memorized the design, specifications and measurements of the Arkwright machines and boarded a ship for the New World in 1789, with the idea of planting the seeds of his knowledge there. Given later developments, Slater probably provided the world with its first case of industrial espionage.

In the same year, Moses Brown of Providence, a member of the wealthy and influential Brown family that had been heavily involved with the triangular trade, built a textile mill in Pawtucket on the bank of the Blackstone River. The mill used home-designed machines that tried to emulate the Arkwright devices, but they did not work very well.

Slater somehow heard about Brown's problems and made him an offer he found difficult to refuse—he would build machines for Brown, but if they were not equal or superior to Arkwright's, there would be no charge. However, if the machines were successful, he would get half the profits. Not a bad deal, as Brown apparently provided all the financing. In 1793, the mill opened for business and was an immediate success.

The mill's success was based not only on the design of the machines but also on what would today be called human factors engineering. The mill was designed to be operated by families brought in from rural areas and provided with housing near the mill. Children performed most of the actual work done with the machines. At first, children as young as seven were employed, but later the minimum age was standardized at ten. Views of child labor were very different in those days.

In a family working on a farm, many children translates into many hands bringing in the crops. If that family, for whatever reason, leaves the farm to move to a more urban area, the hands turn into mouths, and the large family turns into a liability. However, if the whole family, even the little children, can earn a wage, the standard of living can go back up to where it had been on the farm, or even surpass it. Child labor was thus viewed as a means of keeping families together and keeping the children busy and out of trouble. Clearly, this view has changed over time.

Soon, textile mills lined the Blackstone, quickly followed by other factories that made textile machinery and the tools used to make that machinery. As the volume of raw materials and the size and weight of manufactured products increased with the success of these plants, it soon became evident that the horse-drawn carriages and carts that were the dominant means of conveyance for both freight and passengers were no longer adequate. The stage was set for the coming of the railroad.

Chapter 2

THE RAILROAD GEOGRAPHY OF RHODE ISLAND

Although tiny in overall size, the geography of Rhode Island has had a strong influence on its railroads. The dominant feature of the state is Narragansett Bay. Since colonial times, there has been regular east–west ferry service at various points up and down the bay. However, there have never been serious proposals to build a railroad bridge across the bay anywhere south of the Providence River at the bay's northern extremity. Narragansett Bay was partially bridged with a cantilever highway bridge between North Kingstown and Conanicut Island (Jamestown) in 1940, and the connection between east and west bay was complete with the opening of the Newport (Pell) highway suspension bridge in 1969. The old Jamestown Bridge combined transportation with a thrill ride for motorcyclists, because the deck at the apex of the bridge was an open grid that allowed a view straight down to the bay 135 feet below, while having a texture that tended to carry the bike to the right and into the guard rail. This bridge was replaced in 1992 with a less interesting but safer concrete box girder bridge that carried a new name: the Jamestown-Verrazano (variously spelled, each proponent claiming correctness) Bridge, reflecting Verrazano's (possible) discovery of Narragansett Bay. In 2006, the old bridge was demolished in spectacular fashion by explosives.

There are strong differences in microclimate in the state. The lowest temperature ever recorded in Rhode Island—negative twenty-five degrees Fahrenheit—was noted at Wood River Junction, located on the current Amtrak route in southwestern Rhode Island. Wood River Junction is consistently the coldest location in the state. In winter, bitter cold can significantly affect railroad operations, especially on electrified sections, where extreme cold weather can cause the copper overhead wire to contract so much that it snaps. Newport is consistently the warmest location, averaging about seven degrees Fahrenheit hotter than Wood River Junction. North Foster, located in the northwest corner of the state, holds all the records for snowfall in Rhode Island. Its relatively high altitude probably has something to do with it. The snow in Foster became a running joke for many years for a beloved local radio personality named Walter "Salty" Brine. Whenever he announced the winter weather and school closings, almost inevitably he would say, "No school today, Foster-Glocester," and people would ask in mock wonderment if Foster-Glocester kids *ever* went to school in winter. As no railroads of significance ever ran through this part of the state, snow removal from tracks has not been a significant factor for Rhode Island railroads, other than the difficulties posed by snow on station platforms or reduced visibility during the occasional blizzard. Hurricanes have been a different matter.

The highest point in Rhode Island, at only 812 feet above sea level, is Jerimoth Hill, in the town of Foster, right next to the Connecticut border. A railroad built on a straight line from the top of the hill to the closest sea-level point on Narragansett Bay would be twenty-two miles long and would have a ruling grade of 0.6 percent. Mountain railroading it would not be. Similarly, there are no broad rivers to bridge. Far more serious as an obstacle to railroad construction was the existence of large tracts of swampland in the southern part of the state.

These are not the alligator-infested mangrove swamps of Florida. Rather, they are primarily extensive peat bogs originally populated with softwood trees like cedars. The cedars were largely cut for timber by the 1920s, but isolated survivors can be found today. These swamps presented huge challenges for early railroad builders in South County, where most of them are located. A mile or two southwest of today's Kingston Station, the New York, Providence and Boston (Stonington Line) Railroad ran into construction difficulties that almost defeated the technology of the day. The Great Swamp began at that point and extended almost to Westerly. There was no economically practical route around the swamp.

Railroad tracks have for many years not been laid directly on the ground but on a bed of crushed stone called "ballast," which provides stability to the track. In a swampy area, dumped ballast tends to sink through the water until it meets a firm bottom. Local legend suggests that through the Great

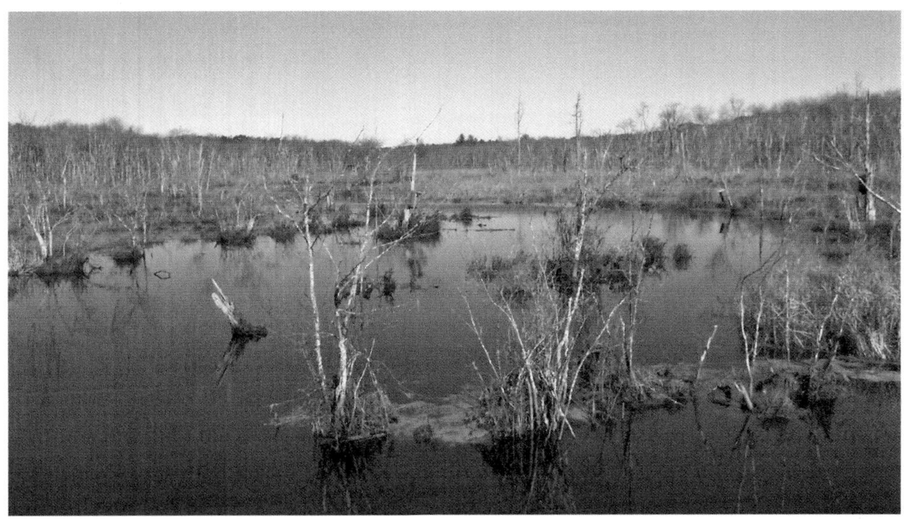

The Great Swamp covers several square miles. Most of it is not quite as wet as this, but certainly a railroad surveyor would be given pause. *Photo by "myeyesonly," panoramio.com.*

Swamp, over seventy vertical feet of ballast were necessary until there was solid footing for the tracks. Construction on the Stonington Line began in 1833 in Stonington, Connecticut, but did not reach Providence, forty-eight miles away, until four years later—roughly a mile a month. There is no record of any extended pauses in the construction.

By contrast, the first transcontinental railroad ran from Omaha, Nebraska, to Sacramento, California, a distance of 1,777 miles over the Rockies, the Utah and Nevada deserts and the Sierra Nevada mountains. It took approximately six years to build—roughly 25 miles a month. On one extraordinary day, April 28, 1869, in Utah, crews of the Central Pacific Railroad laid just over 10 miles of track in one day. So it is not indefensible to say that the Stonington Line presented greater construction challenges than did the Transcontinental Railroad.

The written record is sparse, but there was a narrow-gauge logging railroad in the Great Swamp from 1915 to 1917. An 1889 United States Geological Survey map shows an earlier, short length of track departing the Stonington Line about a mile southwest of Kingston Station and then heading south via a single track for approximately a mile. This may have also been a logging operation. The most probable timber species that was harvested was white cedar, a few surviving examples of which can still be found in South County swamps. There is no evidence of this railroad

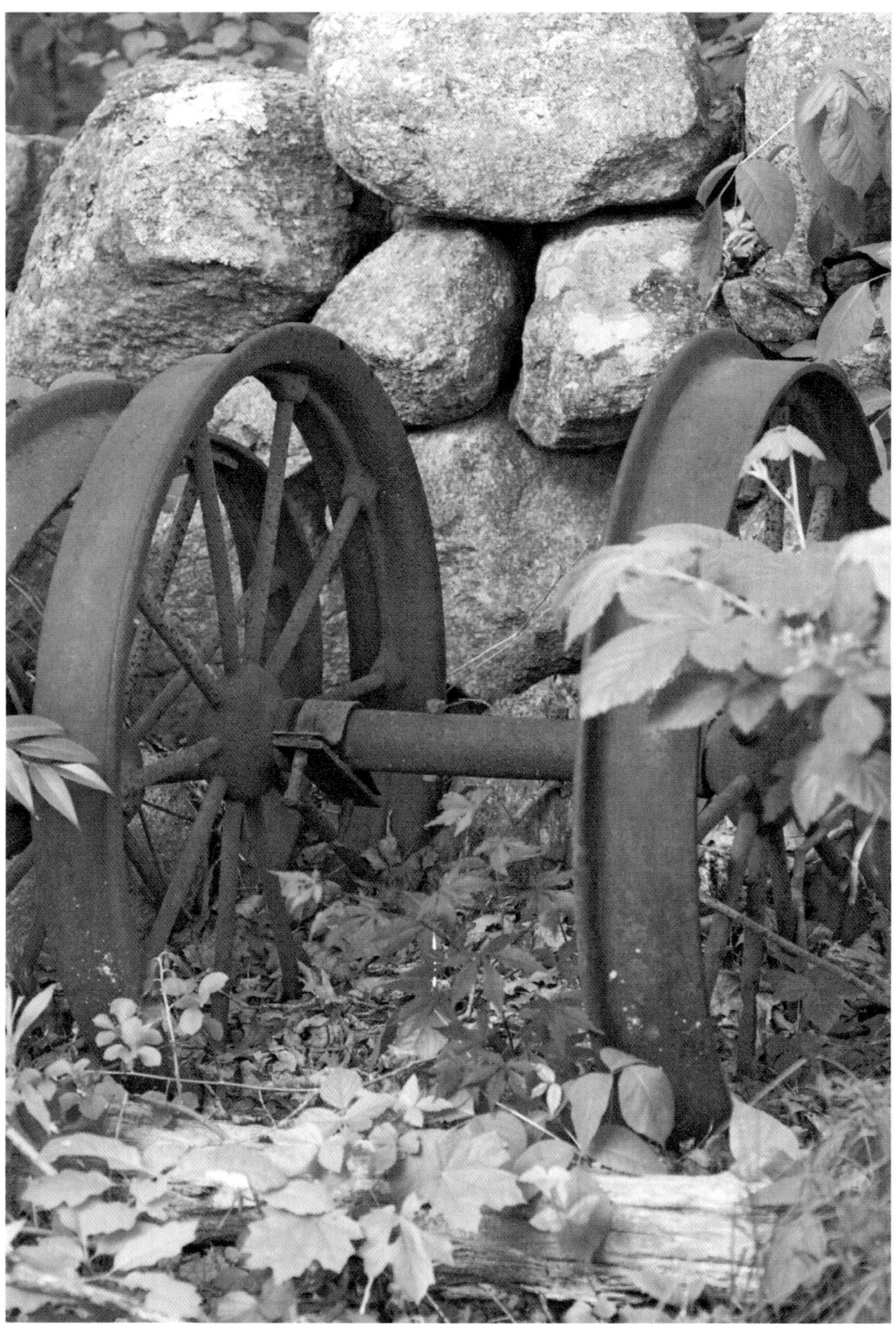

The remains of the Rhododendron Railroad resting in obscurity in the Kinney Gardens, Kingston. *Photo by Frank Heppner.*

today, but local old-timers insist that the single locomotive of the railroad at some point tipped over and was swallowed by the swamp. This is unlikely, because: 1) the few photographs of the 1915–17 operation show that the "locomotive" was a flat car with a marine diesel engine; and 2) according to the 1889 map, the line was not actually built in the swamp itself but on a slightly elevated promontory of dry land projecting into the wetland.

The Great Swamp was also the home of another most unusual railway, perhaps a unique one: the Rhododendron Railroad. One of the dominant plant species in the South County swamps is the rhododendron. Rhododendrons are not native to Rhode Island, but from colonial times they gradually worked their natural way northward, wherever they could find strongly acidic soil. The roots are naturally water-tolerant, and they can be found by the hundreds of acres in suitable areas in South County.

Dr. Lorenzo Kinney Sr., late professor of botany at the University of Rhode Island, became one of the world's foremost experts on rhododendrons and azaleas, growing and breeding new strains at the Lowland Rhododendron Farm in Rhode Island. He started a business exporting rhododendrons, both native and cultivated, to large estates in the East, including Biltmore, the Vanderbilt estate in North Carolina. With his son, the late Lorenzo Kinney Jr., he would gather native rhododendron plants from areas in or near the Great Swamp for shipment to distant points. Kinney Jr.'s home and azalea and rhododendron gardens are now owned by the Faella family, and during the spring they are open to the public. The business grew sufficiently that in the 1920s, Kinney and son were searching for a more efficient way to transport these large-root-ball plants to a loading area on the short-line Narragansett Pier Railroad. For a mile or two, this short line went through one of the drier areas of the Great Swamp. Once loaded into railroad cars, the plants would be taken to Kingston for transfer to the New Haven Railroad, which had absorbed the old Stonington Line.

Their solution to this transport problem, or at least a few remains of it, can be seen at the time of this writing on the grounds of the Kinney home. There, the diligent observer can find a couple of lengths of very lightweight T-rail and a spoked wheel set of perhaps two-foot gauge from some sort of cart. Evidently, the Kinneys bought some rail and a car or two from a mining or industrial railroad and set up a hand-operated railway, in the old British sense, from the Narragansett Pier Railroad tracks near where the railroad crossed RI State Highway 110. History does not say whether these last survivors of the Rhododendron Railroad were surplus to the railway's needs or were brought back to the Kinney property after abandonment.

Waterways and the Railroads

Being essentially flat, and having relatively small rivers with gentle gradients, Rhode Island did not have the abundant supplies of easily extractable water power that Massachusetts or New Hampshire had. Neither were there navigable rivers like the Thames and Connecticut Rivers in Connecticut. The one exception was the Blackstone River, and that was the original center of industry in the state.

The Blackstone runs forty-eight miles from Worcester, Massachusetts, to Providence, winding its way through Woonsocket (pronounced by many natives "woon-*sock*-eht") and Pawtucket (a town whose name is the subject of many bawdy limericks, none of which can be printed here). It has a drop of 438 feet in its run—insufficient to generate significant hydroelectric power but enough to produce mechanical power to operate machines through a water wheel or, later, a turbine. To the south, it joins with the Moshassuck River and then merges with the Woonasquatucket River to become the Providence River, which in turn dumps into Narragansett Bay. In the 1820s, the Blackstone Canal was built parallel to it (more about the canal later in chapter 3). This canal served primarily for transportation of goods on canalboats.

The Blackstone has been associated with industry since the 1790s, and unfortunately, one of the byproducts of that industry has been pollution. For much of its length, the Blackstone is relatively slow flowing. As a consequence, much of the pollution from the textile and machine plants settled into the sediment at the bottom of the river, from which it could diffuse out for centuries. A 1990 report by the United States Environmental Protection Agency called the Blackstone "the most polluted river in the country with respect to toxic sediments." Since that time, a variety of regional restoration projects have largely reduced that distinction.

The Political Geography of Rhode Island

Small as it is, Rhode Island has a very complex system of political subdivisions, which often causes confusion to strangers and sometimes even to Rhode Islanders. To understand how the railroads developed, at least a bit of knowledge of Rhode Island's political structure is helpful.

The level below state in Rhode Island is the county. Rhode Island has fewer counties than any other state save Delaware. Our five counties are

Providence, Bristol, Kent, Newport and Washington. Not included on this list is the unofficial South County, which exists only in the minds of its residents. Once again showing its distinctiveness, Rhode Island is one of two states (the other is Connecticut) that have no county government. The main function of the counties is to serve the judiciary; the counties have both superior and juvenile courthouses. Process servers usually operate out of the county courthouse.

The next unit is the municipality, which can either be a town or a city. The main difference is size and form of government, but both distinctions are fuzzy. There are thirty-nine separate municipalities in Rhode Island, of which eight are cities and the remainder are towns. The chief distinction is that cities (usually) have an elected mayor, and towns (usually) have a town council and an appointed town manager. Eight of the towns still have the ancient New England town meetings. "City" is not correlated with population size. The city of Central Falls has half the population of the town of Cumberland. Like baseball, you can't tell the players without a program.

Within the towns are the villages, which are unincorporated and have essentially no official functions. They often have their own zip codes. However, in the southern part of the state, if you ask someone where he lives, he will rarely say what town he lives in, but which village. So whenever someone asks the author where he lives, the reply is always "Wakefield" (a village) not "South Kingstown" (a town). To make it even more confusing, sometimes the names of the villages can be mixed up with the town. The villages of West Kingston and Kingston are in the town of South Kingstown.

All these subdivisions, although quaint, do not make for an efficient government. The economic crisis of the latter part of the first decade of the new century is prompting discussion of consolidation of municipal functions, but Rhode Islanders dearly love the concept of "local control," and the merging of, say, school or fire districts is proving to be a very hard sell.

Where, Exactly, *Is* Rhode Island?

The boundaries of the states have not always been what they are today. For example, in the original royal charter for Connecticut in 1662, its western border was the Pacific Ocean. As late as 1786, Ohio was still part of Connecticut. The boundaries of Rhode Island have not changed as dramatically since colonial times, but there have been some changes that have been very significant in its railroad history.

The royal charter for the combined Providence Plantations–Rhode Island colonies was granted by King Charles II in 1663. Basically, the outline of the state today is similar to what it was then, but all three land borders—west, north and east—have been contested at various times, and the border between North Stonington in Connecticut and Hopkinton in Rhode Island is *still* in dispute. The discrepancy on the western border arises because there is about a seventy-foot difference between traditional stone boundary markers and lines established by satellite technology from the legal descriptions of the border. There are a few houses located close to this border, and the two towns have made it an issue because there is a question of which town should receive property taxes from the border properties.

In 1663, the border dispute between Rhode Island and Connecticut was considerably more significant. In 1662, in Connecticut's royal charter, its eastern boundary was defined as Narragansett Bay. A year later, Rhode Island's *western* border was defined as the Pawcatuck River, which empties into the ocean in Westerly. A glance at a map quickly reveals the difficulty—Connecticut's defined eastern border is *east* of Rhode Island's western border, thus causing much of Providence Plantations to fall within Connecticut. When this glitch was called to King Charles's attention, he resolved the problem in a rather neat royal way. He simply renamed the Pawcatuck River the *Narragansett River* for legal purposes and declared it to be part of Narragansett Bay. The fact that no one then or since has ever called the Pawcatuck the Narragansett has not proven to be historically relevant, although the estuary that the Pawcatuck River empties into is still called Little Narragansett Bay, even though it is nowhere near Narragansett Bay. Had Charles not resolved this untidiness, both the Kingston and Westerly Amtrak stations might have been in Connecticut today.

The north–south border on the eastern side of Rhode Island and Massachusetts was considerably more complex and enormously significant for later railroad history. In 1747, in response to continuing and annoying conflicting claims between Massachusetts and Rhode Island, King George II granted some land east of the Blackstone River, containing Woonsocket, to Rhode Island. This land had previously belonged to Massachusetts. He also ceded East Providence, Pawtucket and Bristol to Massachusetts. In the same transaction, he also granted Fall River to Rhode Island. In terms of later history, this transfer was to be of enormous significance to the railroads of Rhode Island. The land containing Woonsocket and Pawtucket would later become the center of manufacturing and subsequent railroad development in the state. After the Industrial Revolution, had this border remained intact and these towns remained in Massachusetts, it would be doubtful if Rhode Island could have survived independently, but at the time this significance was not appreciated. Fall River was a significant port to gain, but Rhode Island already had two thriving ports, Providence and Newport.

However, this 1747 deal was not altogether satisfactory to either state, and in 1862, there was a land swap. Rhode Island regained East Providence, Pawtucket and Bristol (and all their industries), and Massachusetts regained Fall River, giving it a south coast warm-water port that was more protected than any in Buzzard's Bay. As it turned out, a good deal for both parties.

With its boundaries now more or less settled, thriving industry and an entrepreneurial population, Rhode Island was ready to welcome its first railroad.

Chapter 3

BOSTON GETS READY FOR THE RAILROAD

By 1820, Boston had a problem. The city that today calls itself (without apparent embarrassment) "the Hub of the Universe" was in danger of becoming an economic backwater. The Louisiana Purchase of 1803 and the British cession of midwestern land near the Canadian border to the United States in 1818 had nearly doubled the land area of America. Ten new states had been added to the original thirteen by 1820. Although the results of the Lewis and Clark expedition of 1804–6 were little known at the time, early travelers to the West returned with tales of Illinois bottomlands rich with three hundred feet of topsoil and prairies with tens of millions of buffalo ripe for the taking. Suddenly, the hardscrabble farmland of New England, with its annual crop of boulders and challenging winters, was beginning to look less and less attractive, and a westward migration of people and capital began that did not slow until the director of the census declared that the "frontier" was closed in 1890.

However, there was one advantage that southern New England had that the frontier would have difficulty competing with: manufacturing and markets. New England had a leg up on the rest of the country with its early adoption of factories, and its proximity to European markets through its numerous ports would be hard to duplicate in Kansas. Moreover, all those folks moving west needed things that New England was happy to manufacture for them. Guns. Plows. Wagons. Trousers. The key to getting goods to customers on the move was the same then as it is now: transportation.

Here, New England had to face the facts of geography. Both the major rivers and the mountain ranges of New England tend to run north and south. The Connecticut. The Thames. The Berkshires. The Whites. Most of New England's manufacturing was done in the very easternmost part of the region. How to acquire raw materials from one direction and ship finished goods in the other was a problem that would challenge visionaries and entrepreneurs for decades.

As if to add geographic insult to injury, the major rivers of New England tended to flow through valleys rather than flatland, as was the case with the Mississippi. An east–west transportation route confronting a river would first have to climb a range of hills (or tunnel through it), cross the river and then make its way through another range of hills on the other side. All of these requirements added time and cost to construction.

Prior to the Industrial Revolution, transportation in New England was handled by riverboats on the few navigable rivers and a network of roads, the most noted of which were the post roads. The first identifiable New England post road was the Upper Boston Post Road, which was so designated in 1673. It ran from Boston to Springfield through Worcester, then down to New Haven, thence to New York. Although not paved in the modern sense, the post roads were graded well, and the postal carriages could be run at a pretty good clip. The Lower Post Road ran from Boston to Providence, through South County to Stonington and then to New Haven and on to New York. This road roughly follows the path of U.S. Highway 1 today and was the post road most heavily traveled by the beginning of the nineteenth century.

The post roads were adequate for the transportation needs of pre–Industrial Revolution society, but by 1790, there was a stark realization that something beyond the barge and the stagecoach was needed. Fortunately, that period was a time that produced an abundance of very bright inventors. The years between 1790 and 1830 brought more changes in transportation than any other period since the invention of the wheel. The Industrial Revolution created, almost overnight, a need to carry large, heavy objects and large numbers of people with a speed that would be unthinkable with animal or human power. Simple machines sufficed to move the giant stones that made up the pyramids or Stonehenge, but their pace could be measured in miles per month. Two inventions appeared almost simultaneously toward the end of the eighteenth century that addressed this issue.

The first of these inventions was the man-made canal. Simple canals had been known since ancient times, and the first canal lock, a section of canal into which water can be pumped in or out to raise or lower the canalboats to a different level, was developed by Greek engineers in the third century BCE in Egypt. The "canals" of Venice were not dug as true canals are. Rather, they were the result of buildings being raised on pilings on flooded land. China had, and still has, an extensive canal system, but the first real national, interconnected canal system was developed in England to support its burgeoning Industrial Revolution, particularly in textile manufacture.

Boston was well aware of these developments, but its first experiment in canal building had not been a happy one. The 27-mile-long Middlesex Canal, started in 1793 and completed in 1803, connected Boston with the Merrimack River, a 110-mile-long stream that originates in mid–New Hampshire, flows to Lowell, Massachusetts, and then runs east to the Atlantic. This canal had been built to bring New Hampshire products directly from the Merrimack to Boston, rather than through the mouth of the river at Newburyport, around Cape Ann in the open ocean and thence to Boston. However, although it was properly engineered, it was poorly built and a commercial failure, dampening the enthusiasm for this new type of engineering marvel—an enthusiasm that was absolutely necessary for generating the capital, both political and economic, for daring new projects.

The experience of nearby Providence was considerably happier. By the 1800s, Rhode Island got most of its agricultural product from central Massachusetts, filtering through the city of Worcester. The Blackstone River ran between Worcester and Providence, but it was scattered with a series of rapids, which although not terribly challenging for, say, a canoeist, were a tremendous hindrance to a flat-bottom cargo boat. A canal would address this problem.

The Blackstone Canal Company was jointly owned and financed by Massachusetts and Rhode Island interests. It obtained a charter in 1823 and started construction on the canal in 1825, and the canal was open for business in 1828. It was an immediate success. Boston commercial leaders noted, not without a little fear, that trade that formerly had gone from Worcester to Boston by road was now diverted to Providence by canal.

In the meantime, farther west, the Erie Canal was started in 1817. It eventually ran from the Hudson River through New York State to the Great Lakes, which, in turn, granted eastern access to the Mississippi and Missouri River drainages and all their riches. The Erie was completed in 1825 to great fanfare and immediately proceeded to enrichen all the communities it passed through. In large measure, it was responsible for the exodus of a good deal of New England's more adventurous population, as they somehow found their way to the Hudson River and then connected with the canal.

Pennsylvania was also struck with canal fever after seeing first the hoopla and later the success of the Erie Canal. Although the first canal was built in Pennsylvania in 1797, canal building did not begin in earnest until the 1820s and was spurred by the opening of the Erie Canal, which Pennsylvania interests perceived as a direct threat to their commerce. By 1840, there were over 1,200 miles of canal in the state, some built by the state government and some through privately raised capital. Ironically, it was in the decade between 1830 and 1840 that railroads started to replace canals for long-distance transport.

The Pennsylvania canal system featured a number of engineering developments that later would prove to be important for railroads. The first canalboats to cross the Allegheny Mountains did so by a series of "inclined planes." The basic principle was something like the cable cars of San Francisco. At the base of a hill, a railroad track dipped into the end of the canal. The canalboat was floated onto a carriage resting on railroad wheels, which in turn ran on a conventional railroad track that went straight up the side of the hill. The carriage had a mechanism that kept the boat level, even though the tracks pitched steeply upward. A cable was attached to the front of the carriage, and the carriage was then pulled up the hill by a steam engine that wound the cable onto a reel. At the top of the hill, the process was reversed, and the boat floated away on a new, higher section of canal. On the Allegheny Portage Railroad, a series of inclined planes that bore canalboats over the Alleghenies near Johnstown, Pennsylvania, the first railroad tunnel in the United States was built. Completed in 1834 (or 1833, the sources vary), the Staple Bend tunnel was 901 feet long and has recently been restored, reflecting its status as a National Historical Landmark.

It was on one of these inclined planes, the Belmont Plane, that in 1836 there was the first demonstration of a steam locomotive pulling itself and a load up a significant grade. Prior to this time, it was thought that a locomotive could only operate on level ground; otherwise, it would simply spin its wheels. This knowledge made it possible to consider railroad routes through mountain ranges. We know today that trains can indeed handle upgrades, but Jeeps they are not. A steep grade for a mainline train would be 3 percent (the tracks rise three feet for every one hundred feet of horizontal distance). The steepest grade for a mainline train in the United States was the Saluda Grade on the Southern Railroad, which for a brief distance pitched up to 5 percent.

Meanwhile, in Massachusetts, both capitalists and the state government were exploring ways to get goods and materials to the Hudson and west without having to go to sea around Cape Cod. In early 1825, the Massachusetts legislature had appointed a group to examine the idea of a canal from Boston to the Connecticut River, a distance of eighty miles. At approximately the same time, a business group in New Hampshire was promoting the idea of a cross–New Hampshire canal from the Merrimack to the Connecticut. Boston would undoubtedly accrue some benefit from such a project, due to an easy connection with the Middlesex Canal, but on the other hand, much New Hampshire traffic that otherwise would have to go to Boston first before continuing west would surely be siphoned off. This latter project fizzled before a spade of earth was turned.

In the meantime, the Massachusetts legislative canal commission hired Colonel Loammi Baldwin, who had been the chief engineer on the Middlesex Canal, to survey a canal route from Boston to Albany in as direct a route as possible. He presented his report in 1826. Colonel Baldwin's route was generally followed many years later by the Boston and Maine Railroad on its way to the Hudson. It followed essentially a straight line from Boston to Fitchburg and then to Athol, where it followed the Miller's River watershed to the Connecticut River, crossed over at Greenfield and then picked up the Deerfield River thence straight to the Hoosac Mountains. Unfortunately, to get a canalboat over the mountains would require 220 locks and would take two days to traverse only eighteen miles. Colonel Baldwin, being a Harvard man, favored a bolder approach. He proposed building a tunnel under Hoosac Mountain, which a canalboat would be able to traverse in about an hour and a half. He provided a construction cost estimate that was a lineal ancestor of the Big Dig original estimate in Boston, in that it was wildly and unrealistically low. By his reckoning, a best case estimate to build the tunnel was $300,000; the worst-case estimate was $900,000. David Henshaw, a contemporary Boston politician, estimated on the basis of Baldwin's report that the tunnel would actually take between 52 and 182 years to complete. This was not an outlandish estimate, given the primitive methods of tunneling available at the time. Many years later, when the Hoosac tunnel was actually built as a railroad rather than a canal tunnel, it opened in 1875 after 20 years of construction and an expenditure of $15 to $20 million (depending on whose accountant you believe).

While all this dithering about canals was going on in Boston, word began to reach America of another British invention that had the potential to resolve most, if not all, of the difficulties presented by canals. It was called the "Rail Road."

What, Exactly, Is a "Rail Road"?

Dictionary definitions for "railroad," or in British usage "railway," leave a lot to be desired because they contain a number of circular definitions. What is a rail? A strip of metal placed atop a tie. What is a tie? A piece of wood or concrete that supports a rail. Whatever the dictionary definition, a railroad has a basic essence. It is two bar-like strips of metal, called rails, bound together to maintain a constant distance between them, upon which rolls a metal wheel assembly that supports a container of sorts into which one puts a load.

The key element to this definition is metal wheel–metal rail, and it is this simple concept that explains why there have been railroads for four hundred years and they show no signs of going away. The friction between a metal wheel and a metal rail is far less than any other combination of wheel and support. For example, a six-thousand-horsepower locomotive can pull 13,000,000 pounds of loaded train; however, the same horsepower distributed among twenty eighteen-wheeler trucks could only pull 1,600,000 pounds of loaded truck. The reason for this is the much lower friction between steel rail and steel wheel, compared to rubber tire and concrete. Only river barges are more efficient than a train, but they are sharply limited in speed.

Primitive forms of railroad were used with push carts in mines in the 1500s. The first recorded above-ground railroad was the Wollaton Wagonway built in 1604 in England. It used horse-drawn wagons to haul coal a distance of about two miles. The rails were apparently made of wood, but not long after, it became universal practice to lay a strap of iron on top of the wood, both to reduce friction and increase the life of the rail. All-iron rails came considerably later.

One problem immediately surfaces. How do you keep the wheels on the rails? There have been two solutions, both appearing in the early days of railroads. No longer generally used, but appearing in the 1700s, was the flangeway. In this system, the wheels were flat at the bottom, like a wagon wheel. Mounted on top of each rail was an L-shaped metal girder, typically with the vertical part on the inside of the rail. This vertical part prevented the wheel from moving sideways off the rail. One of the presumed advantages was that ordinary wagons, provided their wheels were the correct distance apart, could be used either on a regular road or a railroad.

The other system depended on the design of the wheel, rather than the rail, to provide lateral stability. On the inside of each wheel was a raised lip, called a flange, that prevented sideways movement. On modern trains, the distance between flanges is always slightly less than the distance between the rails to reduce friction. A byproduct of this design is a very slight side-to-side movement while the train is running. Okay, here now is the surprising news. The flange isn't what actually keeps the wheel on the track *most* of the time. The *real* stabilizing force is less obvious. Next time you're close to a train car (Not too close! Safety first!), take a look at one of the wheels. Not immediately obvious, but very significant, is the fact that on a train, two wheels opposite to each other are fastened rigidly to a common axle. The resultant assembly is called a wheelset. If something pushed a wheel sideways, the wheel on the opposite side would move an equal distance. Now take a close look at the wheel itself. You'll immediately see the flange, but look at the bottom of the wheel itself. It's not flat, but beveled; the inside of the wheel has a slightly larger diameter than the outside. The same is true on the opposite side. So, what do flanges actually do, if they don't keep the wheel on the track? They're critical in the operation of switches, the devices that enable a train to move from one track to another.

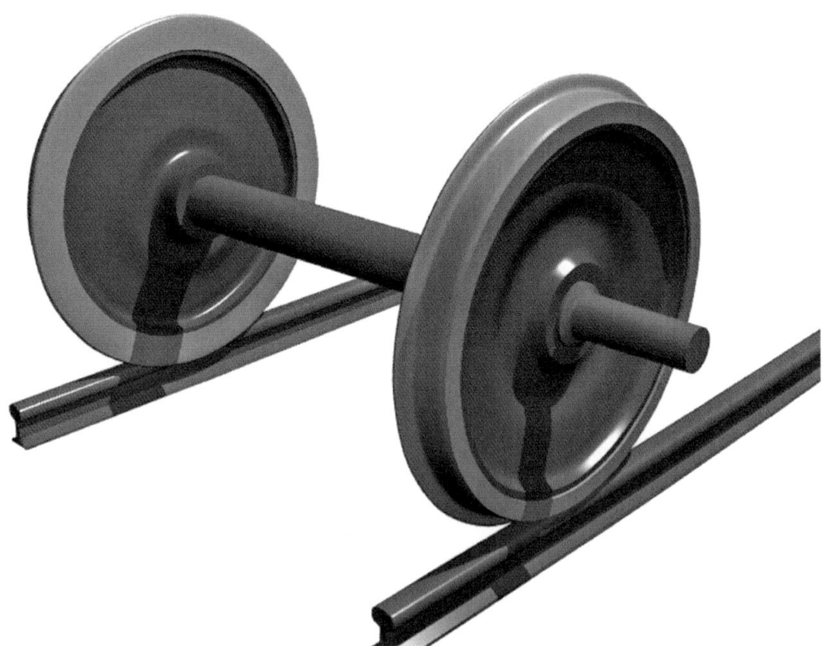

A wheelset with flanged wheels.

All right, let's start the train moving. Say that when we start out, the wheels are contacting the curved top of the rail at the same point—that is, the diameter of each wheel in the wheelset where it contacts the rail is the same. We chug along for a while, and nothing much changes—there aren't any strong forces to move the wheelset from side to side (remember, the distance between the flanges is slightly less than the distance between the rails, so some "slop" is permitted in side-to-side movement). Now we come to a curve. The train wants to keep going straight, but the track curves under it. The result is that the train starts to move sideways relative to the track. Clearly, something has to be done about this, or the train would jump the tracks at every curve. The problem breeds the solution. This outward movement has the effect of moving the wheelset in such a way that the wheel on the outside of the curve is riding on a larger diameter part of the wheel than is the wheel on the inside. Here, the author will show some mercy and skip the several pages of arcane mathematics that serve to explain why what follows *really* happens and just say that a force is thus generated that pushes the wheelset back toward the middle of the curve. The result is that the beveled bottoms of the wheels provide in effect a simple but extraordinarily reliable self-stabilizing system that can keep a train on the tracks with no electronics or moving parts up to a speed of about 140 miles per hour, after which the ride would become uncomfortable due to the rapid back-and-forth movement of the wheels. It is this elegant design, along with the low friction of steel-against-steel, that explains why trains are as efficient and useful today as they were two hundred years ago.

These early railroads used horses as motive power and were limited in top speed by the running ability of the horse. However, toward the end of the eighteenth century, a new device developed by British engineers was beginning to find wide use: the steam engine. The first steam engines were used primarily for pumping water out of mines and were very fuel inefficient. However, James Watt developed a steam engine capable of producing rotary motion that could be used to drive any type of industrial machine. No longer were factories dependent on water power.

It did not take long before some bright person looked at an industrial steam engine with a spinning flywheel and speculated that if such an engine could be mounted on a cart with railroad wheels and placed on tracks, the spinning wheel could be used to move the cart along the tracks. The first person to make such a machine successfully was Richard Trevithick, who was born in 1771 in the mining district of Cornwall, England.

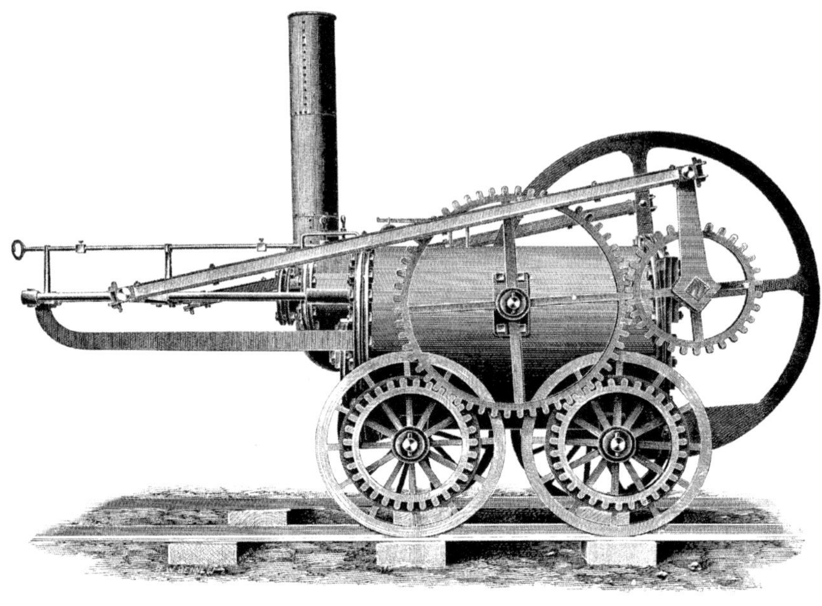

Richard Trevithick's Pen-y-Darren locomotive from 1804. *From* Early American *Locomotives, by John H. White Jr. Courtesy Dover Publications.*

In 1801, using some of his experience building stationary steam engines, he built the world's first self-propelled vehicle, a steam road carriage to which he gave the wonderful name *Puffing Devil.* Unfortunately, three days after her first trial, *Devil* broke down, and while her crew stopped by a pub to discuss the situation and have some libations, *Devil* set herself on fire and went up in smoke.

Several years later, Trevithick took a steam engine he had built to operate hammers in a wrought-iron factory and mounted it on a railway carriage, modifying the engine to drive the wheels. This contraption was then set on the tracks of an industrial wagonway operated by the Pen-Y-Darren ironworks in Wales. This device was not named but is known to history as the Pen-Y-Darren locomotive. On February 4, 1804, this locomotive pulled five connected wagons, ten tons of iron and seventy men a distance of almost ten miles and was thus the first steam-powered train in history.

Over the next twenty years, steady progress was made in England on locomotives, track and railroad cars, and in 1825, George Stephenson opened the Stockton and Darlington Railway, the first publicly subscribed (owned by stockholders) railroad. The railroad had become a practical method of public transportation.

Meanwhile, back in Boston, on June 17 in the same year that Stephenson started his Stockton and Darlington Railway, construction was started on a massive patriotic project that would seem to have nothing to do with railroads but would provide the impetus for the first railroad in the United States. This project was the Bunker Hill Monument. In 1823, the great orator Daniel Webster and six other men convened to discuss building some sort of monument to commemorate the Battle of Bunker Hill, which was actually fought on Breed's Hill, where the monument was eventually built. The design committee included Webster; the Rhode Island painter Gilbert Stuart, who was living in Boston at the time; and Loammi Baldwin Jr., the son of the engineer of the Middlesex Canal. The designer selected was Solomon Willard, a stone carver and architect. The final design was to be a granite obelisk that stood 221 feet tall. But where was the granite to come from?

Willard traveled all over New England and finally identified a vein of beautiful granite in Quincy, Massachusetts. In 1825, a self-taught engineer named Gridley Bryant bought the quarry and secured the contract to supply the building stone. The quarry was three miles from Boston Harbor, and Bryant had to find some means of transporting the very heavy stones from the quarry to the water's edge, where they could then be barged to Charlestown, the site of the monument.

Most of the alternatives available, including canals, were unattractive, but Bryant had read of Stephenson's railway work in England and decided that a horse-drawn railroad would suit his purposes. He approached Willard and a Boston financier named Thomas Handasyd Perkins, who had made the bulk of his fortune in the slave and opium trades, which he had pioneered in China. Perkins agreed to supply the bulk of the capital for the project.

On January 4, 1826, Perkins, Bryant, Willard and three other Bostonians petitioned the Massachusetts legislature to form a corporation to be called the Granite Railway Company. The petition was granted on March 4. This document was to be enormously important for the subsequent history of the railroad in America. It recognized the corporation as an organizational structure for a railroad. Equally important, it established that railroad corporations had the power of eminent domain—the ability to condemn private land and property necessary for the enterprise. Normally this power is reserved for governments. Enormously controversial over its history, eminent domain made it impossible for a single landowner to stop a railroad from being built over his property.

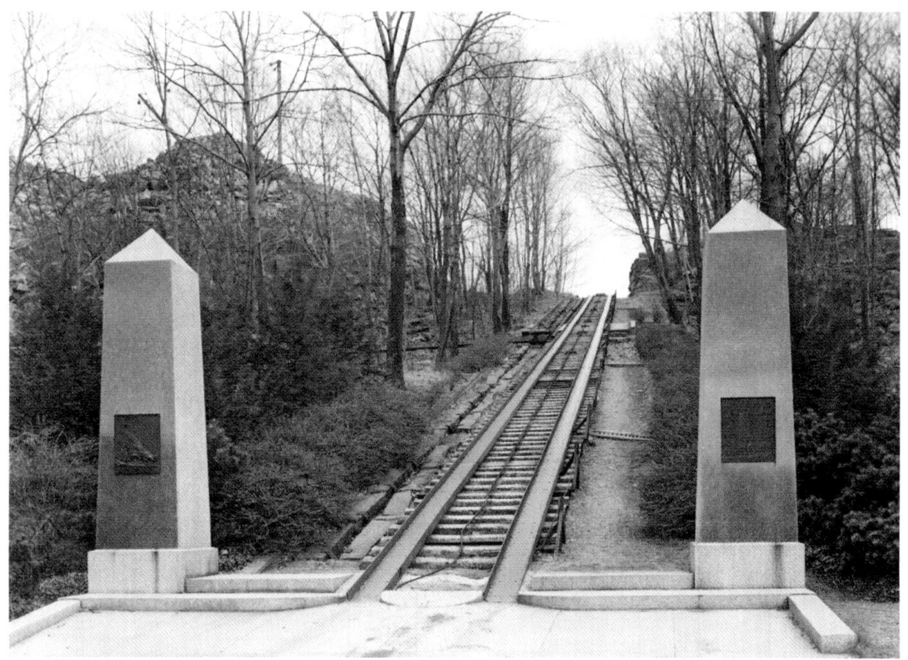

An inclined plane on the Granite Railway. This view from 1934 shows that the track construction was heavily modified from its original configuration. *Library of Congress.*

Charter in hand, Bryant broke ground for his railroad on April 1 (perhaps not the most propitious day to launch a new venture). Construction went quickly, and the line began hauling granite on October 7. Bryant was a brilliant engineer, and he went on to invent many of the devices that were later necessary for railroad development, including the track switch, the locomotive turntable and the eight-wheel railroad car. He never patented any of his inventions, believing that they should be universally applied for the common good.

The Granite Railway became much modified over time, its unique broad-gauge track with granite ties being replaced with conventional railroad track. It survived as a railroad into the twentieth century, and today much of its right of way is a bicycle path. The surviving remnants were placed on the National Register of Historic Places in 1973.

The almost-instant success of the Granite Railway, the first railroad in the United States, led to an explosion of railroad schemes and proposals in Boston in the latter 1820s. By 1830, Boston business interests had started talking about a railroad to Providence.

Chapter 4

THE RAILROAD COMES TO PROVIDENCE

In the late 1820s, Boston was atwitter with railroad plans. The success of the Granite Railroad brought publicity that attracted visitors from all over the East Coast, even though the railroad was firmly linked to the past through its use of horses for motive power. Elsewhere, "firsts" came fast and furious. In 1829, the Delaware and Hudson Railroad in Pennsylvania used the first steam locomotive to successfully operate in America: the Stourbridge Lion, imported from England. Down in Dixie, the South Carolina Canal and Rail Road Company put the Best Friend of Charlestown, the first steam locomotive built in the United States, into service in December 1830. Unfortunately, the Best Friend held another "first" record—the first American steam locomotive to blow up in operation.

Using the model of the Granite Railroad's charter and corporate structure, new railroad enterprises were popping up all over Bean Town. Some were very ambitious, like the plans for a railroad from Boston to Albany to replace the now-defunct trans-state canal plan. Others were more modest but also more practical. Of the dozens of proposals floating about, three actually had received state charters for construction by 1831. It is immediately obvious why two of these railroads were built. The third was a bit more puzzling.

The city of Lowell, Massachusetts, was established as a planned industrial community, consisting not only of textile factories but also boardinghouses for the workers. Its location on the Merrimack River was not an accident. The

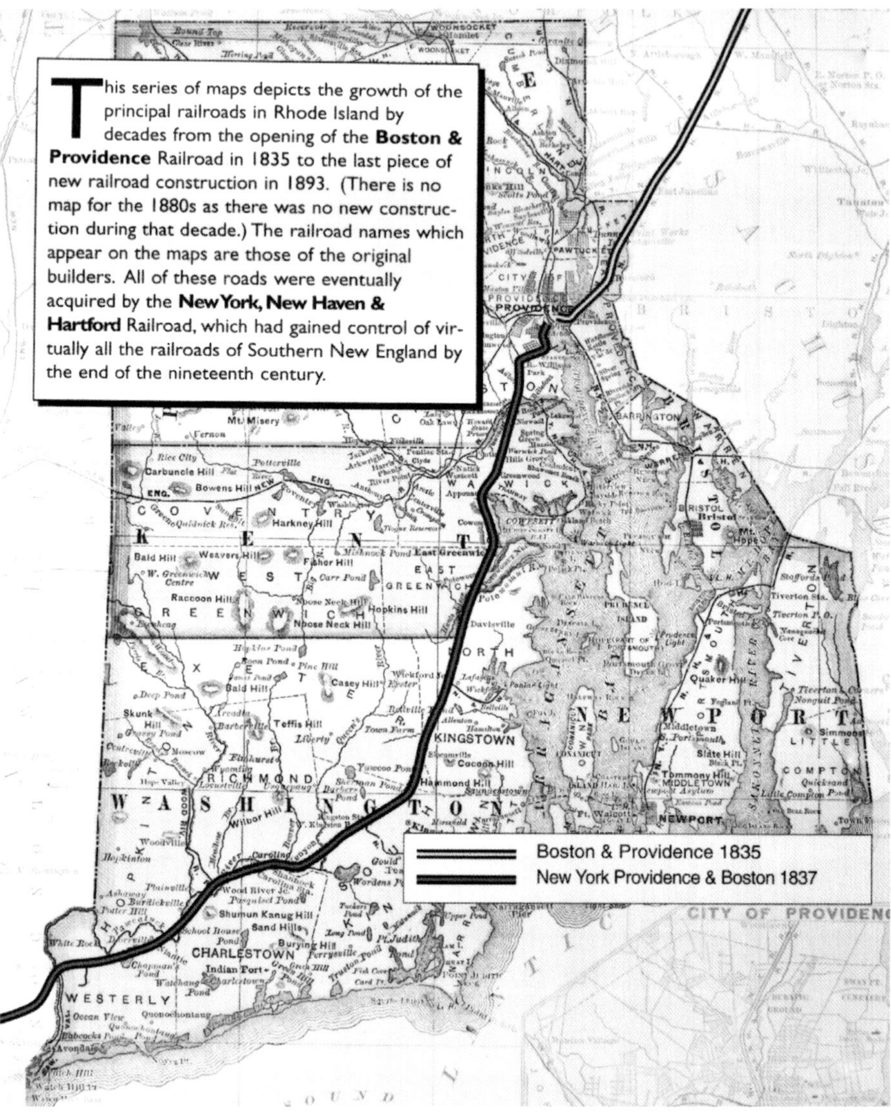

The first two railroads in Rhode Island. The Boston and Providence Railroad went into service in 1835 and the New York, Providence and Boston Railroad (Stonington Line) in 1837. *Rhode Island Railroad Museum.*

Merrimack takes a ninety-degree bend in the old town of Chelmsford and drops thirty-two feet in a relatively short distance, creating the Pawtucket Falls. This relatively shallow drop was compensated for by the breadth and volume of the river at that point, creating ideal conditions for water power generation. A system of power canals fed water to breast wheels when the power system was first built. After 1837, water turbines were used. It was estimated that the Merrimack was able to generate upward of ten thousand horsepower to drive the mills' textile machinery. The Middlesex Canal intersected the Merrimack nearby, providing additional advantage to this location for the first mills.

The early Lowell textile factories were designed around a specific kind of labor force: young single women called "mill girls." They were attracted to Lowell by the high wages (for the time) and primarily came from farm communities scattered over northern New England. However, beginning in the late 1820s, immigrant labor began to displace the mill girls. The first wave of immigrants came in small numbers from Ireland and then in droves after the potato famine in Ireland in the 1840s. Immigrant workers for the mills arrived in the port of Boston, and as 1830 approached, it was clear to both Boston and Lowell financiers that this new invention, the railroad, was ideally suited to bring both raw cotton and raw immigrants from Boston to Lowell.

In January 1830, a group of Lowell textile magnates was called together in Boston by Patrick T. Jackson, one of the founders of Lowell, to discuss the building of a railroad from Boston to Lowell. They met in the parlor of Jackson's town house at 22 Winter Street, only a few steps from the location of the famous Locke-Ober, Boston's third-oldest restaurant. After overcoming opposition from the owners of the Middlesex Canal, the new Boston and Lowell Railroad received a legislative charter and became the first common-carrier railroad in Massachusetts.

While the line was under construction, the owners ordered their first locomotive from Stephenson in England. It was constructed using the track gauge of four feet, eight and a half inches, which was becoming the de facto standard in England, and with the later success of the Boston and Lowell, that gauge became the standard for American railroads as well. The line was open for business on June 24, 1835, and almost immediately, work began to add a second track.

At this point, Dear Reader, we shall have a brief "truth is stranger than fiction" moment. In 1834, Major George W. Whistler became the first shop superintendent for the Boston and Lowell Railroad and was responsible for the building of its first two locomotives. Major Whistler had attended West Point and, while there, befriended a fellow cadet named William Gibbs McNeill. At the time, all West Point students received engineering training. After finishing up, Whistler and McNeill worked on the Baltimore and Ohio Railroad, which was being built in the late 1820s. McNeill went on to become superintendent of the Boston and Providence Railroad and will return to our story again. In the meantime, Whistler married McNeill's sister

Anna, who bore him a son, James Abbott McNeill Whistler, who became a painter best known for a portrait entitled *Study in Grey and Black #1: The Artist's Mother*, otherwise known as *Whistler's Mother*. So without the Boston and Lowell Railroad, there would not have been generations' worth of jokes about Whistler's mom.

THE BOSTON AND WORCESTER RAILROAD

The Boston and Lowell Railroad started with almost everything going for it—a clear reason for being; powerful, wealthy and influential backers; and an easy route. The second of these pioneer routes, the Boston and Worcester Railroad, had virtually nothing in its favor and almost wasn't built.

Whereas the driving force behind the Boston and Lowell Railroad came from Lowell, the reverse was true for the Boston and Worcester Railroad. Worcester had a population a third smaller than Lowell and, since the construction of the Blackstone Canal, felt itself tied commercially more to Providence than Boston. It had a few small factories but nothing like the huge industrial complex that had blossomed in Lowell.

Nonetheless, a few far-sighted souls perceived that a Boston and Worcester railroad might be but a first step toward a Boston and Albany railroad, and they were right, but the baby steps were not accomplished without many preliminary trips and falls. The initial charter was received in June 1831, and construction started about a year later.

There were some significant differences between the Boston and Lowell Railroad and the Boston and Worcester Railroad. The former was very well financed; nothing was too good, whether it be track materials or locomotives. The initial construction of the Boston and Worcester Railroad was done on the cheap. The rails were lighter in weight, causing frequent derailments, and the curves were sharper, to save grading expense, consequently reducing the load the trains could pull.

A telling difference was that the Boston and Lowell Railroad ran through relatively open country between its termini, whereas the Boston and Worcester Railroad had to run through a series of towns: Wellesley, Newton, Natick, Framingham and Hopkinton. In each town, the railroad builders discovered something that is well known today—NIMBY, or "Not in My Backyard." Residents liked the idea of having a swift means of getting to Boston, as long as the tracks didn't pass anywhere near their homes. In addition, although the Boston and Lowell Railroad ran through essentially flat country, the Boston and Worcester Railroad had to climb a vertical distance of five hundred feet, a real challenge for the dinky locomotives of the time.

Unlike the Boston and Lowell Railroad, the Boston and Worcester Railroad opened in stages, primarily to generate a revenue stream during construction. The line was open to paying passengers to Worcester on July 4, 1835, only a few days after the opening of the Boston and Lowell Railroad. Despite its touch-and-go beginnings, the little Boston and Worcester Railroad *did* eventually become the eastern part of the great Boston and Albany Railroad's primary east–west route, and one may still take a passenger train today over the 175-year-old route.

The Boston and Providence Railroad

Finally, we come to the last of the three pioneering lines out of Boston, the Boston and Providence Railroad. But before discussing it, a key question must be asked. Why Providence? Was it because large numbers of people from Providence wanted to go to Boston? Not likely—as we have seen, Rhode Islanders tend to be very self-sufficient. Rhode Island provided for most of their needs, thank you. Was it because large numbers of people in Boston wanted to visit Providence? If you live in the "Hub of the Universe," the answer to that question is self-evident. The actual answer might appear to strike a bit of a blow to the self-esteem of Rhode Island, but looking at the origins of the state, the opinions of others have historically counted for little.

If you lived in Boston in 1830 and you wanted to go to New York, there were three choices. You could take one of the frequent small packet boats out of Boston (if you could get out of the ice pack in February) and sail around Cape Cod, which is one of three locations on the Atlantic coast known as a "graveyard of ships." *If* your vessel didn't join the approximately one thousand ships whose bones lie scattered on the bottom around the Cape, your ship would pass first through Vineyard Sound and then Block Island Sound. Block Island Sound has some of the world's nastiest waters if one is prone to seasickness. The combination of current and quartering winds produces a corkscrewing motion, a kind of pitching and rolling at the same time, that causes many casual travelers to *hope* that their boat sinks, the quicker the better.

If that was not an attractive prospect (and it appears not to have been), one could always take a stagecoach along the Lower Post Road. It was not a particularly fast way to travel, but it had its charms, because it usually involved at least one overnight stay in one of the wayside inns, a number of which are still open and are quite delightful. In winter, it was a whole different story and often an impossible trip for days or weeks.

The third option, and the one that eventually became most popular, was to start out by stagecoach and then head directly to one of the southern port cities, the most important of which was Providence. There, one would transfer to a steamer. In this way, the horrors of the Cape could be avoided, and Block Island Sound did not always represent a dreadful passage. However, this option carried the same liability as the all-stage route. During winter, service became irregular or sometimes cancelled altogether on the Boston to Providence leg.

With Boston's population being 61,000 in 1830, and New York's 202,000, there was a compelling reason to establish an all-year, all-weather rail connection between the two metropolises. Very early on it was perceived that, desirable as it might be, to try to build a rail line in one jump between Boston and New York was both technically and financially impossible to achieve in a reasonable period of time. The next best alternative was to go from Boston to Providence by rail, displacing the stagecoaches, and then have passengers transfer to ships. So, alas, Providence was not the destination but just the place to get off the train.

Like the Boston and Worcester Railroad, most of the early organization and financing for the Boston and Providence Railroad came from Boston rather than the outlying terminus. Somewhat surprisingly today, the initial mention of a railroad from Boston to Providence came in a report to the Massachusetts legislature from its own Board of Internal Improvement on February 15, 1828, that suggested that the state (not a private company) build a horse-drawn railway using granite, instead of wood ties, as was done on the Granite Railroad. The Massachusetts legislature asked its counterpart in Rhode Island for permission to both survey and build the Rhode Island section of the nascent Boston and Providence Railroad. This permission was duly granted, but evidently the State of Massachusetts lost interest in direct financing of the railroad, because we find that on June 22, 1831, the Massachusetts legislature chartered a private stock corporation to construct the Boston and Providence Railroad. Unfortunately, many of the original stockholders bought their stock using financial instruments similar to "margin" in today's stock market, and when it came time to put cash on the line, they defaulted, and the charter was sold at auction less than a year after its formation.

These irregularities evidently made the Rhode Island legislature a bit nervous, because not long after the private charter in Massachusetts was reissued, Rhode Island withdrew its permission to build. This was perhaps not surprising, because feelings about a Boston to Providence railroad were definitely mixed in Little Rhody. First, there was the very real concern that the railroad would cut into the profits of the Blackstone Canal, in which there was heavy Rhode Island investment. Even more important, however, was the feeling that the primary motivation for the railroad, the speeding of passengers from Boston to ships bound for New York, would leave Providence identified even more as a backwater. There was also the knowledge that, at the time, East Providence belonged to Massachusetts, and should the Rhode Island legislature prove difficult, the railroad could simply terminate at docks in East Providence rather than India Point in Providence, which was the intended terminus, and Rhode Island wouldn't even get the crumbs from the construction of the railroad.

Wiser heads prevailed, and on May 10, 1834, the Rhode Island General Assembly passed an act incorporating the Boston and Providence Railroad and Transportation Company and granting it permission to build tracks in Rhode Island to connect with the Boston and Providence Railroad Company, its counterpart in Massachusetts. This rather odd arrangement, the chartering of two separate, state-based companies to build an interstate railroad line, was fairly common in the early days of railroading. National regulation of railroads was in its infancy, and whereas state legislatures were fairly familiar with the chartering of companies that built public access roads, a railroad was a brand-new concept, and it took decades before a single, interstate charter was possible.

The Massachusetts-based Boston and Providence Railroad hired Captain William Gibbs McNeill, whom we met earlier in the chapter, to be its chief surveyor and engineer. His name is little known today, but every Amtrak or MBTA (Massachusetts Bay Transportation Authority) passenger who travels southwest out of Boston should raise a glass in salute to this man, who did one of the most competent jobs of railroad civil engineering in the history of United States.

He began by surveying eleven different possible routes. His overall aim was to have the straightest possible line between the two end cities, but doing so required a potential financial sacrifice by the company. The straightest route involved bypassing several burgeoning towns along the way, which would have provided a significant input of both freight and passengers. One,

Dedham, later succeeded in having a branch line built that later became part of MBTA's Franklin line.

McNeill's line was practically gradeless and had one dead-straight length of sixteen miles. This length of track was many years later incorporated into the Amtrak system, and today, it and two other straight stretches of track in Rhode Island are the only places on the Amtrak system where Acela trains are allowed to stretch their legs to 150 miles per hour.

On McNeill's chosen route, there was only one geological obstacle, but it was a formidable one for the times. Near today's Norwood, at Canton, the Neponset River coursed through a valley that dipped about sixty feet below the surrounding terrain. It would have been possible to halt the tracks on either side of the valley and use inclined planes to transit the cars across, but a spectacular and fatal accident on the inclined plane at the Granite Railroad in 1832 made that alternative unattractive. In addition, inclined planes would have significantly slowed Boston–Providence travel time.

McNeill chose instead to build a viaduct, which is a bridge made of a series of short spans, usually arches. At 615 feet of length and 70 feet of height, it was the longest and tallest railroad bridge in the world at the time it was built in 1835, and it is the only example of its type of construction in the western hemisphere. It is called a blind arcade cavity wall bridge. From a distance, the viaduct appears to be composed of a series of short masonry arches, but these are primarily decorative. The real support for the tracks is provided by two massive parallel stone walls that are essentially hidden by the arches. This type of construction is immensely strong. The locomotives of McNeill's day weighed about ten tons, pulled eight cars of about two tons each and traveled at 30 miles per hour. Today, the Amtrak Regional trains that travel over McNeill's bridge have engines that weigh in excess of one hundred tons and pull eight sixty-ton cars at 125 miles per hour. Scottish stoneworkers who were members of the Ancient and Accepted Order of Freemasons were largely responsible for the masonry work, and Masonic symbols can be seen inscribed in many of the stone blocks in the bridge. The structure has been in continuous service for 176 years. Some idea of the esteem held by the Canton Viaduct in the engineering community lies in the observation that the Canton Viaduct entry in Wikipedia is eleven pages long, but the entry for the Golden Gate Bridge is only nine pages long.

Like the Boston and Worcester Railroad, the Boston and Providence Railroad opened in stages. At the then-current end of line, stagecoaches completed the trip. On July 28, 1835, the first trains ran the whole distance from Boston to Providence. Well, not *exactly* to Providence…

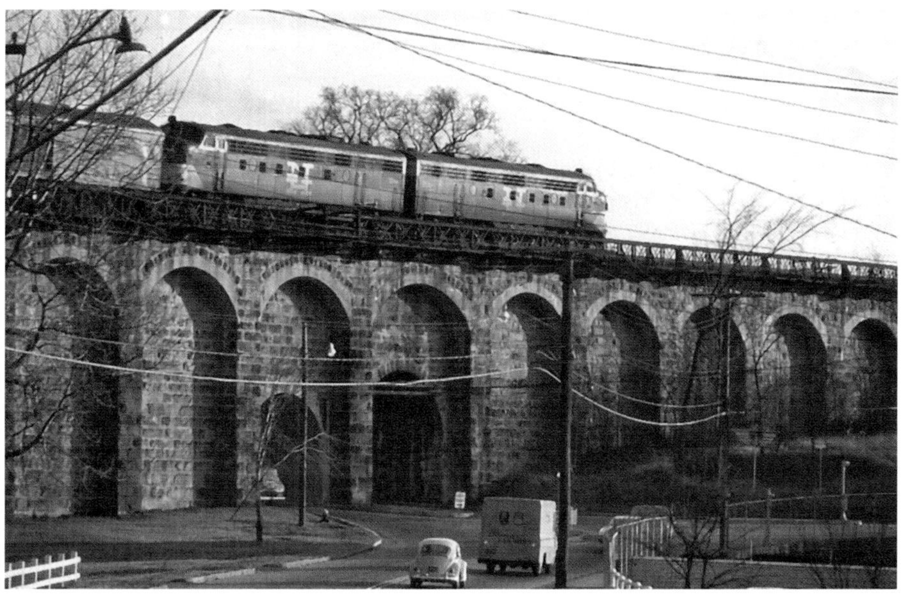

The Canton Viaduct in a view from 1966. The "blind arcade cavity wall" construction can clearly be seen. The arches do not support the weight of the tracks. *Photo by Donald Haskel.*

The original Boston and Providence Railroad line generally followed the current Amtrak line to a point a little south of Attleboro. A few miles beyond Attleboro, at a location today called East Junction, the Amtrak line bends west, and the original Boston and Providence Railroad line, today a little-used freight branch of the Providence and Worcester Railroad called the East Junction branch, continues in a straight line toward Providence. It leaves Massachusetts at North Seekonk and enters Rhode Island (recall, however, that at the time the line was built, East Providence belonged to Massachusetts). Past Rumford, the track bends slightly to the right, crosses a small bridge and, just before King Phillip Road, throws off a track that connects to the Providence and Worcester Railroad's Valley Falls line, which will be discussed later. The end of track is at Dexter Road, but the right of way is easily identifiable, continues under the Henderson Bridge and follows the east bank of the Seekonk River. It continues under Interstate 195, becomes Pier Road and ends at the East Providence Yacht Club, where the remains of the final India Point Railroad Bridge into Providence can be seen. The entire route can be easily traced on Google Earth (www.google.com/earth/index.html).

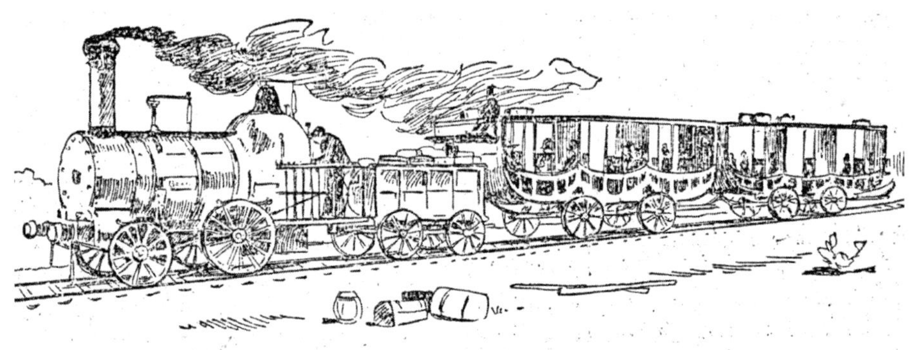

Sketch of a Boston and Providence Railroad train from about 1836. Note that the engine crew has no protection from the elements; it was considered "unmanly" to have same. As train speeds increased, engine crews decided to show their manliness in other ways. *Collection of Edward J. Ozog.*

There is the possibility of some confusion about the actual rail terminus when the line was officially declared open in July 1835. End of track was identified as "India Point (at East Providence)." Today, the geographic nomenclature has changed somewhat. The neighborhood at the southern tip of Providence between the Seekonk and Providence Rivers is called the Fox Point neighborhood. This neighborhood contains two promontories on its southern edge. India Point is on the Seekonk River side, and Fox Point is on the Providence River side. At the time of construction, "India Point" appeared to be a more generic descriptor that included land on both sides of the Seekonk River. So, when the line officially opened, track's end was actually in Massachusetts. So how did passengers get to Providence? They walked or took a carriage. At track's end, there had been a bridge over the Seekonk that could accommodate carriages since 1794. The first *train* did not enter Rhode Island proper until a railroad bridge (one portion of which was covered like the famous New Hampshire covered bridges) was built. Another section was a hand-operated drawbridge, permitting marine traffic to move up the Seekonk. This bridge was completed in December 1835, and Rhode Island was finally connected by rail to Massachusetts. A terminal building was built at India Point near the steamship docks, where India Point Park is today, and was the first railroad station in Rhode Island.

The running time between Boston and Providence was an hour and forty-five minutes, compared to about five hours by stagecoach. The boat service to New York that was the driving force behind the Boston and Providence Railroad began immediately. Commodore Cornelius Vanderbilt

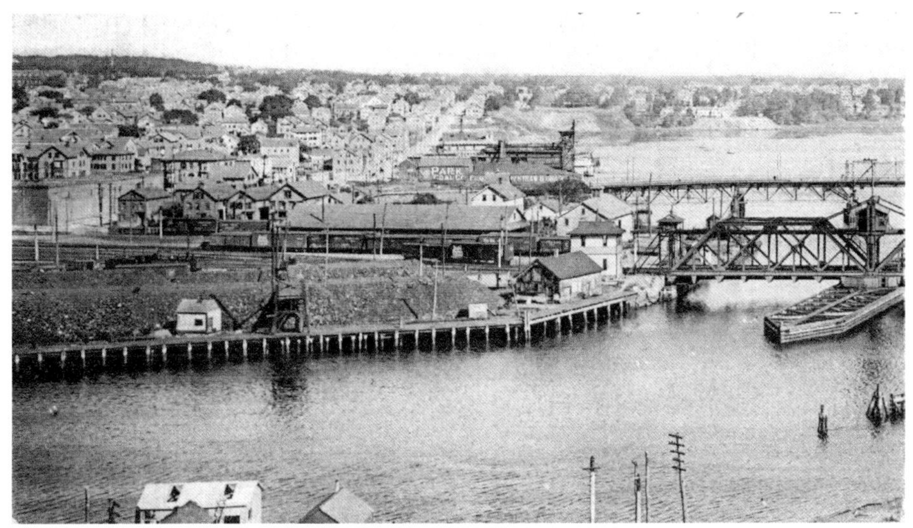

Bridges at the mouth of the Seekonk River in 1906. Inbound Boston and Providence Railroad trains entered Providence from the right. The bridge situation at this location is complex. There have been at least a half dozen different road and railroad bridges over the years. *Collection of Edward J. Ozog.*

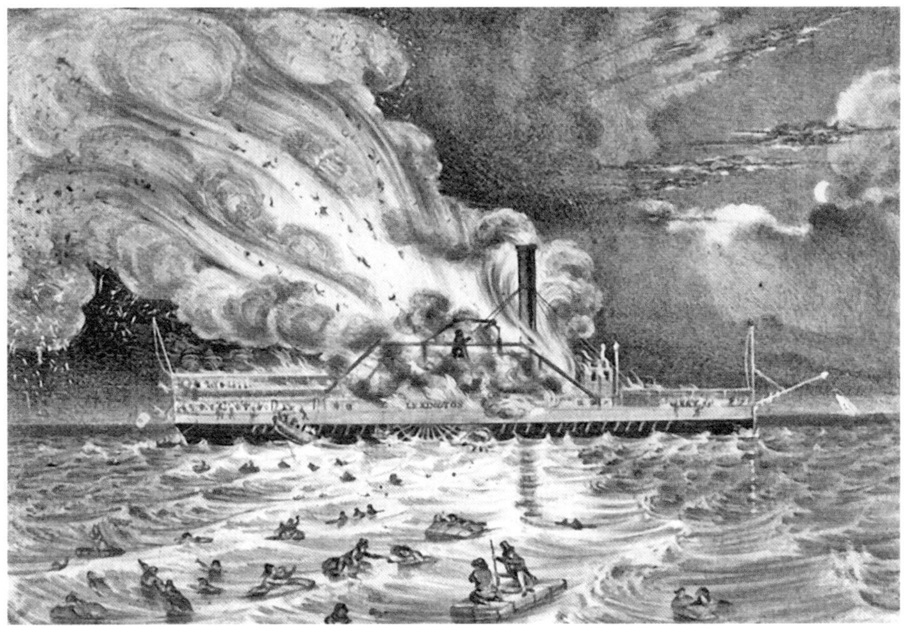

Disaster aboard the *Lexington* en route from New York to Stonington. *Library of Congress.*

commissioned a brand-new side-wheel steamer, the *Lexington*, which made the trip to New York in only eleven and a half hours. Two years later, the *Lexington* was transferred to Stonington after the completion of the Stonington Line permitted train service from Boston to Stonington. Unfortunately, the *Lexington* came to a tragic end in 1840 when she caught fire and sank, with great loss of life.

THE BOSTON AND PROVIDENCE RAILROAD
THROUGH THE YEARS

The Boston and Providence Railroad was an immediate financial success and built several branch lines in Massachusetts. In 1888, the Boston and Providence Railroad was leased for ninety-nine years to the Old Colony Railroad, a large enterprise based in Massachusetts. The New York, New Haven and Hartford Railroad, which eventually became the dominant railroad in southern New England, then leased the Old Colony in 1893. The New York, New Haven and Hartford Railroad itself was merged with the New York Central and Pennsylvania Railroads into the Penn Central Railroad in 1968. The Penn Central Railroad declared bankruptcy in 1970, but before it was liquidated, it legally merged with the Old Colony Railroad in 1972. Subsequently, the MBTA bought the original Boston and Providence Railroad right of way from Boston to East Junction, calling it the Providence/Stoughton Line, and the Providence and Worcester Railroad took over the remainder of track from East Junction to India Point. This complex genealogy is typical of surviving New England railroads.

It is remarkable that almost all of the original 176-year-old right of way of the Boston and Providence Railroad can be traced today, and some of its structures, like the Canton Viaduct, are still in use. With its completion, Rhode Island entered the Railroad Age. But you still couldn't get from Providence to South County by train. That will have to wait until the next chapter.

Chapter 5

SOUTH COUNTY JOINS THE WORLD

Even as ground was being broken for the Boston and Providence Railroad in 1832, the next link in the chain of railroads that would eventually permit an all-rail journey from Boston to New York via Providence was being forged in Connecticut and Rhode Island. This line would go from Providence to Stonington, Connecticut, a distance of about forty-seven miles. As was the case with the Boston and Providence Railroad, two separate state railroad charters were obtained: the New York and Stonington Railroad in Connecticut and the New York, Providence and Boston Railroad in Rhode Island. These names reflected the optimism of their promoters rather than the practical realities of the situation. The two companies were merged into the single New York, Providence and Boston Railroad in 1833, and construction started in Stonington in August of that year and from Providence soon after. Unlike the situation for the railroads discussed so far, most of the original capital for the new railroad came from New York.

From the perspective of the twenty-first century, as we look back at the explosion of railroad building that took place between 1830 and 1875, our initial response might be, "What were those people thinking?" Railroads were being built from Nowhere City to Emptyville all over the USA, and there was often no reasonable prospect of their ever making money. Two and even three railroads sometimes operated parallel tracks between cities, and Chicago had six completely separate train terminals.

Part of this enthusiasm was rational. Railroad trains *did* represent a dramatically improved transportation technology that soon after their introduction were traveling four to five times as fast as their predecessors, the stagecoaches. In contemporary terms, this would be as if the first passenger jet plane in American service, the Boeing 707, could travel 1,500 miles an hour, compared to the 375 miles per hour of its propeller-driven immediate ancestor, the Lockheed Constellation.

However, most of the impetus for this overbuilding of railroads came from the same kind of financial speculation that led to the "Tulip Mania" in Holland, the "South Seas Bubble" in England and, in our time, the recent explosion and crash in the derivatives and subprime markets. Economists argue as to the causes for financial bubbles, but perhaps the most engaging idea is the "Bigger Fool" hypothesis—it doesn't matter what you pay for something, as long as you can find a bigger fool to pay you more. There was much P.T. Barnum–style hucksterism in the promotional literature for railroad stock prospectuses in the nineteenth century. The appeal to potential railroad stock buyers was similar to pitches that today attract people hoping to get in on the ground floor of the next Apple or Microsoft.

The New York, Providence and Boston Railroad did not quite fit into this speculative model. There was a clear and definable market—large numbers of travelers between Boston and Providence and Providence and New York who wished to avoid the over-the-rail, green face–inducing seas of Point Judith. Other than in the formidable Great Swamp mentioned in chapter 2, construction would be straightforward and relatively inexpensive.

The engineers who built the Boston and Providence Railroad (Whistler and McNeill) were engaged to build the new railroad. Construction started from both ends of the line and was completed in 1837. In Providence, there was not a direct connection between the earlier Boston and Providence Railroad, which had a terminal at India Point, and the new line. The New York, Providence and Boston Railroad built its first station at a location that today would be under the west end of the new Iway Bridge, at Collier Point Park. Ferry slips on either side of the Providence River permitted a five- to ten-minute ride between the two termini.

From Collier Point, the line followed the coastline in a southeast direction until the Thurber's Avenue curve on the contemporary I-95 and then bent to the southwest. This curve is near where today's Providence and Worcester Railroad has its South Providence Yard. The line then roughly paralleled the present Providence and Worcester Railroad South Providence branch along I-95, running on the northeast edge of Roger Williams Park. Even

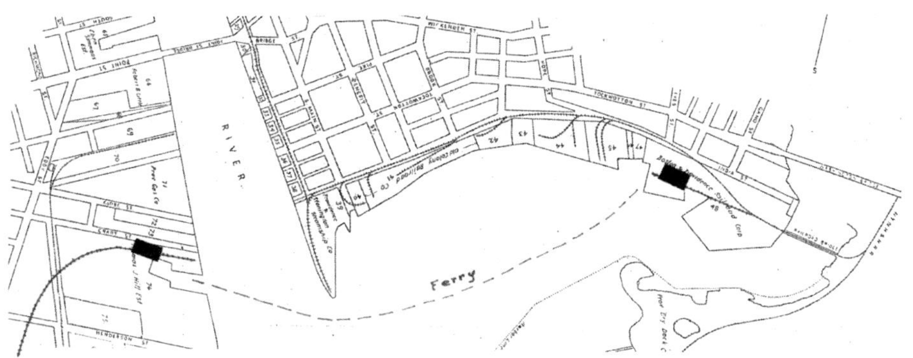

The ferry connection between the Boston and Providence and New York, Providence and Boston Railroads. *Collection of Edward J. Ozog.*

today, in 2012, if you are driving north on I-95 near Providence, you can frequently see Providence and Worcester Railroad locomotives pulling strings of ethanol cars to the terminal at South Providence to meet the mainline just south of Park Avenue in Cranston, Rhode Island, at a place named Cranston Switch (also known sometimes as Harbor Switch).

The Providence and Worcester Railroad's South Providence branch today follows the original New York, Providence and Boston Railroad route from Providence Harbor to Cranston Switch near the Wellington Avenue overpass crossing I-95. Cranston Switch is where today's Amtrak line separates from the Providence and Worcester Railroad South Providence branch, which bears northeast on its way to Providence.

From Cranston Switch, Amtrak follows almost exactly the original New York, Providence and Boston Railroad alignment. It heads southwest to East Greenwich and then continues roughly southwest again to North Kingstown, and it is there that things start getting interesting.

The routing from Providence to East Greenwich made economic sense. At the time, East Greenwich was a thriving community with political, commercial and military interests in the state, and it could be anticipated that a fair number of passengers would board or debark at "East G." The line from Providence more or less followed a southerly direction, as the coast line to the east was heavily incised. If the intent had been, as originally discussed by the founders, to provide the fastest route from Providence to Stonington, from East Greenwich the line should then have followed a direct southwesterly line through the south central and then southwestern part of the state and then on to Stonington. This route would also have avoided the Great Swamp. But that's not the way it went, and the route's peculiarities offer room for some speculation.

In the 1830s, the commercial center of the town of North Kingstown, which lies directly south of East Greenwich, was the village of Wickford. A shipbuilding community, it provided a port for both fishing boats and coastal freight schooners. It was also a market center for the large agricultural plantations that surrounded it.

There was no geographical reason why the abuilding New York, Providence and Boston Railroad could not have headed directly from East Greenwich to Wickford. Many years later, the Seaview trolley railroad did exactly that. But the new line bypassed Wickford by three miles and instead took a ten-mile straight path from East Greenwich to Slocum in South Kingstown and then bent gently toward the west.

WHY DID THE RAILROAD AVOID WICKFORD?

In North Kingstown, as in many places in New England, there were often conflicts between rural, agricultural interests and those of a more mercantile or industrial nature. The opening of trade to the West was a two-edged sword for New Englanders. It offered an inexpensive way to ship eastern manufactured products to the West, but it also permitted inexpensive western agricultural products to compete successfully against eastern farm goods.

Wickford's main business was in the maritime area, and the coming of a railroad would permit the import of less expensive building materials for ships but, at the same time, offer competition for the goods that had previously been brought by sea into the port of Wickford.

Added to this consideration was the fact that agriculture in southern Rhode Island more closely resembled the large plantations of the South than the small, hardscrabble farms of northern New England. A few old families like the Hazards and Tuckers owned huge tracts of land, which remained relatively intact in these families because they practiced primogeniture, the custom of leaving an entire estate to the eldest son, rather than dividing it among the children. The scions of these families saw what was happening to the cities, with their industrialization and importation of immigrants whose religion was distasteful to their Protestant leanings, and many of them wanted no part of it. In their view, the coming of the railroad marked the end of a desirable way of life.

So we might speculate that the route between East Greenwich and North Kingstown was determined by a complex of reasons that might have included an inability to secure a right of way to the west or south from recalcitrant plantation owners and a conflict between commercial interests in Wickford, some of whom wanted the trains to come through the middle of town, and others who would have been happier if the railroad was close, but not too close, to the village.

The Wickford area was bypassed entirely when the line opened in 1837. When local trains were added a year later, the trains stopped at a location called Wickford Junction, where the Newport and Wickford Railroad and Steamship Company eventually built a three-mile line to Wickford village in the 1870s. The proponents of a direct route from East Greenwich to Wickford were ironically vindicated when, over the next forty years, Wickford declined economically in comparison to the nearby communities that had easier rail access.

From Wickford Junction, the New York, Providence and Boston Railroad proceeded arrow-straight through what are today turf farms (turf represents Rhode Island's largest agricultural crop) and what is facetiously called the "Rhode Island Desert," a large sand and gravel operation popular with dirt bikers. After a gentle bend to the right, the tracks proceeded to the vicinity of one of the larger villages in South County, Kingston.

Kingston, which was known until 1825 as "Little Rest" for reasons best left to historical argument, was one of the early villages in the southern part of the state, along with Peace Dale, Wakefield and Narragansett. Kingston was built atop Kingston Hill, which is not much of a hill by Colorado standards, rising merely 170 feet above the future tracks. It was enough of a hill, however, to add to the cost of routing the railroad to the village, should that be the option selected, although if the railroad had headed due south from the area of Slocum, there would have been a very gentle climb up Kingston Hill.

As usual when the topic was railroads, opinions around the state varied as to the wisdom of a particular routing, usually depending on how the opinion-giver perceived that his particular ox was going to be gored by its construction. Kingston, which until the 1820s had been a seat of local government, saw its influence decreasing as the nearby villages of Peace Dale and Wakefield started to take the first steps toward a manufacturing economy. Kingston had been notably unsuccessful in its first few humble steps away from farming. Idiosyncratic as always, Kingston tried making beaver hats and shoes. It started a newspaper, which lasted for only a year. A few tiny textile mills opened but succeeded only in annoying local farmers, who objected to the damming of their fishing brooks to power the mills.

In the meantime, under the guidance of the very powerful Hazard family, Peace Dale, Wakefield and Narragansett were developing into compact textile manufacturing areas, not on the scale of Lowell or Woonsocket, but self-sustaining and capable of making long-term profits. From the point of view of Wakefield business interests, the new railroad should go right through Peace Dale or Wakefield, but Kingston Hill provided a barrier for a direct route. However, it was already becoming evident from experience in Massachusetts that branches from a mainline could serve communities not on a direct route almost as well as being on a mainline, so near was not as good as next to but not a bad compromise if a branch could be built later.

A contrary voice was expressed by a Newport-based member of the ubiquitous Hazard family, Benjamin Hazard, attorney and member of the Rhode Island state legislature. Hazard, speaking for Newport maritime interests, was concerned that a railroad running through South County and being close to its ports would provide significant competition for Newport's coastal shipping trade. The Kingston newspaper, the *Advocate*, made it into a bit of a town-mouse and city-mouse affair, complaining that anytime someone proposed something that would benefit honest farmers (conveniently leaving out that many of these honest farmers were also *rich* farmers), some city politico would squash the idea.

A compromise was evidently reached wherein the line would go through what is called today West Kingston and a station would be built there. Thus, technically, there is no Kingston Station—it should be called the West Kingston Station, but nobody calls it that. The first station in the Kingston area was located about a half mile to the northeast of the present Amtrak station, where Waites Corner Road crosses the track. It would have been about a two-mile stagecoach ride into Kingston up the hill and another two into Peace Dale. More about Kingston Station will be presented in a later chapter.

Once the route had been decided, construction of the New York, Providence and Boston Railroad (or Stonington Line, as it was almost universally called in its day) was slow but uneventful. While it was being built, the rail-steamboat connections at Providence thrived. A new "technology" was developed for this service. Typically, before the 1830s, transportation services didn't operate on a schedule; the stagecoach or ship left when it was full. With the development of combined services, it was essential that the train or ship not be left standing idle while waiting for its counterpart to arrive. This became critical when workers started being paid by the hour rather than the day. The solution was the timetable, and some of the earliest timetables in the United States were published for the Providence train-ship connection.

The Stonington Steamship Line had been formed as the maritime arm of the Stonington rail line. Its first vessel was the *Narragansett*, and on

November 9, 1837, she left New York for the overnight trip to Stonington. Upon arriving, passengers trekked to the railroad-built Wadawanuck House hotel for breakfast. After the meal, the pioneer travelers returned to the pier, where they boarded two eight-car trains for the maiden trip to Providence, which took about two and a half hours. "Eight-car train" sounds a bit more imposing than the actuality. The first railroad passenger cars were just stagecoach bodies suspended on leather springs and held eight to twelve passengers in varying degrees of discomfort. Coincidentally, the Amtrak Northeast Corridor Regional trains, traveling along the same right of way, also have eight cars, but the potential passenger load is over five hundred.

A Ride on the Stonington Line

Downtown Providence in 1837 would be almost unrecognizable to a time traveler from today. Like Boston, most of the downtown area was built on filled ground. The land around today's Route 6-10 Connector was swampy, and there was a circular cove where Citizen's Plaza is presently located.

The nearby Stonington Line terminal was unprepossessing but did have canopies for weather protection. The awaiting train would be minuscule by today's standards. The locomotive would have a tall smokestack flared at the top and a single pair of driving wheels. There was no protection for the engine crew from the elements—it was not considered manly to have such. The cars would be instantly recognizable to stagecoach passengers. They were, in fact, stagecoaches. The cars were connected by lengths of chain, and the resultant slack between cars meant a rather abrupt start for passengers in the final coach, because the engine might have traveled fifteen feet before the final car started moving. There were brakes, of a sort, on the tender of the engine and on each of the cars. These brakes were applied through a wheel and screw mechanism by a brakeman on each car.

Typically, the early locomotives burned yellow pine fuel, which was brought to Stonington by schooner from the South. Yellow pine burned very hot but very fast, so a load of wood on the tiny tenders was good for about twenty-two miles. Judging from the few pictures that exist of the early passenger cars, it appears that they would be subject to a pronounced fore-and-aft pitching movement, and in reality, it might have been a tossup (or throw-up) between a Stonington Line trip or a nasty voyage around Point Judith. Of course, travel by air coach today is not much of an improvement.

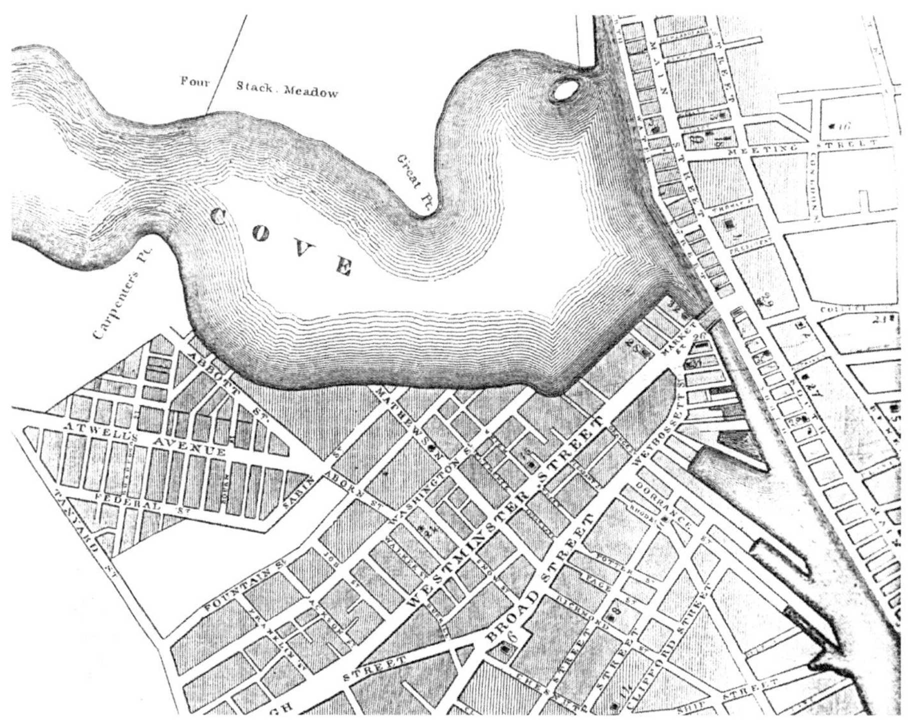

Pre-railroad downtown Providence. Much of the present downtown Providence area was a tidal basin surrounded by marshlands. *Collection of Edward J. Ozog.*

The early engines did not have what the layman calls a cowcatcher but the railroader calls a pilot. This is a device, pointed on the early locomotives, intended to deflect objects on the track, like a cow, and prevent a derailment. They did not exactly *catch* the cow but, more exactly, sped it on its way to becoming steaks. As the locomotives were very light, an encounter with a cow, which could be expected on the open farmlands of South County, was not a trivial matter.

Top speed was in the vicinity of thirty miles per hour, which, given the roughness of the track made by early methods, must have produced an E-ticket ride. Nevertheless, on a nice summer day, young bucks would sometimes ride on the roofs of the cars, which produced the added thrill of the possibility of having your hair catch on fire from the volcano of sparks spewed by the engine.

We can roughly imagine what the trip might have sounded like. Early rails were twenty to thirty feet long and fashioned together with bolted clamps (when steel rails came into general use thirty years later, the length was standardized in the United States at thirty-nine feet). Every time a wheel passed over a rail joint, a sound would be made. And here, Dear Reader, you will be introduced to a piece of trivia that will enable you to amaze your friends if you watch videos of old movies. From the earliest days on American railroads, the joints between rails were staggered by about four feet on each side of the track. On European and English railroads, the joints on the two sides were parallel. With four wheels on each wheel carriage assembly (truck) on either end of the car, what you would hear when riding an American train would be "clikity-clack, clikity-clack, clikity-clack." What you would hear on an English train would be "ta-DUMP…ta-DUMP…ta-DUMP." So, if there was an American movie purporting to show someone riding an English train, if you heard "clikity-clack," you would know the producers were cheap and just recorded a nearby American train instead of the real thing. Alas, for the past thirty years or so, rails have been welded together and then filed smooth, so no more clikity-clack, just a smooth hiss, unless you pass over a switch.

From this description, one might conclude that early rail travel was not exactly luxurious, and that would be a correct observation. It probably explains why Long Island Sound steamboat service survived well into the

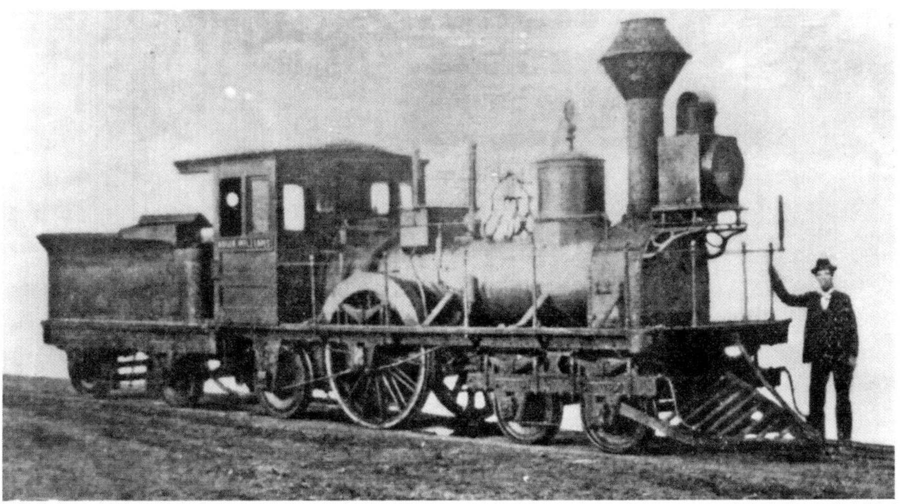

One of the New York, Providence and Boston Railroad's earliest locomotives, built in 1836 as the *Pawcatuck*. It was rebuilt in 1846 and became almost unrecognizable, gaining four wheels in front and two wheels in back of the massive driving wheels. It was renamed the *Roger Williams*. *Collection of Edward J. Ozog.*

Announcement of the first trains on the New York, Providence and Boston Railroad. Notice that a definite time of departure is not indicated. Timetables would appear a few years later. *Rhode Island Railroad Museum.*

twentieth century, despite the later availability of all-rail service from Boston to New York. This was true especially on the Fall River Line boats that went in service in 1847 and lasted until 1937. The later boats were big (over four hundred feet long), fast, comfortable, relatively inexpensive and, at least in first class, very luxurious. Rail travel did not begin to come to this standard until the end of the nineteenth century, and by that time, many people were cemented into the steamboat habit. Another reason for the longevity of steamboat service may have been arrival time at the termini for business travelers. If you lived in Boston and wanted to be in New York for a nine o'clock business meeting, an overnight train that took four to six hours would have to leave past midnight for a reasonable morning arrival time. A steamship might leave around dinnertime, offer spacious sleeping quarters and abundant on-board entertainment and arrive around eight o'clock the next morning. Speed wasn't always the cardinal virtue.

WHERE DO WE GO FROM STONINGTON?

Stonington was never intended to be the permanent end of the line for rail service from Boston. The first rail connection beyond Stonington was provided not by a rail line along the Connecticut shore but with the Long Island Railroad, which completed its line from New York City to Greenport at the tip of the North Shore of Long Island in 1844. A ferry service between Greenport and Stonington opened in that same year.

Rail service along the Connecticut shore proceeded in fits and starts. The first segment of what eventually would be a continuous rail line from Stonington to New York was provided by the New York and New Haven Railroad running east from New York City. It was chartered in 1844 and put into service in 1849. The next section was the New Haven and New London Railroad, which was completed in 1850. Trains crossed the Connecticut River at Old Saybrook by means of a car ferry, which could carry the entire train with its passengers across the river. Needless to say, this was a costly and time-consuming procedure.

The next portion ran east from New London to Stonington. Another car ferry provided the crossing of the Thames River. This line was completed in 1858 under the name of the New Haven, New London and Stonington Railroad. For a few years, dockage of the Long Island Sound boat connections was moved to Groton in anticipation of more business with connections from Norwich, but after disappointing results, dockage returned to Stonington. The Stonington Line eventually bought the Groton and Stonington segment from the New Haven, New London and Stonington Railroad. Thus, by the mid-1800s, it was possible to journey by rail from Boston to New York (albeit with a few delays due to river crossings, necessitating a ferry ride).

All of these lines were eventually absorbed by the New York, New Haven and Hartford ("New Haven") Railroad, which was chartered in 1872 and eventually swallowed over one hundred smaller railroad lines in New England and New York. The New Haven was also known at the time as the Consolidated Railroad. In the last decade of the nineteenth century, J. Pierpont Morgan and William D. Rockefeller, titans of American banking and industry, joined the board of directors of the New Haven and began a twenty-year program of expansion, improvement and exploitation that resulted in near-bankruptcy in 1913, the result of an assumption of an insupportable debt.

Two physical barriers prevented an uninterrupted rail trip along the shore. The Thames and Connecticut Rivers presented obstacles that were more political than geographical. Both the Thames and Connecticut were navigable, and the shipping interests that ran the river service were astute politically. Although bridges were feasible and even relatively easy to construct (though the Thames River bridge presented some difficulties with its piers), the owners of the riverine ship lines quite reasonably pointed out that bridges presented a hazard to navigation. At the Thames, the U.S. Navy had a large facility upriver of any proposed bridge, and it, too, objected to a rail crossing. To elevate the bridges high enough to clear any river shipping would have been prohibitively expensive. As a result, trains crossed both rivers by car ferries, which interrupted the trip and added time to the journey. It was not until the technology of the drawbridge was adapted to the long-span requirements of railroad use that it became possible to bridge the Thames and Connecticut Rivers with assent from objecting parties. The Connecticut was bridged with a drawbridge in 1870, and the Thames was not bridged, incredibly, until 1889.

THE STONINGTON LINE DERAILS

The Stonington Line was in financial trouble almost from the day the first train ran. Like most railroads of the day, its property was heavily mortgaged, and faith in the value of its bonds was a function of overall confidence in the national economy, as well as perception of the value of the property itself. Unfortunately, just as Pets.com was introduced right as the dot.com bubble burst, the Stonington Line chugged into view just in time to get caught in the Panic of 1837.

This economic collapse bears eerie resemblance to the situation in the United States in 2008. Some of the factors that contributed to the Panic of 1837 were extravagant speculation in land; easy, unrestricted credit; government-sponsored low-interest rates; state government indebtedness; unbridled personal spending; and a belief that prosperity would last, if not forever, at least for a very long time. Finally, there was a collapse in the value of financial instruments like bonds, mortgages and stocks, especially those that were, to use today's term, heavily leveraged. It would appear that the more things change, the more they stay the same.

In 1839, the Stonington Line went into what would today be called receivership. The property was not returned to its stockholders until 1843, and the original bondholders took a financial bath, losing 50 percent of their investment.

It is sobering to recognize that the chilling effect of the Panic of 1837 lasted a decade. There was not a new railroad constructed in Rhode Island until 1847. But then railroad construction restarted with a vengeance, and the first new line to be built was one that still runs today: the Providence and Worcester Railroad.

Chapter 6

THE OTHER SURVIVOR

The Providence and Worcester Railroad

The Panic of 1837 had three primary causes: 1) the cutting off of funds to the United States from Great Britain, which was having financial problems of its own; 2) the calling in of loans by American banks that had extravagantly extended credit; and 3) a contraction of the money supply by the federal government's insistence that it be paid for federal land sales in "hard" (gold and silver) money. The panic was followed by six years of depression. By 1843, the depression had started to lift, and Rhode Island again began to feel the stirring of railroad lust.

This feeling was expressed most strongly in the northern part of the state, which by that time had been firmly established as the center of manufacturing and industry. The small city of Woonsocket had been built on the Blackstone River at one of two sites where there was a significant change of elevation in the riverbed, thus opening the possibility of water-powered mills. Samuel Slater built his mill at Pawtucket Falls, and Woonsocket developed around the thirty-one-foot drop at Woonsocket Falls.

To the north, across the Massachusetts line, the city of Worcester was beginning to develop as a railroad junction. The earlier Boston and Worcester Railroad had connected the city with Boston, and in 1839, the Western Railroad opened to Springfield, where connections were later made to Albany, New York. In 1840, the Norwich and Worcester Railroad opened, connecting Worcester with the head of navigation of the Thames River in Norwich. In 1848, the Worcester and Nashua Railroad linked the two manufacturing cities and established a gateway for tourism, which would begin in earnest in the 1850s in the mountains of New Hampshire. There was even a real oddity in New England: a narrow-gauge steam railroad. The Worcester and Shrewsbury Railroad (which never reached Shrewsbury) was a 2.7-mile-long railroad that ran from downtown Worcester to a popular amusement area, Lake Quinsigamond. The locomotive was affectionately called the Dummy because it looked like a streetcar and was muffled so it wouldn't scare horses. This line led an astoundingly long life, outliving many of the "real" railroads that dwarfed it. It lasted until the late 1920s.

During the early part of this period, the Blackstone Valley didn't have a railroad, but it did have the Blackstone Canal, which was an asset to those who used it but not a profit generator for its owners because its construction costs were much higher than anticipated and its maintenance costs were also high. However, in yet another example of the law of unanticipated consequences, the very success and utility of the canal caused its primary users, the mill owners, to ultimately rise against it and urge construction of a railroad. Why? The mills on the Blackstone River were all water powered, and the canal tapped a significant amount of that water to float its boats, as it were. That meant less water available for power generation, hence less output from the mills.

In 1844, discussions began in Providence about the possibility of building a railroad between Providence and Worcester. As was the case with the Boston and Worcester Railroad, most of the capital (and political influence) originated from the larger of the terminal cities. Following the practice of the time, charters were obtained from the two state legislatures, and in 1845, the two charters merged into a single corporate entity, the Providence and Worcester Railroad. In 1845, before the charter was obtained, an engineer named Willis Pratt was hired to survey a possible route.

Pratt's report was a model of clarity, and he explained for his nontechnical readers a fundamental concept in the laying out of a railroad, what is today called the ruling grade. The ruling grade is the steepest portion of a line, and it is the steepness of the ruling grade that is one of the most important determiners of the cost of hauling, say, a ton of freight. The energy cost to raise a carload of potatoes over a hill is very sensitive to the steepness of the steepest part of the railroad grade. For example, let's say that between Providence and Worcester, you could build a line that had a gentle, constant grade. All well and good, but suppose there was a single hill along the way that couldn't be avoided. To get over the hill, you would have to add to each train a second (or third) locomotive that would only be needed on the hill. Or you might have to use a much bigger, hungrier single locomotive.

As a result, by building around the hill rather than over the hill, your initial cost might be a bit higher due to construction expenses, but your long-term operating costs would be lower.

Pratt suggested following the route of the old Blackstone Canal all the way from Worcester to Providence. By the 1840s, the canal had fallen into almost complete disuse, and it would be abandoned totally in 1848. In fact, in the mid-1840s, the organizers of the railroad bought the canal to secure a right of way. In some locations, Pratt actually recommended building over the old canal. He noted in his report, however, that another survey suggested an alternate southern approach to Providence that would not follow the route of the canal exactly. This alternative route would be slightly longer and have a steeper ruling grade than the canal-following route, but it would be closer to the developing population centers immediately north of Providence, offering the possibility of more passenger traffic. This route, which was eventually adopted, branched off from the canal at the long-forgotten but delightfully named village of Sinking Fund, Rhode Island. (Perhaps only Toad Suck, Arkansas, has a greater "What on Earth?" factor.) From Sinking Fund, the line went roughly north of Lonsdale, through Valley Falls, Pawtucket and then into Providence. From Pawtucket south, this is basically the Amtrak line into Providence today.

One huge issue had to be resolved before the route of the line could be finally determined. What would happen when the railroad reached Providence?

Providence has undergone several dramatic makeovers, in each case altering the landscape in such a way as to make the previous version almost unrecognizable. By the early 1840s, the Boston and Providence Railroad had a large station in the area of today's India Point Park, and the New York, Providence and Boston Railroad's trains continued to terminate at Collier Point. It was still necessary to take a ferry between the two stations. Both of the existing stations were located in areas that were becoming increasingly industrialized and were about a mile south of the center of the city's commercial and residential area.

The focus of this commercial area was an embayment of the Providence River called the Cove. It's difficult to visualize today, but the area bounded by Exchange Street to the south, the Pleasant Valley Parkway to the west, Promenade Street and Finance Way to the north and Canal Street to the east was all under water, with marshlands on the border.

With the Providence and Worcester Railroad approaching the city from the north, and the city's other two railroads having termini distant from the population center, the time was ripe for discussions about a new, single-rail terminal for Providence. The Providence and Worcester Railroad took the initiative and requested both permission and a subsidy in the form of a land grant from the City of Providence to build a new Union Station—the first in the United States. The new station would be located on the southern border of the Cove, most of which would be filled in. Needless to say, in addition to enthusiasm from predictable commercial quarters, there was opposition from the ancestors of today's environmentalists, who objected to the loss of open space and the pleasant walking areas on the boundaries of the Cove, like today's Promenade Street. Progress was not to be denied, however, and a compact was entered between the three railroads and the City of Providence to build the new station. Before the station could be built, however, there would have to be some dramatic realignments of the existing railroads. In the meantime, with assurance of a terminal location, final corporate organization and construction of the Providence and Worcester Railroad could begin.

Issued in 1845, the original charter of the Providence and Worcester Railroad was highly unusual for the times and tells us much about the mixed feelings communities and the financial establishment had about railroads at the time. The first odd component was a specification that the maximum annual stockholder dividend was to be 12 percent. This sounds generous by today's terms, but not so for the day. What this meant in practical terms was that if there was profit generated above the dividend maximum, those funds were to be put back into the railroad rather than into the shareholders' pockets. The implication of this is clear—the Providence and Worcester Railroad was to be built to provide a service rather than to maximize profit for investors. In an era of unbridled and largely unregulated capitalism, where did this seeming altruism come from? A look at the list of chartered stockholders suggests an answer. They were mostly men who had industrial interests along the route of the railroad, and it was to the advantage of their primary businesses to have a well-built and well-run railroad serve their industries.

The second component is highly unusual and may provide the first known example of a "Poison Pill" stockholder protection plan. The Poison Pill structure is usually attributed to Martin Lipton, a corporate lawyer who described it in 1982, during the era of the "hostile takeover." The idea of a hostile takeover was explored in the 1991 movie *Other People's Money* starring Danny DeVito. In a hostile takeover, a corporate "raider" looks for a company that has a lot of tangible assets like cash, inventory or plant but a low stock price, perhaps because the company is in an unglamourous area of business. Secretly, the raider buys enough shares to secure sufficient seats on the board of directors to gain control of the company. Once achieving control, the captive board votes to liquidate the company and distribute the profits to the shareholders, who make bundles of money. (The fictional company in the movie was called the New England Wire and Cable Company, and the exteriors were shot at an actual wire mill in Georgetown, Connecticut, called the Gilbert and Bennet Mills. Ironically, subsequent to the movie, Gilbert and Bennet, the real company, was subject to a hostile takeover by Kuwaitis, and the company was dismembered in 2001.)

The Providence and Worcester Railroad's Poison Pill provided a complex mechanism that ensured that if outsiders tried to buy into the company, the price of the stock would automatically be jacked up enough to repel the attack. In the case of the Providence and Worcester Railroad, the idea of this structure was to keep the railroad intact to service its area and rebuff the predators who might buy a local railroad to milk it dry. So it appears that the original directors of the Providence and Worcester Railroad were about 140 years ahead of their time.

Construction of the Providence and Worcester Railroad began in 1847 and was both swift and relatively uneventful. At about the same time, work started on the new station, and the other two railroads that would share it began their track realignments. Both roads independently decided that it would be inefficient and costly to extend their lines north from their existing terminals. For the Stonington Line, an extension would require running a line through what had become very expensive real estate. For the Boston and Providence Railroad, College Hill would force the tracks right down to the edge of the Providence River along a major thoroughfare. Something more drastic would be needed.

For the Boston and Providence Railroad, the decision was made to build a four-and-a-half-mile extension from the existing mainline at Dodgeville, Massachusetts, a bit south of Attleboro, to a junction with the new Providence and Worcester Railroad line in the north end of Pawtucket. The point of origin of this line in Attleboro is known as East Junction, and the intersection with the Providence and Worcester Railroad in Central Falls is called Boston Switch. These names are used today by the railroaders operating trains over these lines. The original Boston and Providence Railroad line to East Providence survives and is owned today by the Providence and Worcester Railroad in its Rhode Island portion and by the Massachusetts Bay Transportation Authority (whose trains today

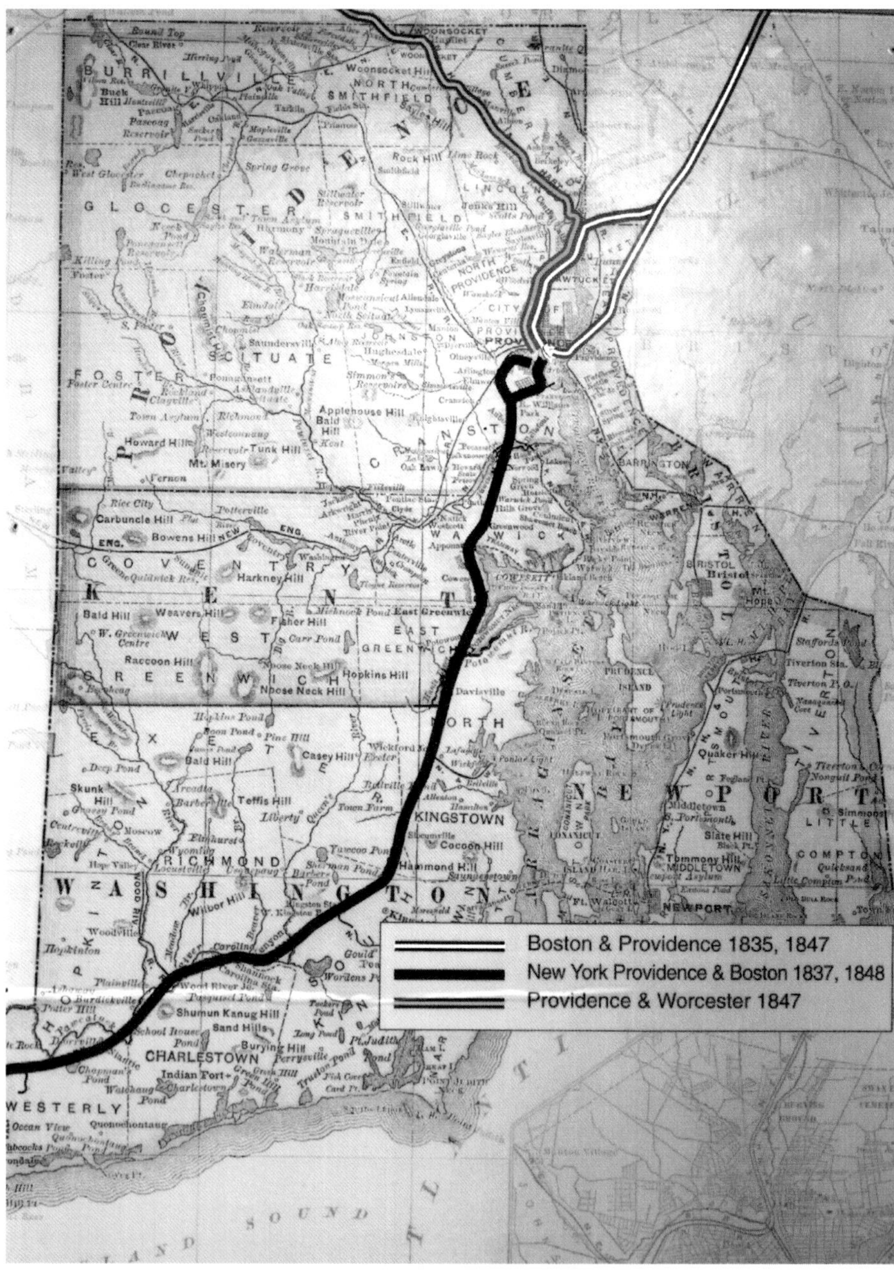

The construction of the Providence and Worcester Railroad and the new route into Providence by the Boston and Providence Railroad. Also shown is the rerouting of the New York, Providence and Boston Railroad into Providence's new Union Station. *Rhode Island Railroad Museum.*

are operated by the Massachusetts Bay Commuter Railroad Company) in Massachusetts. Collectively, it is now known as the East Junction Branch. Originally, ownership of the Pawtucket-Providence section of the mainline was shared by the Boston and Providence Railroad and Providence and Worcester Railroad, but today the co-owners are Amtrak and the Providence and Worcester Railroad.

The process of building a new entrance to Providence for the Stonington Line was a bit more complex. From the south, the new line branched off the old main (which is today's Providence and Worcester Railroad's Harbor Branch line) at Cranston Junction (Harbor Branch Junction) near the baseball field in Roger Williams Park. From there, the line bent to the west until it intersected the route of today's 6-10 Connector highway into Providence. The original line in Providence was located to the south of today's Amtrak line.

The First Union Station

Providence has experienced bouts of civic boosterism ever since its beginnings, most recently in the late 1970s to '90s, when it dubbed itself the "Renaissance City." In the 1840s, it viewed itself as a serious rival to New Haven, and it wanted its new train station to reflect its ambitions. Here we are introduced to a quaint and long-forgotten measure of "big-timeness" in cities: a stub-end train station.

There are two basic designs for a large train station. In a through station, the building is built by the side of the tracks. The incoming train comes from wherever it came, stops and then moves on to its next destination. In a stub-end station, the tracks end at the station. The train stops, discharges its passengers, backs out of the station, turns around, backs into the station, picks up a new load and returns to its origin. In other words, the station is the end of the line. Most of the great stations of the United States—Los Angeles, Washington, Chicago Union and Grand Central—are all stub-end stations; therefore, Providence needed to have a stub-end station. There were a few technical problems with this idea, however.

The Stonington Line trains would approach the proposed new station from the west. The Boston and Providence Railroad and Providence and Worcester Railroad trains would approach from the north, but there was a possibility that the tracks could bend around what was left of the Cove after it had been mostly filled so they could approach the station from the east. There was no room at the Cove location for a stub-end terminal whose tracks ran north and south. What to do? In a fit of wacky brilliance, the station was designed as *two* stub-end stations facing east and west, joined by a common roof. In railroad parlance, the headhouse is the portion of the station containing the ticket offices, waiting rooms, baggage rooms, etc., separate from the tracks. The new Providence station would have two separate headhouses, the western one serving the Stonington Line and the eastern one the Providence and Worcester and Boston and Providence Railroads. Between the two would be a north–south roadway leading to the promenade road around the remainder of the Cove. However, this road crossed the two through tracks that were provided for nonstop freight trains, and horses and buggies were regularly clipped by these trains, so the road was eventually closed and the space enclosed to make a common headhouse between the two sides of the station.

The first Union Station building was quite remarkable. It was a perfect demonstration of how civic pride sometimes trumps practicality. It was located approximately at the corner of today's Exchange and Washington Streets, next to Kennedy Plaza (formerly Exchange Place). It was the longest building in the country at the time (some historians dispute this assertion; none of them is from Rhode Island). It was designed by a

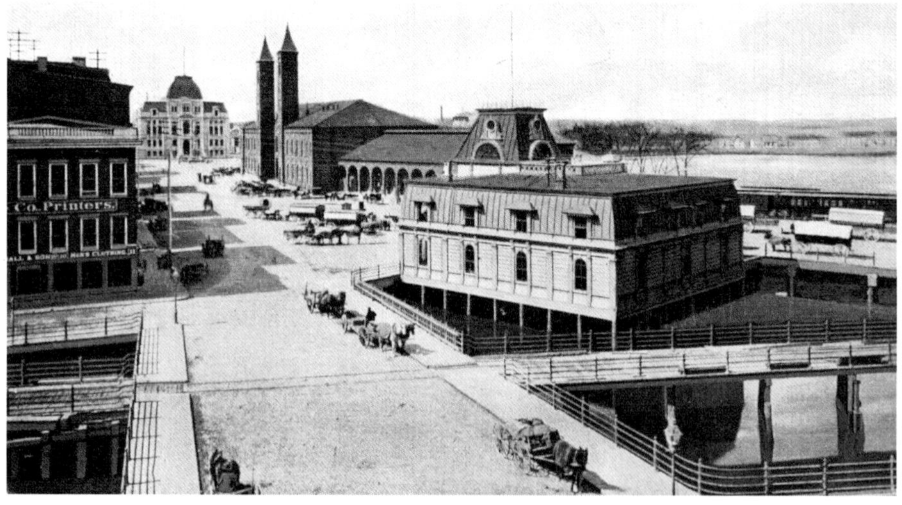

The Tefft station, with Providence City Hall in the background. The Cove, still quite large at this time, is back of the station. The conjoined-stub-end nature of the station can clearly be seen; it is really two separate stations butted end to end. The track in the foreground is a short-lived freight track of the Providence and Worcester Railroad running by the docks on the west side of the Providence River. *Collection of Edward J. Ozog*

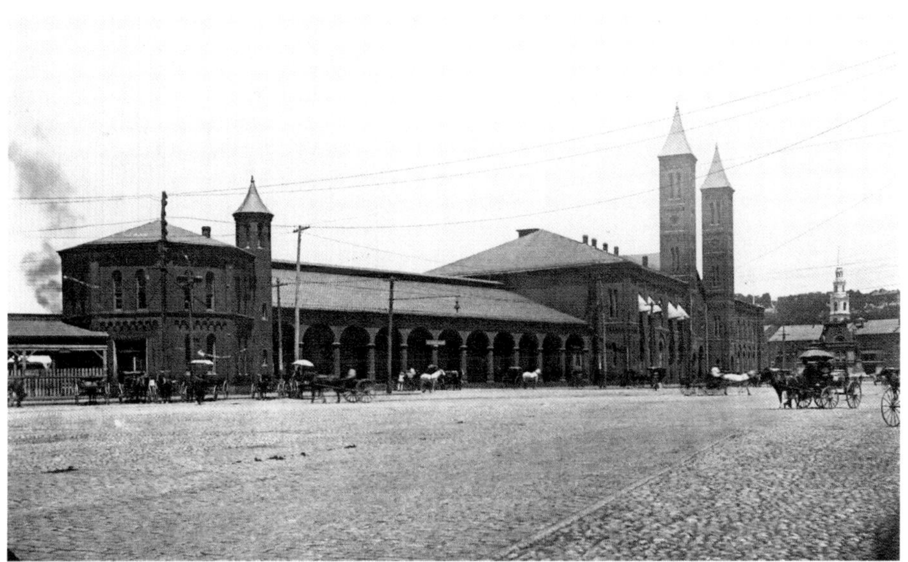

Tefft station with the Old Central Fire Station in mid-background and the spire of the First Baptist Meetinghouse in far background. This was the first Baptist church in America. The statue of General Ambrose Burnside can be seen, dating the photograph after 1886. The statue cost a whopping $10,000—approximately $1 million today. General Burnside was evidently held in high regard. *Collection of Edward J. Ozog*

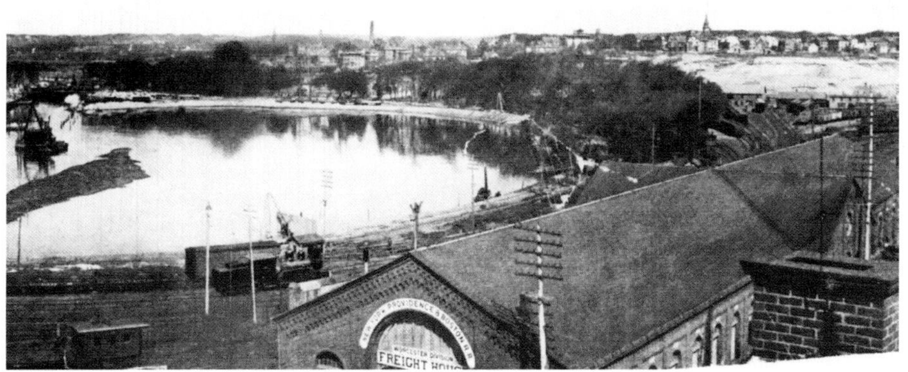

Filling in the Cove for the new Union Station. This view looks roughly to the west. Smith Hill, where the new statehouse will be built, is on the right. *Collection of Edward J. Ozog*

twenty-one-year-old Brown University student named Thomas Alexander Tefft, who at the time worked for the architectural firm of Tallman and Bucklin in Providence. By a strange coincidence, the Tefft family were large landowners in South County. It was designed in the Lombardic form of Romanesque architecture. Tefft also designed the beloved St. Paul's Episcopal Church in Wickford.

The first trains operated on the Providence and Worcester Railroad in 1847, and the Union Station was opened in 1848. Several years later, the line built freight-only tracks on the west side of the Providence River on River Street to Dorrance Street, where a connection was possible with the harbor tracks of the Stonington Line. Slightly later, a second, freight-only track was laid down Water Street to Fox Point, enabling a freight connection with the original Boston and Providence Railroad line.

THE SECOND UNION STATION

The first Union Station was so successful that by the end of the Civil War, discussions were started about a new station that could accommodate not only the original three railroads but also other short lines that were added over the next few decades. These discussions were sometimes acrimonious

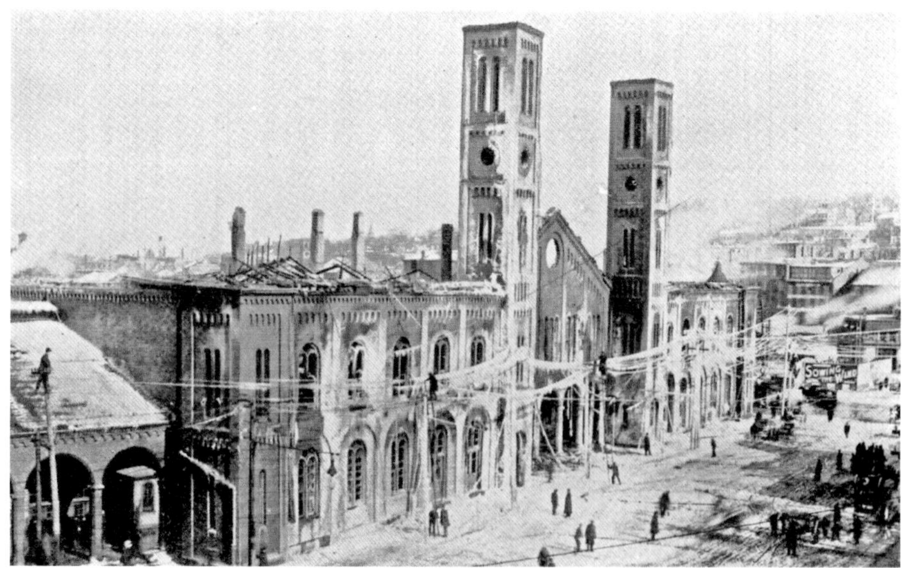

The Tefft station after the fire in 1896. *Collection of Edward J. Ozog.*

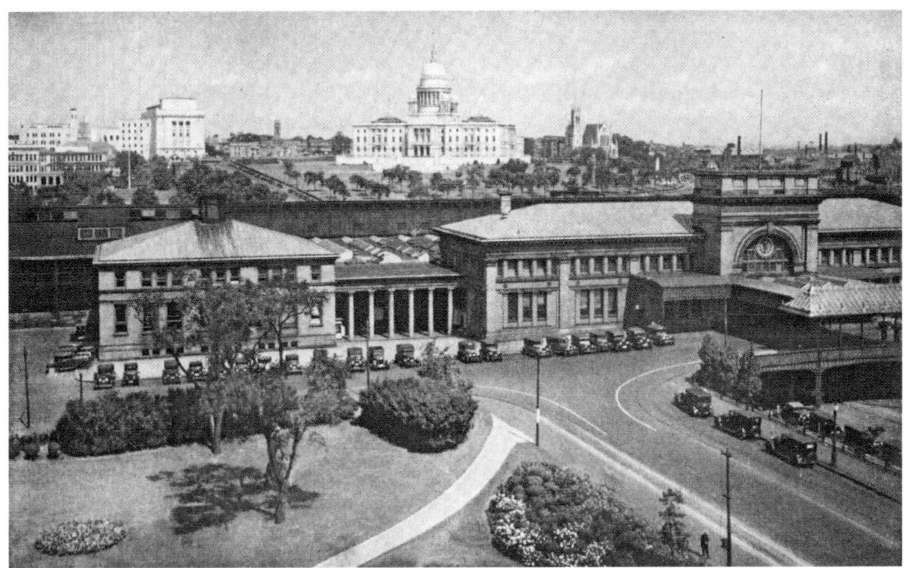

The second Union Station in the late 1920s or early '30s. In the background can be seen the statehouse and the never-completed Masonic Temple. *Collection of Edward J. Ozog.*

because the railroads and the City of Providence did not always see eye to eye on matters of location, size and funding. By 1890, these disagreements were resolved, and work was started on a new through station that would be northwest of the old station, on land created by the filling in of the Cove. The new station was called a "union" station, but in reality, by the time it opened, all the railroads entering Providence were controlled by the New York, New Haven and Hartford Railroad. Whereas the Tefft station had been at ground level, the new station was elevated and reached through a series of viaducts. Critics argued that these constituted a "Chinese Wall" dividing the city, but the viaducts were penetrated frequently by city streets, so the criticism was more aesthetic than functional.

Construction was still in the early stages for the new station in February 1896 when a fire broke out on the second floor of the old Tefft station, and within hours, it was a gutted shell. Completion of the new station was still two years away, but temporary station arrangements were quickly made, and service was uninterrupted. The new station opened in 1898 and remained in service until 1986, when it was replaced by a much smaller station when the viaducts were removed and the tracks lowered below grade in a tunnel.

Success of the Providence and Worcester Railroad

During its original incarnation, the Providence and Worcester Railroad had few expansionist tendencies. It built only one real branch line (still in operation today), the East Providence Branch, in 1875. This branch separates from the mainline at Valley Falls, heads east and then southeast, crosses I-95 on a bridge and then proceeds at street level through Pawtucket. Folks waiting in traffic to see a Pawtucket Red Sox game at McCoy Stadium might well encounter East Providence Branch tracks in the vicinity. The line then heads roughly south and connects with the East Junction branch at King Philip Road in East Providence. The tracks continue for about a half mile southwest of this junction and end at the Henderson Bridge. At one time, the branch was busy carrying coal from the docks in East Providence, but it has seen little use in recent years.

Business was good on the main Providence and Worcester Railroad line right from the beginning, and money was plowed back into the railroad in the form of continual improvements. Traffic warranted putting in a second, parallel track along the length of the line, and the decision to add the track was speeded by a horrific head-on collision at Boston Switch in 1853 that killed thirteen people. This was the first train wreck ever to be photographed and printed in a newspaper. Bridges were strengthened, smaller stations were added and electrical track signals were implemented as soon as they became available, and by the 1870s, another period of great expansion in the American railroad system, the Providence and Worcester Railroad was indeed a first-class line, all out of proportion to its size.

Connections with the Providence and Worcester Railroad

By the mid-nineteenth century, railroads were radiating out of Boston like spokes from a wheel. Most of these lines had modest ambitions; they were content to remain essentially commuter railroads. However, a few rail visionaries had noted that the shortest distance between Boston and New York lies not along what had come to be called the "Shore Line" but inland. Amtrak also noted this in its 2010 "Next-Gen" high-speed rail Boston–New York proposal, which suggests a routing from Boston to Woonsocket to Hartford to New York.

The completion of the Providence and Worcester Railroad stimulated several attempts to provide an alternate, northerly route to Boston that might permit a future more direct connection to New York through central Connecticut. Two of these attempts started at Valley Falls.

When one thinks of "mining rushes," gold in California in the 1840s and silver in Nevada in the 1850s come to mind, but there was a bit of mining fever in the early 1870s in Rhode Island. Since Revolutionary War times, small quantities of a rare kind of iron ore called Cumberlandite were mined from surface deposits in Cumberland, Rhode Island, and used to make iron for cannons. It was not an easy ore to process, but in 1865, a charter was issued for the Rhode Island Mining Railroad Company to build a short railroad from Valley Falls, connecting with the Providence and Worcester Railroad, to the mining area in Cumberland about eight miles away. This line was never built, but that didn't prevent the promoters from proposing, in 1871, an extension of this line from Valley Falls to Narragansett Bay through East Providence (the astute reader will recall that this route is the one the Providence and Worcester Railroad eventually followed for its East Providence branch in 1875). There was at least one man, Harvey Chace (of the Rhode Island family that established Berkshire Hathaway of Warren Buffet fame), on the board of directors of both the Rhode Island Mining Railroad and the Providence and Worcester Railroad companies, and the complex series of developments that followed might be explained by this common interest.

Although the mining company proposed building the East Providence Line, which would have been very advantageous to the Providence and Worcester Railroad had it some sort of leasing arrangement, the mining company was not able to produce financing, and the line was eventually built by the railroad. Undaunted, the mining company took advantage of the fact that its original railroad charter permitted building through Massachusetts to reach East Providence. It changed directions entirely, and in 1872, it changed its name to the Rhode Island and Massachusetts Railroad and consigned mining to memory.

In 1877, the Rhode Island and Massachusetts Railroad built a line branching off from the Providence and Worcester Railroad just north of the bridge over the Blackstone River, to Adamsdale, just over the Massachusetts border, and thence to Franklin, Massachusetts, where there were rail connections to Boston. The line was initially operated by the New York and New England Railroad, a line with an incredibly complex history that aspired to operate an "air line" route between Boston and New York.

Passenger trains were operated over the line briefly, but most of the traffic was local. When the line was later absorbed by the New York, New Haven and Hartford Railroad, the route was sometimes used when the Shore Line was blocked for some reason.

From Adamsdale, in 1903, the New York, New Haven and Hartford Railroad built a short connector to North Attleboro, where a connection was available to Norwood, Massachusetts. There were now two alternate routes available to Boston from New York via the Providence and Worcester Railroad, starting in Valley Falls.

Today, thanks to Google Earth, you can easily trace the routes of these long-abandoned rail lines. Starting in Valley Falls, just north of the junction between the Providence and Worcester Railroad mainline and the East Providence Branch, you can see a single track curving off to the right at Titus Street. The track ends just after the line crosses the street, but if you zoom out, you can follow the old line as it traces a path to the left of a stream and a series of small lakes. The line becomes a little hazy at this point but follows a northeasterly direction to Depot Street in Adamsdale. From there, the Franklin line branched left and roughly followed Mendon Road and then ran to the right of Abbot Run Valley Road. The most dramatic remnant of the line is a pair of bridge abutments that mark the crossing of the line across Diamond Hill Reservoir on Quaker Street. The line to North Attleboro is much more difficult to follow, but at the intersection of Mendon Road and Lowe Meadow Lane in Adamsdale, you can see a curved path that almost certainly was a railroad roadbed.

CONNECTIONS WITH THE PROVIDENCE AND WORCESTER RAILROAD AT WOONSOCKET

Woonsocket is well worth a visit from railroad enthusiasts because of its beautifully restored station; the Museum of Work and Culture, which has much of railroad interest; and some intriguing railroad archaeology. The Providence and Worcester Railroad mainline today passes through the center of town.

In the 1850s, Brookline was one of the fastest-growing towns near Boston. The Boston and Worcester Railroad, one of the three original lines in Massachusetts, chartered a subsidiary, the Charles River Railroad, which reached Woonsocket in 1863. This line was visualized as one link in a chain of railroads that would eventually provide an inland route to New York. The

Charles River Railroad was eventually absorbed by the New York and New England Railroad, which we earlier saw building a line from Franklin to Valley Falls, thus hedging its bets in its effort to provide an inland competitor to the Shore Line.

There is some uncertainty in the historical record about the provenance of the next link in this chain, from Woonsocket via Slatersville to Pascoag, a mill town in the northwest corner of Rhode Island. We will meet Pascoag again in a later chapter. Some authorities say that the line was built in 1891 by a locally chartered group, the Woonsocket and Pascoag Railroad, and it was later taken over by the New York and New England Railroad. Other sources say the New York and New England built the line directly. In either case, the line beyond Slatersville was abandoned in the 1930s, but against all probability, the line between Woonsocket and Slatersville survives today as a freight branch of the Providence and Worcester Railroad that primarily serves a single customer, a steel supplier called Denman and Davis.

Google Earth again enables us to resurrect the lines around Woonsocket very nicely. Start at Depot Square to admire the Providence and Worcester Station, and then take an imaginary drive west to Arnold Street and take a right. Just before you turn, you will see the Providence and Worcester Railroad mainline curving off to the left. From Arnold Street, you will be able to see a switch on the main track and a siding curving back toward Arnold Street. At

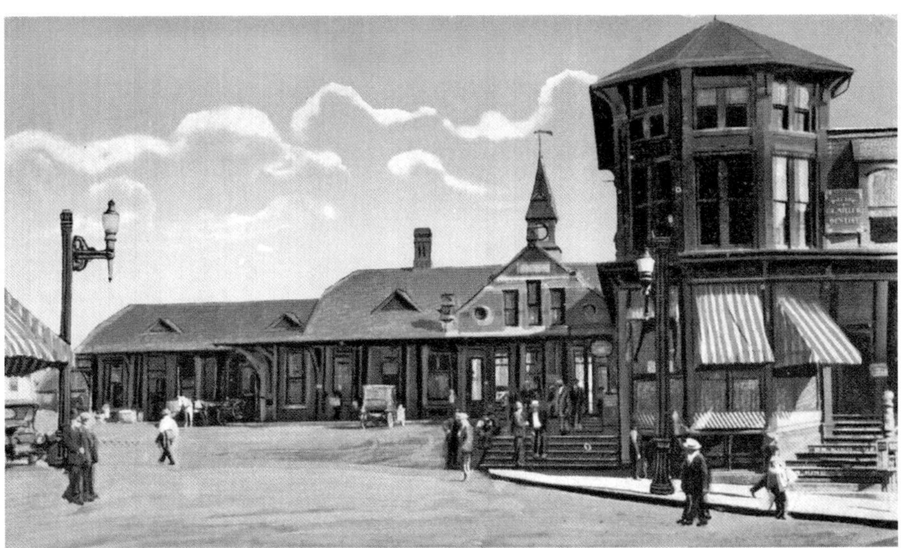

Woonsocket Station in the 1920s. The restored station looks very much like this today. *Collection of Edward J. Ozog.*

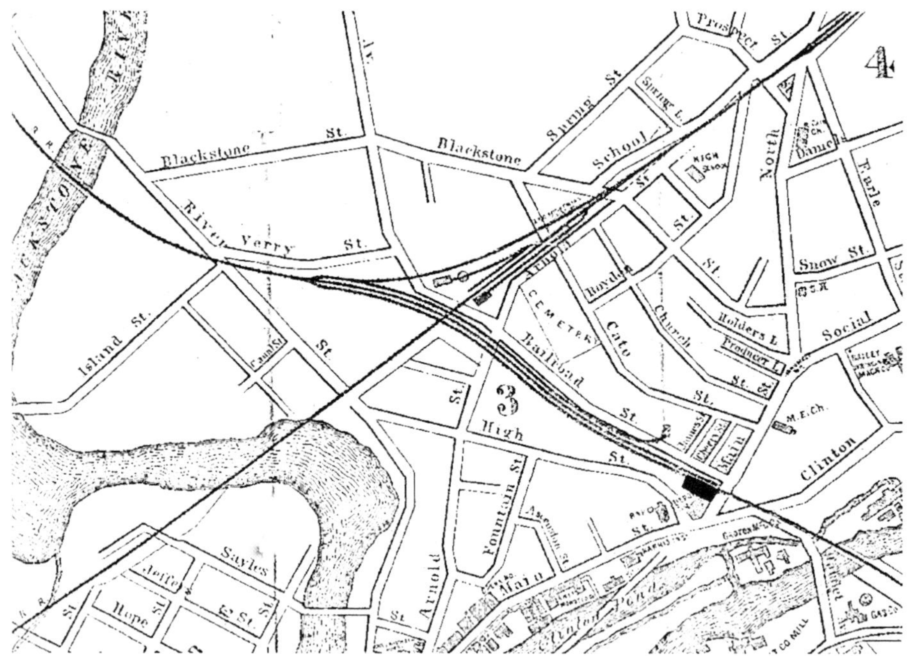

Downtown Woonsocket. The Slatersville-Pascoag branch goes from the center of town to the lower left of the map. The old New York and New England Railroad line to Franklin heads to the upper right. *Collection of Edward J. Ozog.*

about the intersection of Cato Street with Arnold, this siding meets a track traveling northeast to southwest and extending northeast for about 1,000 feet. This is the remains of the New York and New England Railroad line to Franklin. Going in a southwestern direction, this track crosses over the Providence and Worcester mainline and becomes the Slatersville branch. In practice today, if the Providence and Worcester Railroad wants to send a locomotive to pick up some cars at Slatersville, the locomotive switches off the mainline, backs up the curved siding and, once on the Slatersville branch, proceeds to its destination. The return trip involves a reverse movement. Typically, only four to five cars are handled in this way. If you then travel to the northeast on River and Canal Streets into Blackstone, Massachusetts, you will be able to see a few of the surviving bridges and other structures of the New York and New England Railroad's Air Line route between Franklin, Massachusetts, and Willimantic, Connecticut. At its closest point, this line is within 150 feet of the Rhode Island border, and today it is a hiking trail.

THE PROVIDENCE AND WORCESTER RAILROAD TODAY

The Providence and Worcester Railroad survived as an independent railroad much longer than most New England railroads, but in 1889, it was leased by the New York, Providence and Boston Railroad, until that line was swallowed (leased) by the behemoth New York, New Haven and Hartford Railroad (New Haven Railroad) in 1892. However, due to the distinctiveness of its original stockholder protection plan, the New Haven Railroad was never able to milk the Providence and Worcester Railroad for its resources, as it did with most of its other properties. In 1969, when the ill-fated Penn Central Railroad took over the New Haven Railroad, the New Haven Railroad refused to extend the Providence and Worcester Railroad lease unless the protective clauses put in place in the 1840s were removed. In the meantime, fate intervened when the Penn Central Railroad itself went bankrupt in 1970. In the confusion and turmoil, a group of the then-current holders of the ancestral Providence and Worcester Railroad stock petitioned the Interstate Commerce Commission to operate the Providence and Worcester Railroad as an independent line for the first time in eighty-four years. The petition was granted in 1973, and today, the Providence and Worcester Railroad, after acquiring some former Penn Central Railroad lines itself, is a modern, thriving 545-mile-long regional railroad serving three states.

In Rhode Island, it services the Quonset Point industrial park with its auto import facilities and the Port of Providence. The railroad owns a complete 1950s passenger train, which it regularly operates in excursion service. It has freight trackage rights on Amtrak's Northeast Corridor line, and approximately once a week, freight train PR-3 originates in Valley Falls and serves customers in the Port of Providence and a couple of line-side industries in Warwick. It continues on to South County, where there is a single customer, Arnold Lumber of Kingston. Typically, at this end-of-the-run point, there is but a single car of building materials to be dropped off or picked up empty. Rhode Island is the littlest state, so it is entirely appropriate that it have one of the littlest freight trains.

Chapter 7

GO WEST, YOUNG MAN

By the mid-1800s, Rhode Island was well supplied with rail lines to Boston and north to central Massachusetts and New Hampshire. The Shore Line was not yet complete to New York, but there were abundant rail-steamship connections from Fall River, Providence, New London, Stonington and Groton. However, there was still no easy way to go west, and increasingly that deficiency became the focus of rail entrepreneurs. The drive to the west was speeded by a relatively new technological development, one that would have almost as much effect on New England as the original Industrial Revolution itself. This new technology was the use of coal to power both stationary and mobile steam engines.

Due to the seemingly limitless availability of harvestable trees in the United States, wood was the first choice of fuel for early steam engines. Wood, however, didn't contain much energy per pound, so enormous quantities were needed to provide fuel for hungry boilers. With the development of stationary and locomotive engines in the early 1800s, it was clear that a new fuel source was needed to provide America's mobility. That fuel would be coal.

The first commercial mining of coal occurred in Pennsylvania in the mid-1700s. The early center of coal mining was in the Wilkes-Barre and Scranton areas, and the majority of the coal mined was anthracite, or hard coal. Anthracite has the advantage of burning hot and almost smoke-free, but it is hard to ignite and requires a lot of air to sustain combustion. These qualities slowed the adoption of anthracite coal as a fuel for locomotives. Most of the inventions that permitted anthracite coal use for railroads naturally came from the railroads that served the coal areas, like the Reading, Erie and Pennsylvania Railroads.

In addition to technical difficulties with coal use in locomotives, central New England was about 250 miles from the Pennsylvania coal fields, and the cost of transport inhibited the development of coal-burning steam engines until the middle of the nineteenth century. George S. Griggs, a master mechanic for the Boston and Providence Railroad, developed two inventions that made anthracite coal a practical fuel for railroad engines, one of which, the diamond-shaped smokestack, became the visual trademark of mid-nineteenth-century locomotives. By 1860, coal use was widespread in New England locomotives.

With its well-established manufacturing base, Rhode Island soon developed prominence in steam engine construction. George Henry Corliss, a prolific inventor of mechanical devices and machinery, came to Providence in 1844 and soon built a plant on Charles Street to make stationary steam engines, which were used to power machine tools directly and, later, to turn generators for making electricity. Corliss's engines were noted for two things: their high quality of manufacture and their enormous size. Some of his later engines had flywheels thirty feet in diameter. The New England Wireless and Steam Museum (www.newsm.org) in East Greenwich, Rhode Island, has the only Corliss engine still operating under steam in the United States. The museum is open to the public once a year in the fall and is worth a special trip.

In 1865, Earl Philip Mason Jr. (not to be confused with William Mason, who built locomotives in Taunton, Massachusetts) established the Rhode Island Locomotive Works on Hemlock Street in Providence, a building of which still stands. Mason and his sons built over 3,500 locomotives before the company merged with six other firms at the beginning of the twentieth century to become the American Locomotive Company (ALCO). After the merger, the Providence plant built automobiles and trucks after 1909. These trucks were advertised as being built with the same steel as ALCO locomotives. Most Rhode Island Locomotive Works engines were small. The enormous ALCO steam locomotives, like the legendary Big Boys built for the Union Pacific Railroad, were built in Schenectady, New York.

With all this steam engine activity, where was the coal to fire them to come from? From the earliest times, the collieries in Pennsylvania were in the practice of shipping their coal in river barges to the major city markets like Philadelphia and New York. This practice was expanded to serve New

England markets in the latter part of the nineteenth century. In fact, the Providence and Worcester Railroad's East Providence branch was primarily built to service the new coal pier owned by the Lehigh & Wilkes-Barre Coal Co. At the peak of its coal service, the Providence and Worcester Railroad loaded more than fifty cars of coal a day.

This system of shipping coal was not terribly efficient. The coal had to first be loaded onto river barges and then transferred to oceangoing barges and then to railroad cars. Each transfer cost money. A quick glance at a New England map reveals that if one built a rail line in a straight line from Wilkes-Barre to Providence, one would pass through Newburgh, New York (close to where I-84 crosses the Hudson), and Waterbury, Connecticut. A straight line between Boston and Wilkes-Barre would pass through Springfield, Massachusetts, and cross the Hudson at Poughkeepsie, New York. A look at the path of the railroads going west and southwest from both Providence and Boston clearly suggests the objective of the original builders.

THE LURE OF THE WEST

The Hudson River provided both obstacles and a destination for New England railroad magnates (real or would-be) who were seduced by the enormous potential profits available by connecting with the many railroad lines that were developing west of the Hudson. The obstacles were both technical and political. To head due west from Boston, one would have to cross both the Berkshire and Taconic mountain ranges, and then, after breasting the Taconic summits, one would face the unpleasant reality that much of the Hudson south of Poughkeepsie was bordered with formidable cliffs, such as the Jersey Palisades. Once the routing difficulties were met, there then emerged the problem of getting a train across the river. There was far more river shipping on the Hudson than on either the Connecticut or Thames, and the Hudson shipping interests were adamant that there be no railroad bridges blocking their vessels or diverting their cargos. The first railroad bridge to cross the Hudson was built in 1835 at Troy, New York, where the river is relatively narrow and there was not much upriver boat traffic. Until more bridges could be built, the railroads that reached the river from eastern origins had to be content to move their cars across the river by car ferries.

There were three lines that proceeded more or less directly west from Boston to the Hudson. They are of significance to Rhode Island because the dense network of railroads in and around the state permitted connections with these through lines, and in their eastern portions, they provided an alternative to the Shore Line to Boston. Two of the lines operate today almost along the routes they had more than one hundred years ago. The third is no longer whole, but significant portions of it survive.

Most of the major intercity railroad lines in New England were not built as a single entity, as was the case with most of the principal western lines like the Union Pacific Railroad. Rather, they were an assemblage of shorter lines that were pieced together through sale, lease or absorption. That was certainly the case for the northernmost of the Boston-Hudson lines, which in its later years was referred to as the Boston and Maine (Fitchburg) line. Its sections were Boston to Charlestown as the Charlestown Branch Railroad, Charlestown to Fitchburg as the Fitchburg Railroad and then continuing west under that name to Gardner, Greenfield and the Hoosac Tunnel near North Adams. From there, the original connection was made to the Hudson River via the Troy and Greenfield Railroad to Troy. Later, the western routing was changed to the Boston, Hoosac Tunnel and Western Railroad line terminating at Mechanicville, New York, which is the functional end of the line today. In 1900, the Boston and Maine Railroad took over the entire line and held it until 1984, when the Boston and Maine Railroad was bought by Guilford Transportation Industries, which changed its name in 2006 to Pan Am Railways (this company used the logo of the legendary Pan American World Airways, which it bought in 2004). Ironically, Pan Am Railways tried to restart an airline business with the Pan Am name. It flopped. In 2009, Pan Am Railways paired with the Norfolk Southern Railroad to form a holding company called Pan Am Southern, whose avowed purpose was to rebuild the old Boston and Maine line into a modern, efficient, freight-only railroad to be called the Patriot Corridor.

The organizational structure and history detailed here represents only a sample of the actual corporate history, which is almost mind-numbing in its scope. This level of complexity is typical rather than unusual for the major New England routes. In the interest of reader alertness, in subsequent discussions of corporate history, an effort will be made to simplify as much as possible.

The second Boston-Hudson line, which also survives today, is generally known as the Boston and Albany line, after the railroad that controlled it during most of its existence. Today, it's the line that Amtrak follows for the Lake Shore Limited passenger train from Boston to Chicago. The original section of this line was the old Boston and Worcester Railroad. The line continued as part of the Western Railroad through Palmer, Springfield and then through the Berkshires to Pittsfield and the New York state line, where it originally joined with the Albany and West Stockbridge Railroad to complete the line to the Hudson in 1842. The separate lines were merged to become the Boston and Albany Railroad, which was bought by the New York Central Railroad in 1914, and the latter railroad joined with the Pennsylvania Railroad to form the Penn Central Railroad in 1968. When that line went belly-up in 1976, the former Boston and Albany line was taken over by a private/government hybrid named Conrail. Conrail, in turn, was broken up in the late 1990s, and the Boston and Albany line finally came to rest with the CSX Transportation company, which is today's operator.

The final Boston-Hudson line is one we were introduced to in the last chapter: the Air Line route of the former New York and New England Railroad. It was this line's ambition not to go due west from Boston to the Hudson but to cut diagonally across Massachusetts and Connecticut eventually to New Haven via Middletown, where it would connect with the Shore Line route and thus reach the Hudson. From Willimantic, Connecticut, a branch also permitted access to Hartford and points due west.

The Air Line route was in its organization the most complex of the three Boston-Hudson lines. It was composed of dozens of smaller lines, repeatedly went into receivership and was eventually taken over by the New York, New Haven and Hartford Railroad. It languished under this ownership, as the Shore Line, also owned by the New York, New Haven and Hartford Railroad, received the bulk of the parent railroad's attention.

There was one brief, shining moment of glory for the Air Line route. From 1891 to 1895, the Air Line's crack train, the New England Limited, was painted all white with gilt lettering and received some ultra-luxe dining and parlor cars from the Pullman Company, the dominant passenger car builder of the era. The new incarnation of the New England Limited was quickly dubbed the White Train and, later, because of its spectral appearance, the Ghost Train. So, for a very few years, the Shore Line had some real competition in the Boston to New York trade, until the train, and the railroad itself, fell victim to financial manipulations, in which the names Morgan, Gould and Vanderbilt played a role. Today, the tracks are gone from Willimantic to the northeast, replaced by the Air Line hiking trail all the way into Massachusetts, but Willimantic still has freight rail service from the Providence and Worcester Railroad and an excellent small railroad museum, the Connecticut Eastern Railroad Museum (www.cteastrrmuseum.org).

The Hartford, Providence and Fishkill Railroad

Today, Hartford would not seem to be a destination capable of exerting a siren call on otherwise sensible Rhode Island capitalists, but in the 1840s, its lure appeared irresistible. It had a large manufacturing base and offered the possibility of an almost limitless number of actual or potential connections to the Hudson. From 1846 to 1849, following the custom of the times, separate state charters were obtained to build a line from Providence west and Hartford east, meeting at Plainfield, Connecticut. But the ambitions of these early organizers were not limited to Hartford. Plans were quickly made to extend the line west to Fishkill Landing (today called Beacon) on the Hudson, from whence car ferries would move the trains across the river to Newburgh, where a connection would be made with the New York and Erie Railroad. The railroad ultimately would be called the Hartford, Providence and Fishkill Railroad. At least, that was the plan.

Construction started in 1847, and the line opened in stages, starting with the Hartford to Willimantic, Connecticut section. Unfortunately, the company started to run out of money, and with a technique of creative financing that appears to be alive and well today, a transfusion was obtained by appealing to the municipal governments of Providence and Hartford for a bailout. Each city took out a first mortgage on the tracks in its own state. Today, this would be called "economic development." The transfusion worked—in a sense. The line was actually completed, and in 1854, the first trains traveled between Hartford and Providence. In 1855, the line was extended to Waterbury, Connecticut.

Alas, by 1857, the line went toes-up and defaulted on its bonds. This was partly a product of the times, as well as a faulty business plan. Twenty years after the Panic of 1837, another great national economic paroxysm took place, and even great railroads like the Erie and Illinois Central Railroads shut down. The trustees for the bondholders of the Hartford, Providence and Fishkill Railroad took over its operations. Coveting its access to Providence, the Boston, Hartford and Erie Railroad—a line that was to become synonymous with financial shenanigans, chicanery and outright fraud—picked up the Hartford, Providence and Fishkill Railroad in 1863, but so complex and murky were the financial arrangements in this acquisition that clear title was not finally obtained until 1878, by which time the Boston, Hartford and Erie Railroad itself had been swallowed by the New York and New England Railroad, which also absorbed the Air Line

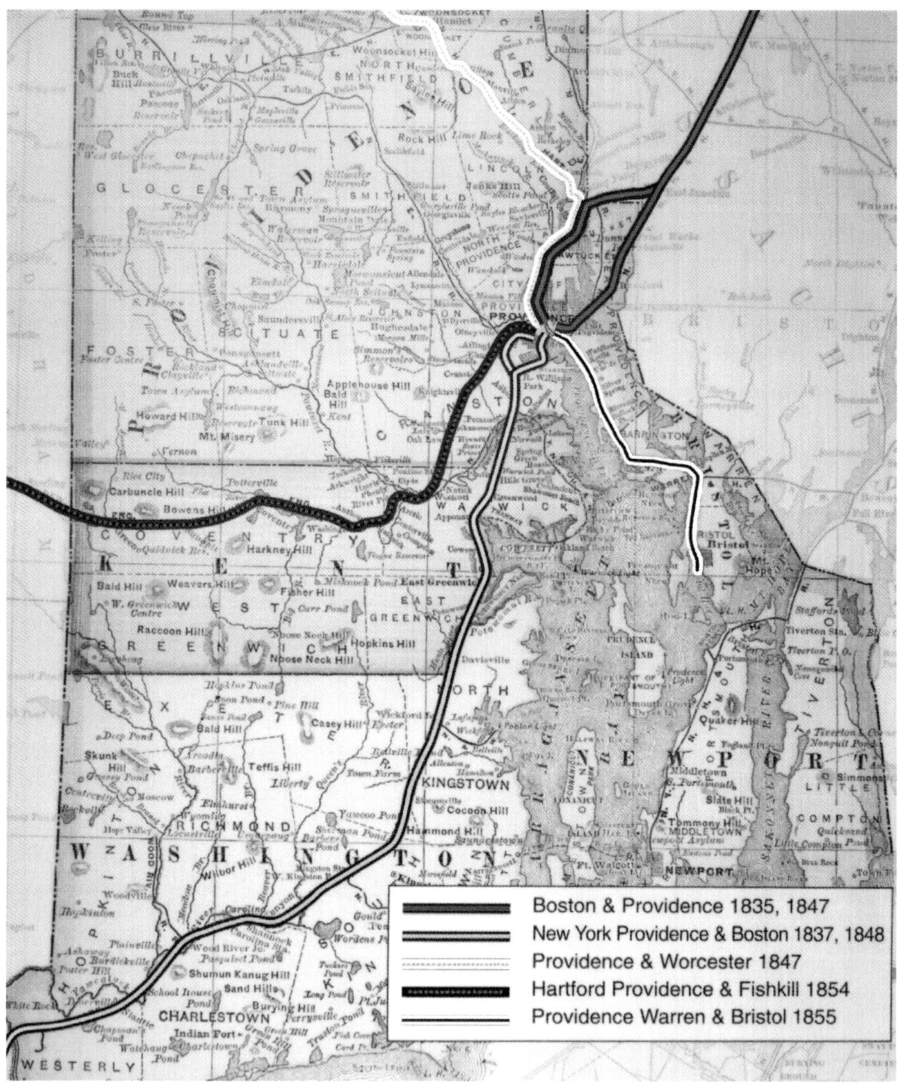

The Hartford, Providence and Fishkill Railroad entered Rhode Island in 1854. Also shown on this map is the Providence, Warren and Bristol Railroad, which will be discussed in a subsequent chapter. *Rhode Island Railroad Museum.*

route. This company was gobbled up in turn twenty years later by the New York, New Haven and Hartford Railroad, which eventually devoured almost all the shorter rail lines in New England south of the Boston and Albany Railroad line. This entire series of transactions was so loaded with bribery, bamboozlement and corruption that its closest contemporary parallel was the Enron debacle and disaster of 2001.

During its reign, the New York and New England Railroad hedged its bets on routes to the Hudson from mid-Connecticut. While it was assembling the previously seen Air Line route, it started building or absorbing smaller lines that would take the Hartford, Providence and Fishkill from Waterbury to the Hudson. Under the New York and New England Railroad name, it built from Waterbury through Danbury, Connecticut, and Brewster, New York, to Hopewell Junction, New York, where it used a short railroad, the Newburgh, Dutchess and Connecticut Railroad, to reach the river. Finally, in 1881, the Hartford, Providence and Fishkill Railroad reached its namesake destination.

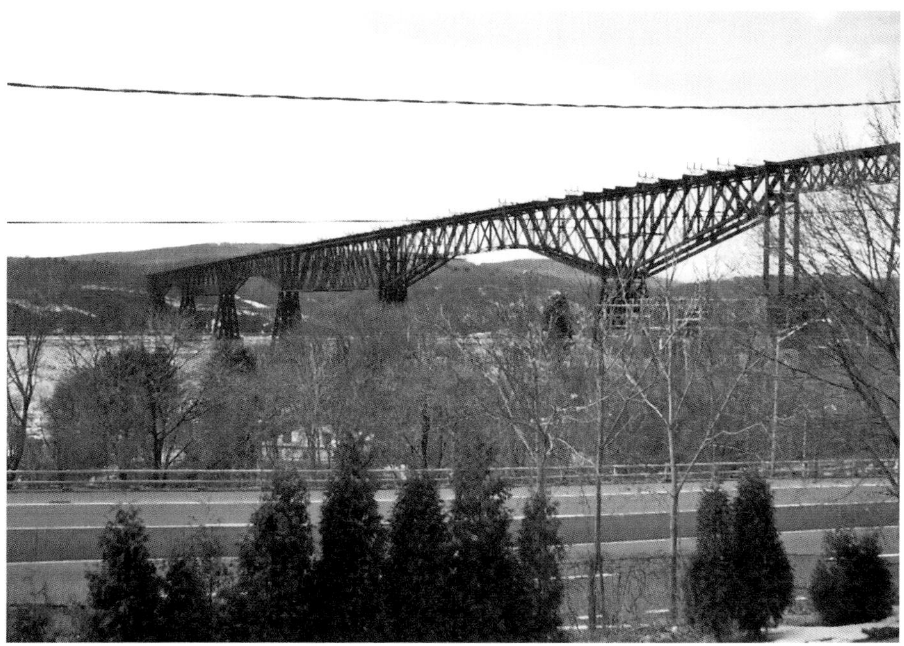

A contemporary view of the Poughkeepsie Bridge, which was rebuilt for pedestrians. *Photo by David Shankbone.*

Unfortunately, all that effort would quickly prove to be for naught. This line from the Hudson to Providence was the longest and steepest of all its competitors, and the completion of the magnificent Poughkeepsie Railroad Bridge in 1888 permitted a nearby, direct and much straighter route from the Pennsylvania coal fields and western railroad lines to central Connecticut. As the Poughkeepsie Railroad Bridge was the only example of its kind south of Albany until 1928, competing lines faced the economic and temporal hurdle of ferrying their cars across the Hudson. The poor little Hartford, Providence and Fishkill Railroad, after earlier becoming cannibalized by the New York and New England Railroad and later the New York, New Haven and Hartford Railroad, became marginalized, serving primarily local traffic until its demise in the latter part of the twentieth century. The last passenger train serving Providence creaked to a halt in 1932, although local freight service persisted until 1988.

THE HARTFORD, PROVIDENCE AND FISHKILL RAILROAD IN RHODE ISLAND

The rights of way granted railroads for the construction of their lines were often wide enough for multiple parallel tracks. This was not so much in anticipation of an eventual four-track speedway like the Pennsylvania Railroad's mainline between New York City and Washington, D.C., but in preparation for the installation of side tracks to service industries that were expected to sprout up along the tracks. The Stonington Line's right of way out of Union Station in Providence to the south was easily able to accommodate the single track of the Hartford, Providence and Fishkill Railroad until it branched off on its own south of Providence, and the two railroads came to agreement on a lease.

The Hartford, Providence and Fishkill Railroad's line followed the Stonington Line's tracks from Union Station to a point about where today's Union Avenue passes over the Route 6-10 Connector highway. As the Stonington Line bent to the southeast, the Hartford line's track kept straight in a southwest direction. It kept going in that general direction until it met Cranston Street, which it then paralleled through Oaklawn to the general area of today's Community College of Rhode Island, at which point it bent gently to the west and, following that direction, passed through West Warwick and the villages of Washington, Coventry, Summit and Greene, just before the Connecticut state line.

In its later years, the Hartford, Providence and Fishkill line passed through a series of owners. Conrail took over from the New York, New Haven and Hartford Railroad in 1969. Conrail acquired operating rights in 1976, but that service was transferred to the Providence and Worcester Railroad in 1982. Somewhere around this time, the line was degraded to the status of a spur called the Washington Secondary (the term "secondary" was not generally used by railroaders in the Penn Central and Conrail era, the term "branch" being preferred). In the 1980s, the occasional Providence and Worcester Railroad locomotive could be seen pulling a few freight cars at a leisurely fifteen miles per hour near the malls in the center of the state. The Rhode Island Department of Transportation acquired the right of way from the Providence and Worcester Railroad in 1996 for the purpose of converting the railbed to a bicycle path. The railroad retained certain rights, however, and in 2001 entered an agreement with Vitreum Networks LLC to lay fiberoptic cables along the old right of way.

Fortunately, almost the entire line is available today for inspection. Very nearly the entire fifteen miles of roadbed from Depot Avenue in Cranston to Coventry is now paved and called the Washington Secondary Rail Trail. It is suitable for walking or unmotorized wheeled recreation. West of Coventry, the trail is unpaved and called the Trestle Trail (Coventry Greenway), where it continues past the Connecticut border. TrailLink (www.traillink.com/trail/washington-secondary-trail.aspx) has a good description of the path.

Connections with the Hartford, Providence and Fishkill Railroad in Rhode Island

Industry in New England developed primarily along the banks of medium to large rivers like the Merrimack and Blackstone because early factories depended on water as a source of power and transportation. As the steam engine took over these functions, water took on additional roles that could be satisfied by smaller rivers. Many of the more sophisticated industrial processes that developed from the mid-nineteenth century on used water for cooling, cleaning, waste disposal and as an ingredient in chemical operations. These functions could usually be satisfied by the smaller volume of water available in modest rivers. Thus, after 1850 or so, factories began to pop up all over Rhode Island along the banks of rivers whose names were often almost as long as the stream, like the Woonasquatucket. As these smaller rivers were usually unnavigable, there was increasing demand for rail transportation.

These small, feeder railroads often were originated by mill owners themselves rather than railroad entrepreneurs, much as was the case with the Providence and Worcester Railroad. Many of these smaller railroads were designed from the start with a limited role: to provide connection with an established railroad.

THE PAWTUXET VALLEY RAILROAD

This tiny line, eleven miles long at its greatest extent, probably had more corporate complexity per mile than any other railroad in Rhode Island. When completed, it ran from a junction with the Stonington Line at a station called Auburn, in the city now called Cranston, through the villages of Sockanosset, Howard, Pontiac, Natick, River Point, Phenix, Arkwright and finally Hope. The railroad was not built as a whole, nor was it built under the same ownership.

The first three-mile section was built in 1874, from a stop on the Hartford, Providence and Fishkill Railroad at River Point to the village of Hope. This line was operated by the latter railroad and was called the Pawtuxet Valley Railroad. It roughly followed the course of the Pawtuxet River, and one of its best customers was a mill now called the Arkwright Company. The original mill produced textiles and uniforms, but today, in a startling adaption, the company produces ultra-high-tech coatings for printing papers and the graphic arts industry. Only four years later, the New York and New England Railroad absorbed both the Hartford, Providence and Fishkill Railroad and its branch, the Pawtuxet Valley Railroad.

A year later, the Stonington Line built a branch southwest from Auburn to Pontiac Mills. This five-mile-long railroad was called the Pontiac Branch. At their closest approach, the Pawtuxet Valley Railroad and Pontiac Branch lines were but a mile apart. In 1879, the Stonington Line leased the Pawtuxet Valley Railroad and built a short connector track between it and the Pawtuxet Valley Railroad so that it was possible for a train to go from Providence, via an admittedly torturous route, to Hope. In fact, passenger trains did operate on this line until 1922. In 1892, the New York, New Haven and Hartford took over all the lines mentioned above. With the end of passenger service, bits and pieces of the line were abandoned. By 1991, it was but a memory.

In 1921, this little branch line acquired its own branch. The general contractor building the dam for the Scituate Reservoir, the largest construction enterprise the state had yet seen, built a temporary 2.1-mile-long track connecting with the Pawtuxet Valley Railroad near the end of the line in Hope. A single locomotive was leased to service the line, which eventually operated over the top of the dam, and it was in operation at least through 1925.

A trip via Google Earth is revealing. The beginning of the Hartford, Providence and Fishkill Railroad line can easily be found where Union Avenue crosses the Amtrak tracks in Providence. It then passes through Cranston, West Warwick and thence more or less straight to the Connecticut border.

The Pontiac Branch Railroad is a bit more challenging. Find where Park Avenue crosses the Amtrak tracks in Cranston. Follow the tracks for 4,200 feet, and you will see where the Pontiac Branch Railroad line switched off the Amtrak main in a southwesterly direction and then crossed I-95 by a still existing bridge. You can roughly follow the line until it crosses RI 37, and then it disappears into suburbia. It can be picked up again roughly at the intersection of Pontiac Avenue and Kenney Drive. A short distance later, it ends at the Pontiac Mill. Everything beyond has been swallowed by malls and suburbia.

PROVIDENCE AND SPRINGFIELD RAILROAD

The final line to travel in a western (in this case, actually northwestern) direction from Rhode Island was the Providence and Springfield Railroad (not to be confused with the little-known Providence, Webster and Springfield Railroad, which was chartered in 1882 in Massachusetts and never reached either Providence or Springfield). It was organized in 1871 by factory owners whose mills were along the banks of the Woonasquatucket River in Providence and was chartered as the Woonasquatucket Railroad, but the name was quickly changed to reflect a more ambitious goal: to service the many mills in the northwestern part of the state that were not on major rivers and possibly extend into Massachusetts and reach Springfield.

Most of the names of the towns along the right of way would not be recognized by anyone outside Rhode Island, but one town name would be instantly recognized by anyone who was a child in the 1920s through 1940s. The Esmond Mills made baby blankets and, in a stroke of marketing genius, published a little book in 1924 designed to be read aloud to children. Called *The Tale of Bunny Esmond*, it was about an adorable bunny that was always cold until somebody wrapped him in a Bunny Esmond blanket.

By a strange coincidence, Esmond Mills made a baby blanket that had Bunny's image printed on it. Bunny Esmond was the Elmo of his day. The Esmond blankets were softer than most, and in 1943, the author would have killed with his tiny fists anyone who tried to take his Bunny Esmond blanket away from him.

The Providence and Springfield Railroad's routing into Providence reflected its Johnny-come-lately status in the Rhode Island railroad scene. Technically, the line started in Olneyville, south of Providence, about where Dike Street met the Stonington Line's tracks. However, there was about as much of interest to the casual visitor in Olneyville then as there is now, and the Providence and Springfield Railroad soon leased trackage rights on the Hartford, Providence and Fishkill Railroad's track into Union Station in Providence. By 1874, it had its own track into Providence along the same right of way, but because Union Station was becoming crowded, the City of Providence forced the line to build its own small station at Gaspee Street in 1880.

The Providence and Springfield Railroad never paid a dividend, but on the other hand, it never lost money and continued to provide a valuable service to its line-side shippers, many of whom were stockholders. Alas, after only seven years, the poor little Providence and Springfield Railroad attracted the attention of the New York and New England Railroad, which had assimilated the Hartford, Providence and Fishkill Railroad. The New York and New England Railroad began demanding back rent for its use of the Hartford, Providence and Fishkill Railroad's tracks. The ensuing financial confusion depressed the small line's stock price, and the New York and New England Railroad was able to buy the stock cheaply and assume a majority interest. That road did only one constructive thing for the Providence and Springfield Railroad—it built a seven-mile extension from Pascoag to Douglas Junction in Massachusetts, where it met the Air Line route. This short piece of track had one distinction. The only station on the extension, Wallum Lake, was also the highest in elevation in Rhode Island, at 570 feet. The Wallum Lake station, which was as close to the middle of nowhere as you can be in Rhode Island, actually did a rather good business bringing visitors, staff and materials to the Rhode Island State Hospital for Consumptives, the building of which still stands and is today the Zambarano Unit of the Eleanor Slater Hospital, which specializes in chronic care for patients with severe neurological conditions.

Like the other railroads in this chapter, the Providence and Springfield Railroad was eventually taken into the New York, New Haven and Hartford

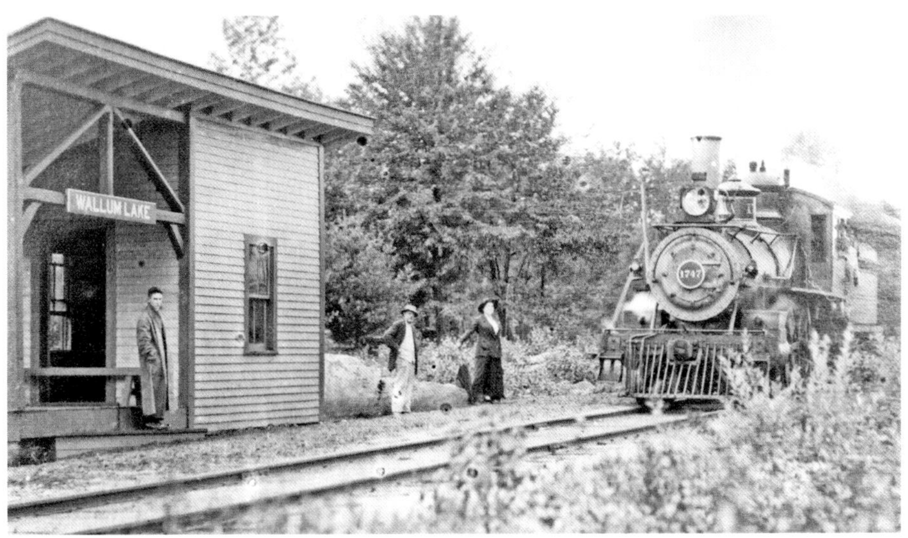

This photograph of the Wallum Lake station suggests just how far out in the boondocks it was. *Collection of Edward J. Ozog.*

Railroad system and suffered the same fate: amputation in stages. Passenger service was phased out, the Douglas Junction extension was abandoned in 1937 and the rest of the line to Providence was abandoned in 1967.

Unfortunately, Google Earth is not as helpful in following the old right of way as it was for the other lines in this chapter. There is one physical survivor right near the point where the line branched off the Hartford, Providence and Fishkill Railroad line in Olneyville. Where Pilsudski Street dead-ends at Route 6, there is a rusted-out railroad deck girder bridge crossing Route 6. (Pilsudski was a Polish patriot often regarded as the George Washington of his country. This neighborhood seems to fancy odd street names—paralleling Pilsudski are Huldah and Judith Streets, both Jewish prophetesses.) There is no identifiable right of way leading either to or from the bridge. The Woonasquatucket Greenway/bike path follows the line from about the location of the footbridge over RI 6 at Sheridan Street to a little past Manton Pond. From there to Smithfield, you can identify sections that *might* be the old roadbed, but they are so disconnected that one cannot be sure.

WHY DID THE WESTERN LINES FAIL?

The primary reason is "too little, too late." By the time the lines going west or northwest were built, they were in fierce competition with other lines, like the Providence and Worcester Railroad, which had far better physical plants than they did. They also didn't have enough local traffic, especially after the decline of the textile industry, to support themselves. For the railroad enthusiast, however, they had the charm of quaintness and rural operations, and in some ways, it is rather amazing that they lasted as long as they did.

Chapter 8

THE EAST BAY MAKES TRACKS

Communities separated by the width of a river or bay may not be physically far apart, but they are often very unlike in character. San Francisco is different from Oakland. Manhattan is different from Hoboken. The communities on the western and northern shores of Narragansett Bay are not at all like those on the fringes of the east bay, and those differences are reflected in the development of their railroads.

Whereas the towns and cities to the west and north of the bay had their economic origins in agriculture and then manufacturing, east bay communities were more closely linked to maritime interests like shipping, shipbuilding, support of the navy and, eventually, summer seaside tourism. Due to their geography, the east bay communities closest to Providence very early on developed a commuter relationship with the city.

THE GEOGRAPHY OF THE EAST BAY

The topography of the east bay is complex, and referral to a map will be helpful. The upper end of Narragansett Bay is long and narrow, bordered on the west by Providence and the east by East Providence. South of East Providence lies Riverside and then Barrington, which is today one of the most affluent of the Providence suburbs. Barrington dead-ends to the south

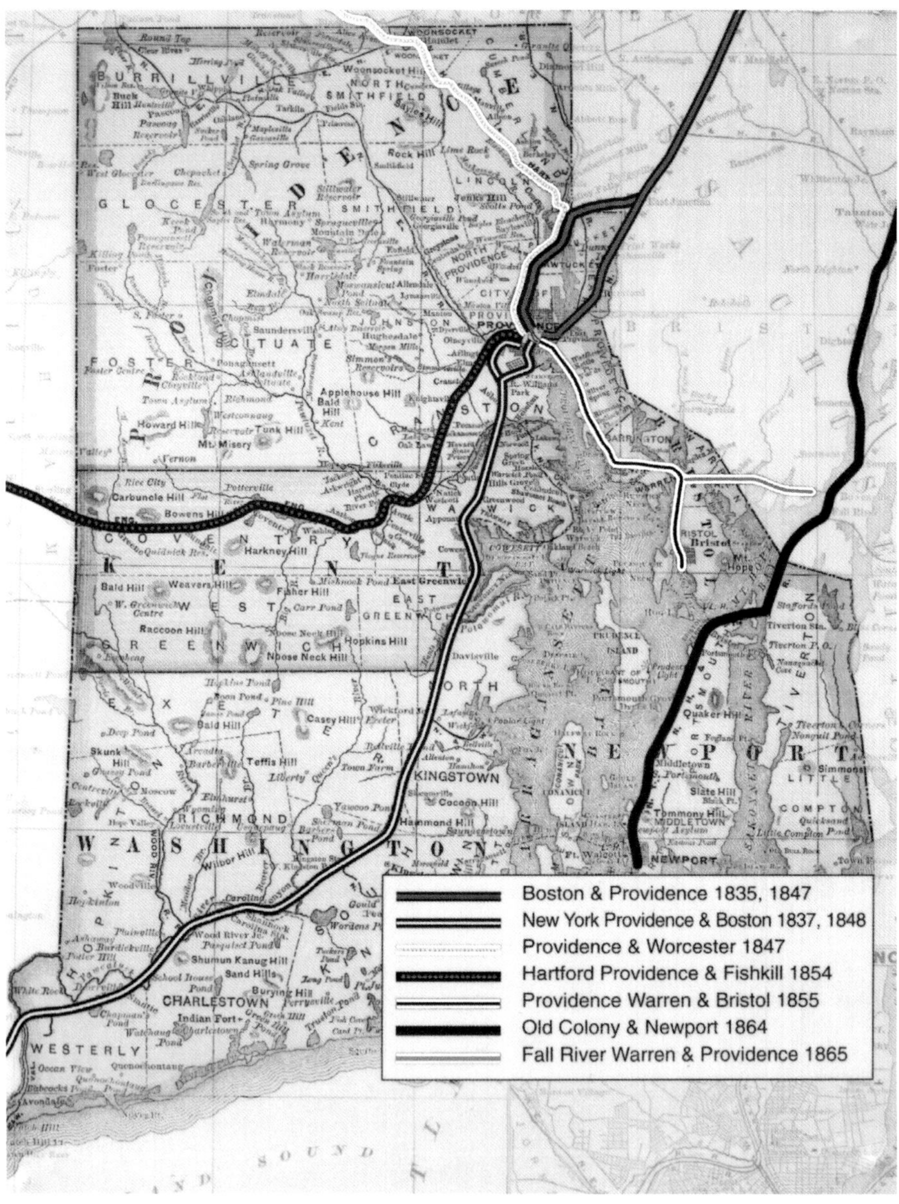

The east bay lines were primarily constructed between 1855 and 1865. Note the gap between the Providence, Warren and Bristol Railroad and the Old Colony and Newport Railroad line. This was caused by the Taunton River, which was originally crossed by ferry but was later bridged. *Rhode Island Railroad Museum.*

at Rumstick Point, and to proceed to the next community, Warren, one must head east and cross over first the Barrington River and then, a short jaunt later, a bridge over the Palmer River. On the east side of the Palmer is a long peninsula running north–south that has the town of Warren on the north end and Bristol to the south. At the southern tip of the peninsula is the Mount Hope Bridge, which continues to Aquidneck Island. If one takes an immediate turn to the east after crossing the Mount Hope Bridge, a small bridge leads to the town of Tiverton, which lies at the head of a narrow strip of Rhode Island land that culminates in the rural (and affluent) town of Little Compton. If, instead, one headed due south on Aquidneck Island, he would pass through the towns of Portsmouth, Middletown and finally Newport. Fall River, Massachusetts, is the closest city of note to the east bay. From Fall River, it is a straight shot of only forty-five miles to Boston and sixty-two miles to the outer shore of Cape Cod.

Topography, Demography and the Railroads

Other than the actual entrance into Providence, which presented hellish problems that will be discussed later, building a railroad south from East Providence to Bristol through Riverside, Barrington and Bristol presented few technical difficulties. The significant issue was: why bother?

Barrington had no significant industry other than a brickworks. Warren had a more complex industrial history. From Revolutionary times, it had heavy involvement with shipbuilding, fishing and whaling. It was the latter two commerces that attracted its largest immigrant population, the Portuguese. The Portuguese first came to America in large numbers during the 1840s, due to the ascendancy of the whaling industry in Nantucket and New Bedford (which has an outstanding whaling museum, www. whalingmuseum.org). As these populations grew, they spilled over into nearby Warren and Bristol, and today, these are the only two communities in Rhode Island that have a Portuguese plurality (a hint to the gastronomic tourist—the best chouriço *anywhere* can be found in Warren and Bristol).

As whaling declined, some textile manufacturing developed in Warren, but it was largely small scale. The shipbuilding industry continues today. Blount Marine, which manufactures small- to medium-sized ferries and tour boats, is a significant employer.

Bristol also maintains its marine tradition. Nathanael Greene Herreshoff, the famous sailing yacht designer, had his manufactory in Bristol, and his memory is enshrined in the Herreshoff Marine Museum (www.herreshoff.org). Very conscious of its Revolutionary history, Bristol has the oldest Fourth of July parade in the United States.

At the southern tip of Bristol, the entrance to Mount Hope Bay separates the town from Aquidneck Island. If there was a railroad from Providence to Bristol, it would seem to make sense to continue it through to Newport, which had more population than Bristol and Warren combined. Although there has been a ferry at this point since 1680, the passageway presented formidable problems for early to mid-nineteenth-century bridge builders. A bridge was not built over Mount Hope Bay until 1929, and it was the longest highway suspension bridge in New England until the completion of the Pell (Newport) Bridge in 1969. The Mount Hope Bridge started another Rhode Island bridge-building tradition—over budget and behind schedule. Not long after the cables were spun for the bridge, it was discovered that the steel was inadequate for the load, and new cables had to be installed at a cost of $1 million (20 percent of the whole bridge budget), producing a five-month delay in completion. When the Pell (Newport) Bridge was built years later, the original paint job was faulty, and the entire bridge had to be repainted within two years after construction, at a price of 21 percent of the original cost (borne by the contractor, fortunately). When the low bid for the new Jamestown-Verrazano Bridge was accepted in 1985, it was for $63 million. When the bridge was opened in 1994, the final cost was $161 million (the author, a transplanted San Franciscan, reluctantly points out that the beloved Golden Gate Bridge was built in only four years, under some of the most difficult bridge-building conditions in the world, for $1.3 million under budget).

Thus, the practical end point for a railroad built extending south of Providence was not Newport but Bristol. But with little manufacturing for line-side traffic, and limited opportunities for freight, what was the point? It is difficult to visualize today, but one of the primary motivators for building railroads in the mid-nineteenth century in New England was passenger service. In the case of a Bristol-Providence line, this would not be through or long-distance passengers but local traffic. A railroad from the tip of Bristol to East Providence would be less than fifteen miles long, have relatively low construction costs and pass through areas that were densely populated for the times. The economics were compelling, and at about the same time the Hartford, Providence and Fishkill Railroad was starting in the west bay area, a new railroad began construction in the east bay.

The Providence, Warren and Bristol Railroad

The Providence and Bristol Railroad was organized in 1851–52 and quickly reorganized into the Providence, Warren and Bristol Railroad. Like most of the early railroads in Rhode Island that crossed a state line (recall that at the time, East Providence was in Massachusetts), it was organized separately in the two states and then quickly merged before construction. An interesting and portentous note was a clause in the original Massachusetts charter of 1851 that specifically granted the new railroad the right to connect with the Boston and Providence Railroad's East Providence line, which would have provided a direct connection to Boston, bypassing Providence's new Union Station. This connection was never really exploited. The line was opened in 1855, one year after the direct connection was established between Providence and Hartford via the Hartford, Providence and Fishkill Railroad. The line from East Providence to Warren was double-tracked, suggesting anticipation of heavy traffic. The stations were often as little as two miles apart, indicating commuter business.

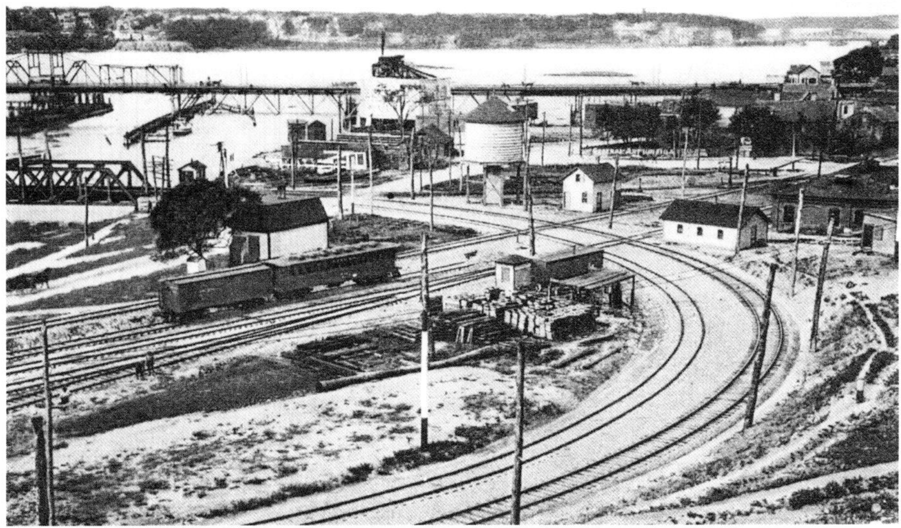

The "sharpest curve in the world." The view of the picture is from Fort Hill in East Providence. Beyond the water tower, the tracks coming in from Boston on the Boston and Providence Railroad can be seen. The tracks going to the lower left are the Providence and Worcester Railroad's freight tracks to the East Providence piers. *Collection of Edward J. Ozog.*

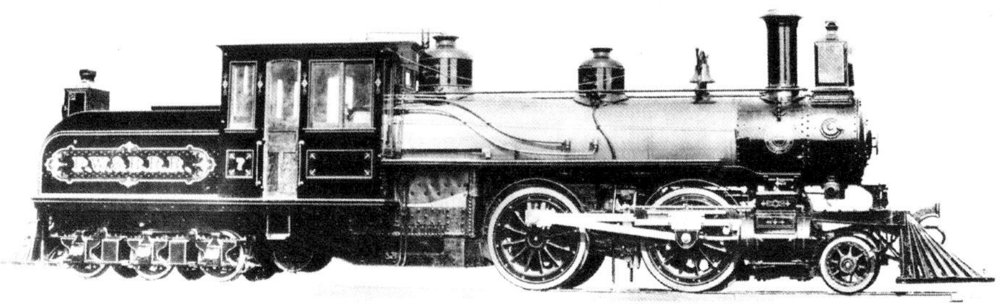

Locomotive *Pokanoket*. What made this engine unusual was that the frame holding the four large driving wheels was not fastened rigidly to the boiler. Rather, it pivoted, making the locomotive behave more like a boxcar in negotiating curves. *Collection of Edward J. Ozog.*

The Providence, Warren and Bristol Railroad gained access to Providence by using the East Providence bridge of the Boston and Providence Railroad at India Point, thence its own tracks running west to Fox Point and a new terminal building at what today would be the intersection of South Water and India Streets. During the active life of the Providence, Warren and Bristol Railroad, the south shore of Fox Point and the banks of the Providence and Seekonk Rivers were lined with piers servicing both passenger and freight boats, and the southern part of the Fox Point neighborhood quickly filled with railroad tracks, becoming a major rail yard that even had separate tracks for storage of railroad cabooses.

As the line of the Providence, Warren and Bristol Railroad approached the India Point Bridge from the south, a problem immediately presented itself. The tracks hugged the shoreline, but in the vicinity of the bridge, a steep bluff, Fort Hill, hemmed the tracks into a narrow strip along the bay. To approach the bridge straight on, without tunneling into or cutting away the hill, the railroad had to make an extremely tight radius curve, only 211 feet. No regular mainline steam locomotive could negotiate this curve without derailing, so the Providence, Warren and Bristol Railroad ordered from the Mason Locomotive Company an unusual steam locomotive, one of fewer than two dozen made of its wheel arrangement. Having an official designation of "2-4-6T," the *Pokanoket* was used until an alternate route into Providence was built and the line electrified at the beginning of the twentieth century. Locomotives were not the only kind of equipment experiencing difficulties with this curve. Standard-length passenger cars would bind between cars, causing derailments, and shorter-than-standard cars were used in the early days.

Fall River, Warren and Providence Railroad

The success of the Providence, Warren and Bristol Railroad suggested that a new commuter market might be tapped by an extension to Fall River. The population of Providence in 1870 was sixty-eight thousand and that of Fall River twenty-seven thousand, and both cities were experiencing rapid population growth. In 1865, the Fall River, Warren and Providence Railroad built a seven-mile connection between Warren and Fall River. The railroad proceeded in a generally easterly direction from Warren, crossed several small inlets of Mount Hope Bay, ran along what is now Swansea's town beach and ended at the west bank of the Taunton River, approximately at the location of today's Braga Bridge. Access to Fall River was initially gained by a ferry, but in 1875, the Slade's Ferry Bridge was built. This was a double-decker swing bridge that carried railroad tracks on the top deck and first carriages and then automobiles on the lower deck. It served almost one hundred years, living much longer than the railroad for which it was built. At approximately the east landing of the old bridge, there is a small railroad museum, the Old Colony and Fall River Railroad Museum (www. ocandfrrailroadmuseum.com).

Electrification and the Tunnel

By the beginning of the twentieth century, the Fall River and Bristol lines were under the control of the New York, New Haven and Hartford Railroad. A new Providence Union Station had been completed in 1898 (this building still stands but has other functions), and the volume of traffic on the lines and the bottleneck provided by the approach to the India Point Bridge led to a series of steps that dramatically changed the nature of the railroads.

The first step was the electrification of the lines all the way to the two destinations of Bristol and Fall River. This permitted the use of electric-powered passenger cars, which were much more efficient than steam trains for short, frequent runs. The trains run during the electric era were typically two double-ended cars long. Freight was still hauled by steam engines. Electrification was in place by 1900.

To permit the Fall River and Bristol trains to enter Providence more directly, a major change in track alignment was made. About a half mile north of the India Point Bridge, a new two-track, rolling-lift drawbridge was built. The tracks from the Providence, Warren and Bristol Railroad lines

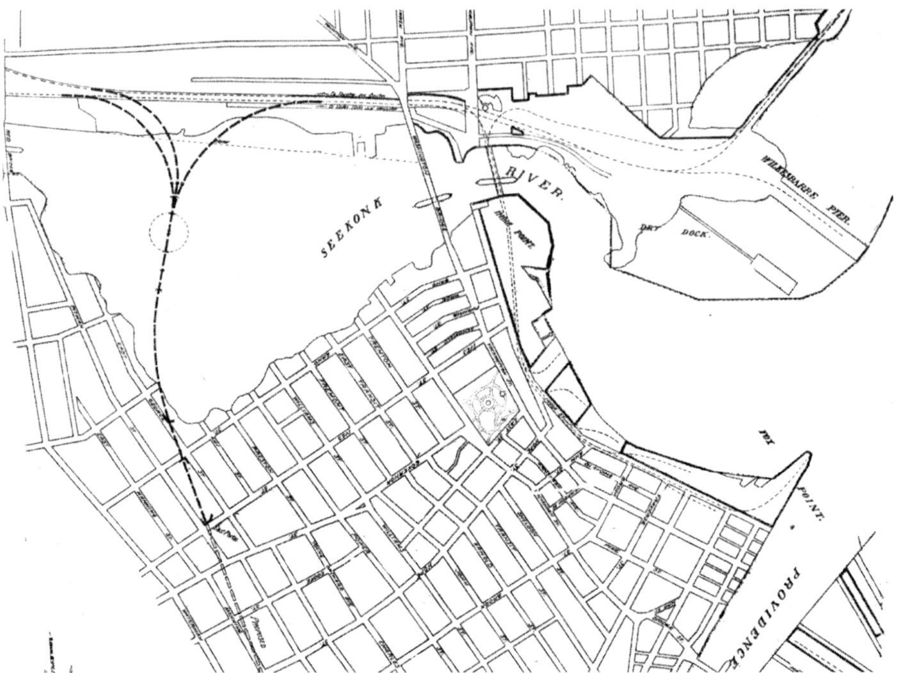

Track diagram of East Providence at the end of railroad development. The new railroad bridge for the Providence, Warren and Bristol Railroad (which still is in place) is shown at the left. Three railroads converged in this area: the Boston and Providence; the Providence and Worcester; and the Providence, Warren and Bristol Railroads. *Collection of Edward J. Ozog.*

gently curved into the bridge from the south. In addition, tracks from the Providence and Worcester and Boston and Providence Railroads' Valley Falls and East Junction lines curved into the bridge from the north, forming a "wye" on the east side of the Seekonk. On the west side of the river, the pair of tracks led to the east portal of a new, mile-long tunnel passing under College Hill from Gano Street on the east to North Main Street on the west (this East Side Tunnel should not be confused with the double trolley tunnel a few blocks south, which is still used by buses). From the west entrance of the tunnel, a viaduct (now demolished) led to the complex of tracks at Union Station. Originally, both tracks were electrified, but by the end of passenger operations, only the south track was electrified for use of the Fall River and Bristol trains. The other track was primarily used to bring freight to Providence from eastern points without having to go through Pawtucket. The bridge and tunnel were placed in service in 1908.

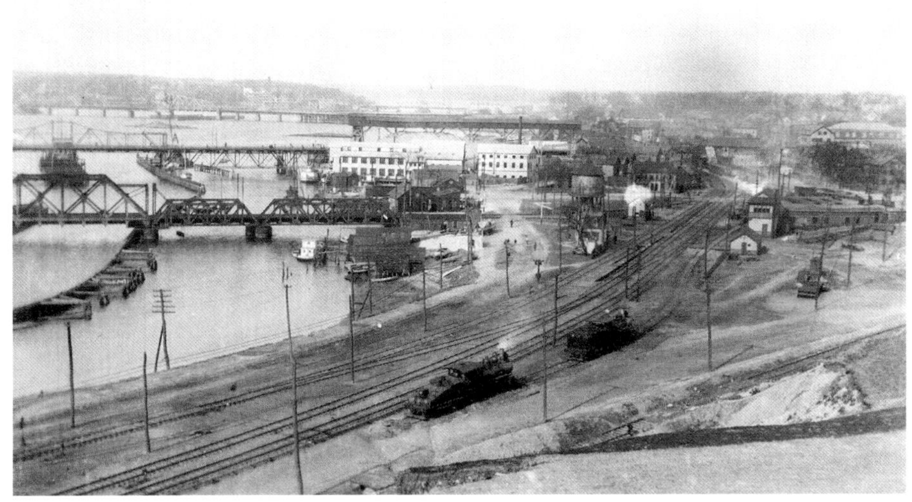

East Providence at the mouth of the Seekonk River after the construction of the new Providence, Warren and Bristol Railroad bridge. The "sharpest curve in the world" is now gone. *Collection of Edward J. Ozog.*

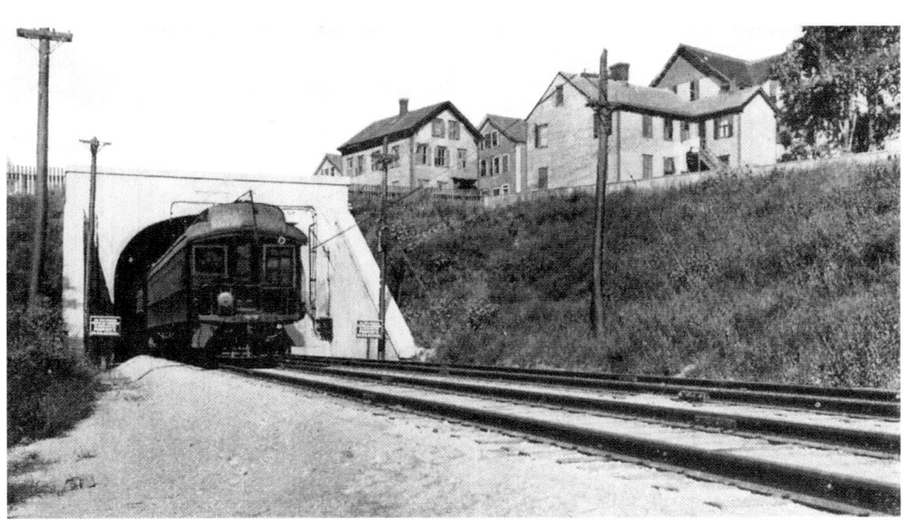

The east portal of the East Side Tunnel during the period of New York, New Haven and Hartford Railroad ownership. *Collection of Edward J. Ozog.*

Electric train service is not economical unless there is a high volume of service, and by the 1920s, the automobile had begun to eat into commuter patronage. By 1934, it was insufficient to support electric trains, and gas-electric commuter cars were substituted. Even these were not enough to keep passenger service alive, and by 1938, the last passengers were carried. The line to Bristol itself survived with bits of freight until 1986, and the last train traveled through the tunnel in 1981, when ownership passed to the State of Rhode Island for unspecified potential future use.

The post-railroad career of the abandoned tunnel would have bemused the builders. Young teenage boys discovered it was a wonderful rite of passage to walk through it—by yourself without a flashlight. Brown University and Rhode Island School of Design students used the tunnel as a staging place to launch assaults on the sensibilities of the good burghers of the East Side by nocturnally flying from the west entrance in outlandish costume, beating drums and bearing torches. Alas, this fun was ended when the tunnel entrances were sealed in the 1990s.

CONSOLIDATOR RAILROADS

The fates of the Providence, Warren and Bristol and Fall River, Warren and Providence Railroads would eventually entwine, but to understand the mechanism by which this marriage took place, it's necessary to look at the evolution of the railroad industry in New England during its middle period, from about 1850 to 1900.

The earliest railroads were primarily built to serve the end destinations of their corporate names (Boston and Providence, Boston and Worcester). Typically financed locally, their purpose was to accommodate the population and industry of their namesake communities.

After the success of these early efforts, railroads expanded primarily by linear extensions from one or another of their endpoints. For example, the Boston and Providence connected directly with the Stonington Line, creating in effect an operationally singular line between Boston and Stonington, even though there might still be separate corporations operating the segments. In another example, the Boston and Worcester Railroad connected directly with the Western Railroad, giving Boston access to the Berkshires.

Not all of these early lines survived, but those that did began to expand, not necessarily by building new lines but by buying, leasing or gaining stock control of existing lines, sometimes as extensions of their mainline and other times as branches. For example, in 1859, the Stonington Line leased the New Haven, New London and Stonington Railroad only a year after it was built to give it access to New Haven. When one looks at some of these acquisitions from the perspective of 150 years of history, not all of these "deals" seem to make sense, but we must remember that in the 1900s, railroads were essentially an unregulated industry, and very clever people soon figured out that there were a lot of ways to make money from a railroad, and not all of them involved building railroads and running trains.

Perhaps the most spectacular of these operations was the Crédit Mobilier of America scandal associated with the building of the great Union Pacific Railroad from Omaha, Nebraska, to Promontory Summit, Utah. When this affair was revealed in the early 1870s, the names of many individuals at the highest level of the federal government were tainted.

The organizers of the railroad figured out that the cost of building the railroad would be high because of the terrain, as would the eventual expense of maintenance. On the other hand, the eventual possibility of a large revenue stream was low. How, then, to make money? The principal source of capital to build the railroad was the United States government. So the officers of the railroad formed an ostensibly separate construction company, the Crédit Mobilier of America, which secretly had the same directors as the railroad, who were also the principal stockholders of Crédit Mobilier. The Crédit Mobilier would bill the railroad with inflated charges. The railroad would pay the bill, using funds obtained from the government, and the Crédit Mobilier would immediately buy stock in the railroad at "par value," which was lower than the market value. It would then turn around and sell the shares of stock in the open market for a handsome profit. These profits more than compensated for the inflated bills the railroad received for construction costs. This complex procedure was necessary to conceal the fact that the railroad (hence the government) was being charged far more for construction than the actual cost, and the difference represented pure profit to the railroad owners. This operation could not have taken place without compliant government officials, and railroad representatives often visited Washington with bagsful of cash. Readers who follow financial news will note some similarities between this operation and the Enron financial disaster.

This example suggests that once the obvious railroad lines were built, there was more profit to be had by financial manipulation than in building or operating new lines. Thus, there gradually emerged in New England a class of railroads whose primary goal was to form a network of railroads (with some new construction, to be sure) and seek profit in the financial markets rather than railroad operations. These will be called "consolidator railroads" here.

These consolidator railroads were to have a huge effect on the railroads of Rhode Island, and we'll look at three of them: the New York and New England Railroad; the Old Colony Railroad; and the ultimate consolidator, the New York, New Haven and Hartford Railroad.

NEW YORK AND NEW ENGLAND RAILROAD

The New York and New England Railroad, which we were introduced to in earlier chapters, had multiple parents, but perhaps the most important was the Hartford, Providence and Fishkill Railroad, which went into service between Hartford and Providence in 1854. It ran into financial difficulties immediately and declared bankruptcy in 1857. In 1863, the Boston-based Boston, Hartford and Erie Railroad, headed by a banker named John Eldridge, gained title to the Hartford, Providence and Fishkill Railroad. Eldridge's intent was apparently to use the Boston, Hartford and Erie Railroad, which existed only on paper, as bait to persuade the Erie Railroad to finance the construction of an actual railroad that would have the existing Hartford, Providence and Fishkill Railroad at its core and would extend to a connection with the Erie Railroad at the Hudson.

This action put Eldridge and the poor little Hartford, Providence and Fishkill Railroad square in the middle of one of the most titanic Wall Street battles of the nineteenth century, in which such luminaries as Cornelius Vanderbilt, Jim Fisk, Daniel Drew and Jay Gould struggled with one another for control of the Erie Railroad. Their purpose was not so much the operation of the railroad as the opportunities for leveraging capital that stock manipulation offered.

When the dust settled, the Boston, Hartford and Erie Railroad lay in bankruptcy and ruin somewhere between 1873 and 1875. The uncertainty arises because most of the land titles of the predecessors were called into question due to various irregularities and frauds, and it was decades of litigation before matters were finally settled.

However, as matters were being argued in court, there were a number of viable railroad properties still running, and the Boston, Hartford and Erie Railroad was reorganized as the New York and New England Railroad to operate these railroads. It, too, went bankrupt in 1895, and all of its lines were taken over by the "ultimate consolidator," the New York, New Haven and Hartford Railroad.

Rhode Island railroads that eventually came under the control of the New York and New England Railroad included the Hartford, Providence and Fishkill Railroad and its branches; the Providence and Springfield Railroad; the Rhode Island and Massachusetts Railroad; the Charles River Railroad going to Woonsocket; and the Woonsocket and Pascoag Railroad. The New York and New England Railroad was more of a holding company than an operating railroad—not an unusual situation among the consolidator railroads.

Old Colony Railroad

The Old Colony Railroad was established in 1845 to run a line between Boston and Plymouth, Massachusetts. In 1854, it merged with the Fall River Railroad to form a new company called, appropriately, the Old Colony and Fall River Railroad. This was a Y-shaped line with the junction at South Braintree. The next logical extension was with the Newport and Fall River Railroad (described in more detail later). The name of the line was again changed, this time to the Old Colony and Newport Railroad, not without hearty objection from Fall River interests. This expanded company proceeded to merge with, buy, lease or build new lines all over southern Massachusetts and Rhode Island until it eventually controlled over six hundred miles of track and fifty-six railroad and steamship companies, including the fabled Fall River Line of steamships. In 1872, the company decided that its name was too restrictive, and it reverted back to the original Old Colony Railroad name.

What is striking in looking at historical accounts of the New York and New England and Old Colony Railroads and the people who owned or ran them is the difference of opinion about their contributions to their areas. In his definitive book on New England railroads, *Steelways of New England*, Alvin F. Harlow characterizes the New York and New England this way:

> *Throughout its entire career, it was living not only on borrowed money—all railroads did and do that—but on borrowed time; for it was born with the seeds of death in its blood stream. Looted by pirates in its infancy, with a main line as crooked and hilly as a snake-trail, unable to obtain any sound outlet to west or southwest, menaced by so well entrenched an antagonist as the New Haven, its eventual demise was as certain as the sunset.*

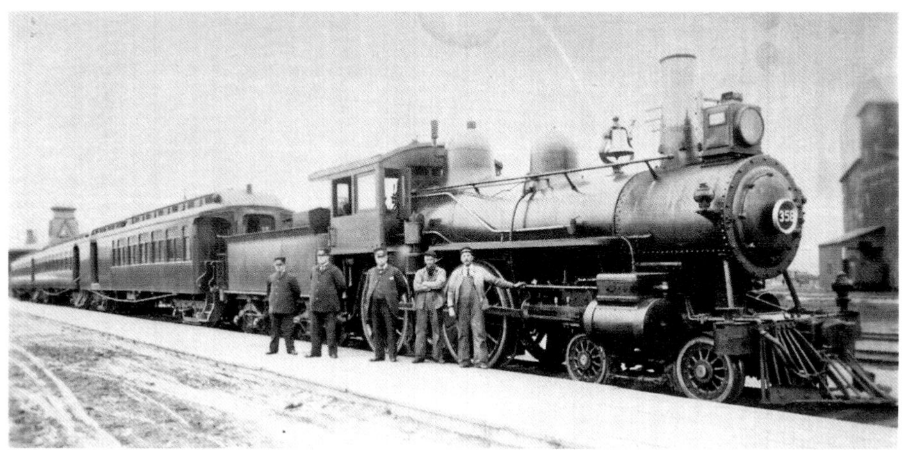

The *Dandy*, a first-class Old Colony and Newport Railroad train, bringing the swells from Boston to Newport. *Collection of Edward J. Ozog.*

In language even more colorful, Charles F. Adam's Jr.'s *Chapters of Erie and Other Essays* refers to the early organizers of the New York and New England Railroad's ancestor, the New York, Hartford and Erie Railroad, in these scathing tones:

> *A faction made its appearance composed of some shrewd and ambitious Wall Street operators, and certain persons from Boston who maintained for the occasion the novel character of railroad reformers. This party, it is needless to say, was as unscrupulous, and as the result proved, as able as either of the others; it represented nothing but a raid made upon the Erie treasury in the interest of a thoroughly bankrupt New England corporation, of which its membership had the control. If the Erie was of doubtful repute in Wall Street, the Boston, Hartford & Erie had long been of worse than doubtful repute in State Street.*

This may be contrasted with the glowing description of the Old Colony Railroad by its historian, Charles E. Fisher, in his *Story of the Old Colony Railroad*:

> *Those who were incorporators and who gave the Old Colony Railroad its name builded [sic] better than they knew for they could not have selected a name more appropriate to the territory it covered. That very name, as solid as Plymouth Rock, stood, and always will stand, for all that is upright, honorable, and progressive in railroading.*

The Old Colony Railroad eventually came to control in Rhode Island the operations of the Boston and Providence Railroad and its subsidiaries, the Providence, Warren and Bristol Railroad and the Newport and Fall River Railroad.

New York, New Haven and Hartford Railroad

The behemoth New York, New Haven and Hartford Railroad started, as did most consolidator railroads, as a single line, between Hartford and New Haven. It became the eponymous New York, New Haven and Hartford Railroad when it joined with the New York and New Haven Railroad in 1872.

The next twenty-five years represented a scale of amalgamation previously unseen in New England. Over one hundred separate rail lines were acquired by sale, stock control, merger or lease. A man named Charles P. Clark became president of the New York, New Haven and Hartford Railroad in 1887, and during his reign, the New York and New England and Old Colony Railroads were absorbed, giving the New York, New Haven and Hartford Railroad a monopoly of almost all railroads longer than a few miles in New England, including all those in Rhode Island.

In 1903, a group of New York investors headed by John Pierpont Morgan gained control of the New York, New Haven and Hartford Railroad. Morgan placed Charles S. Mellen in the presidency, and there began a process of expansion and reorganization called "Morganization." Morgan loathed the idea of competition, while at the same time being a proponent of efficiency. Once having achieved control of the New York, New Haven and Hartford Railroad, his objective became control of *all* transportation in New England—railroads, ship lines, streetcar lines, etc.—using the railroad as a vehicle. Some of his famous quotes offer mute testimony as to how he went about this business:

> *A man generally has two reasons for doing a thing. One that sounds good, and a real one.*
>
> *If you have to ask how much it costs, you can't afford it.*
>
> *Well, I don't know as I want a lawyer to tell me what I cannot do. I hire him to tell how to do what I want to do.*

(These quotes are un-sourced and may be apocryphal.)

Under Morgan and Mellen, the railroad properties experienced great improvement. The lines between New York and New Haven, and many of the New York suburbs, were electrified. New trains, bridges and stations, some very grand, were built. Larger, faster and more powerful locomotives were ordered. The M&M team, unfortunately, did not watch the cost of these improvements too closely and financed them chiefly by borrowing (something very familiar to Rhode Islanders) or issuing more shares of stock, a phenomenon known as diluting the stock. Morgan and Mellen's attempts to gain control of all transportation in New England led to the drafting of the first antitrust laws and much attention from the federal government, which, after World War I, was its largest creditor. The line finally went bankrupt in 1935, both due to the Great Depression and its own excesses.

The New York, New Haven and Hartford Railroad left a mixed legacy in Rhode Island. It is the only name several generations have associated with mainline trains. It made tremendous improvements in the physical plant of the railroads, especially in the early days. After the 1960s, however, it became synonymous with "falling apart" and "shabby," and its passage was scarcely noted when it was reluctantly absorbed by the Penn Central Railroad in 1968.

NEWPORT, AH, NEWPORT

The small city of Newport is on an island, and island communities are almost always different in character than nearby mainland areas, and often a bit eccentric. True, Aquidneck Island is a "courtesy" island, being only 613 feet from the mainland at its closest point. However, that distance might be the English Channel for the psychological difference between folks living in Newport and those living in Tiverton across the channel.

From the very beginning, Newport has had a strong maritime tradition through privateering, slave trading, intercontinental shipping, shipbuilding and an important naval presence. In the past, the U.S. Navy was Rhode Island's largest single employer, and much of that employment was on Aquidneck Island, in Newport, Middletown and Portsmouth. The largest of these naval units was Cruiser Destroyer Fleet Atlantic (CruDesLant), located in Newport for many years. However, immediately after the 1972 presidential elections, in which Rhode Island was one of the two states that gave the smallest plurality to President Nixon (Massachusetts was the only state that voted for George McGovern), the fleet would soon depart and deploy elsewhere. In 1973, CruDesLant sailed off to Norfolk, Virginia, and in 1974, Quonset Naval Air Station on the other side of the bay flew off into the sunset, taking with them twenty-three thousand jobs. Newport in the old days was very much a navy town, with all its pluses and minuses, and the author fondly remembers barhopping the sailor bars with his larger and tougher graduate students on a Saturday night.

In addition to its advantageous location for marine interests, Newport had something else going for it that led to the ultimate construction of a railroad: a salubrious summer climate. From the 1840s until the Civil War, Newport was the summer residence of wealthy southern plantation owners who came north to avoid the fetid summer vapors of their homes. After the war, that trade was over but was quickly replaced by northern nabobs who decided that Newport would become the summer location of New York society. New York City was often stifling in the summer, and Newport's long association with wealth led to the construction of the first of the huge homes on Newport's Bellevue Avenue, Château sur Mer, in 1852. The peak of Gilded Age construction occurred during the 1890s, and a number of the owners of these houses made their fortunes in railroading, particularly the Vanderbilt family of the New York Central Railroad and the streetcar royalty of Philadelphia, the Wideners.

The Old Colony Railroad completed its line from Boston to Newport via Fall River in 1864. It opened Newport to affluent visitors from Boston coming for extended stays at the many fine hotels that opened up after the Civil War and, then as now, day-trippers intent on dropping a few bucks on souvenirs and chowder. Rail access to New York was a different story. The shortest all-rail route from Newport to New York involved going first to Fall River, changing trains to Providence and then changing again in Providence for a through train to New York. The mansion owners, however, tended not to go back and forth from their base in New York City. They would bring their families and servants up at the beginning of the summer "season," which might only be six weeks long, and then leave the mansions to caretakers for the rest of the year after their departure. For those folks, they could attach their private railroad cars to the end of Rhode Island–bound trains from Manhattan and have the cars detached at either Kingston or Wickford Junction, where they would be attached to one of the short-line railroads that will be discussed in a later chapter. The cars would be parked at one of the private car storage tracks at Wickford or Narragansett, and the owners would take one of the little ferries to Newport. Not too much of a hardship for a twice-a-year trip.

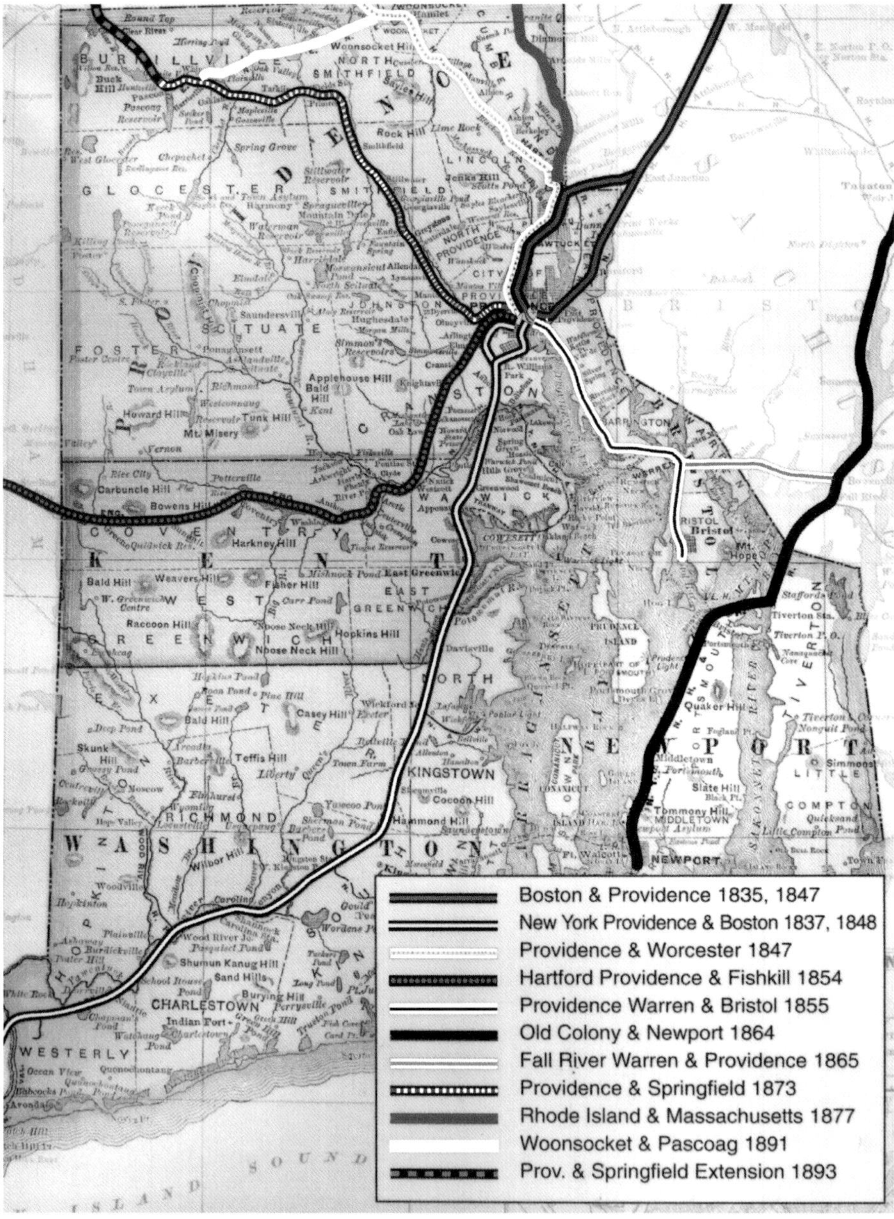

The final limit of railroad construction in Rhode Island. After 1893, there were no new independent railroads or significant branches built. *Rhode Island Railroad Museum.*

After the beginning of the twentieth century, like most of the other railroads in this chapter, the Old Colony Railroad line to Newport suffered a gradual decline and slide into oblivion. The last regularly scheduled passenger train departed, without much notice, in 1938. Freight service continued on a sporadic basis. In 1976, the line south of Portsmouth was sold to the State of Rhode Island, which in turn leased it to a tourist line, the Old Colony and Newport Railway (www.ocnrr.com), which had assumed the name of the old mainline railroad, and the Newport Dinner Train. A collision between a train and a barge knocked out the railroad bridge between Portsmouth and Tiverton in 1988, so as far as railroads are concerned, Aquidneck Island is truly an island again.

THE EAST SIDE LINES TODAY

The harried commuter sweating through jammed I-195 traffic on his way from Barrington to Providence might reflect that had things turned out a bit differently, he might today be riding to work on a fast, comfortable electric train, undoubtedly equipped with WiFi, which would get him to his destination in about half the time as his present commute by car. As long as we're dreaming, he might even be savoring a martini in the parlor car, as he would be able to on the Long Island Railroad's *Cannonball* to Montauk, were he riding that train today. Looking up from his iPad, he would have been able to see one of the prettiest coastlines on the eastern seaboard. As he sipped away, he'd watch the sun set over Narragansett Bay. Unfortunately, because his ancestors fell in love with the automobile, he can't do that and must contend with fumes, traffic and texting, tailgating fellow drivers.

There is one category of traveler who can still enjoy much of the original east bay routes—the bicyclist. Almost the whole of the Providence, Warren and Bristol Railroad is today the East Bay Bicycle Path.

Our friend Google Earth reveals almost the entire extent of the old lines. Starting at the northern end of the bicycle path in East Providence, across Fort Hill from the original India Point railroad bridge, the bike path follows almost exactly the railroad right of way to "downtown" Bristol. In Warren, at Croade Street, you can see in the aerial view where the Fall River line branched off. Much of the old line is submerged in suburbia, but there is enough left to trace the line all the way to the bank of the Taunton River.

On Aquidneck Island, the tracks are intact to the defunct bridge crossing at the north end of the island. On the Tiverton side, the tracks are mostly gone, but with a bit of imagination, one can trace the line up the coast to a few miles south of Fall River, where the tracks pick up again. Out of Fall River, the original Old Colony line to the northeast survives in freight service.

It is tempting to think "what might have been," and certainly there have been some "rails to trails to rails" conversions, but with the passage of time, such reconversions become more difficult because there is now a twenty-first-century constituency, the bicyclists, who do not easily give up their wonderful trails—and who could blame them?

Chapter 9

LITTLE GUYS

Every state has a collection of tiny railroads whose histories are often longer than their lines, and Rhode Island is no exception. Most of these have been abandoned, shrunk or converted to other uses, but a few are more interesting than the big boys.

Westerly Granite Railroads

In 1840, Orlando Smith discovered an outcropping of granite near what is now the location of the Babcock-Smith House in downtown Westerly. It proved to be of superb quality, fine grained, very hard and having a variety of colors, mostly reddish or pinkish. It was used to make monuments and sheath buildings all over the country. Other deposits were found in nearby Bradford and Ashaway. The granite was not only quarried there but also made into cemetery monuments and public sculptures.

The granite was quarried in open pits, which often filled with water after their abandonment. These locations around Westerly can easily be identified on Google Earth. The industry survived until the early 1950s, and Westerly's large Italian population started with stonecutters who were brought over from Italy to work the granite. They were primarily from Sicily and Calabria. (Culinary note: This is heresy, but the best Italian charcuterie is not to be found on Providence's Federal Hill but in Westerly. You have to hunt for it, though.) Over 30 percent of the population of Westerly is of Italian origin.

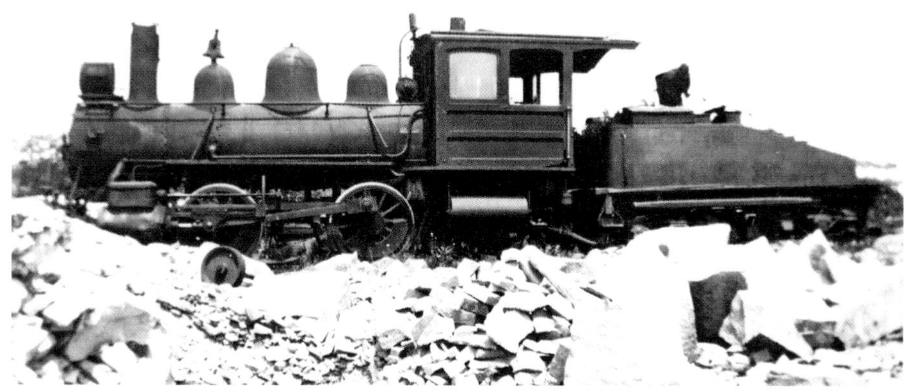

Smith Granite Company No. 1, bought from the Moshassuck Valley Railroad. *Collection of Edward J. Ozog.*

Railroads linked several of these quarries with the Stonington Line mainline in or near Westerly. The first of these connected the New England Granite Works in 1870 and was then extended to the Smith Granite Company in 1892. Another line went to the Sullivan Granite Company in nearby Bradford. Also in Bradford, the Bradford Dyeing Association, a fabric printer that today is the largest American manufacturer of military battle dress uniform fabrics, once had an extensive network of industrial sidings, a few remains of which can still be seen near both the plant and the current Amtrak mainline. Most of these lines were, strictly speaking, industrial railroads, serving only a single industry, and typically were less than a mile long. In some cases, they were operated by industrial locomotives owned by the quarries. New England Granite Company operated an adorable little 0-4-0 tank switcher that would have looked at home on a Lionel model railroad. Smith Granite Company operated a slope-back tender 0-4-0 that in 1932 looked like it hadn't been updated since the 1890s.

WOOD RIVER BRANCH RAILROAD

Between Kingston Station and Westerly, today's Amtrak line passes through country that is almost as rural as it was a century ago. About halfway between Kingston and Westerly, on the old Stonington Line, lies the tiny village of

Wood River Junction, in the town of Richmond. Wood River Junction has a disproportionate amount of tragedy associated with it. In 1873, one of the most horrific accidents in Rhode Island railroad history occurred at Richmond Switch, as Wood River Junction was then known.

The rains had been heavy in April of that year, and in the village, water had backed up behind a small dam across the Pawcatuck River, only about 150 feet from the Stonington Line tracks. There was a short railroad bridge, about 20 feet long, over the river. Sometime between midnight and 3:00 a.m., unbeknownst to neighbors, the dam broke, completely washing away the bridge.

At 3:00 a.m. on April 19, the Boston-bound boat train from Stonington hurtled across the gap at forty miles per hour. The engine flew across the opening, burying its nose in the opposite bank. The tender followed suit, spilling coal, which immediately caught fire from the embers pouring from the ruptured firebox. Engineer and firemen were both killed instantly.

The cars immediately following the engine piled into one another, some catching fire from spilled flammable oil from the oil lamps and flaming coal

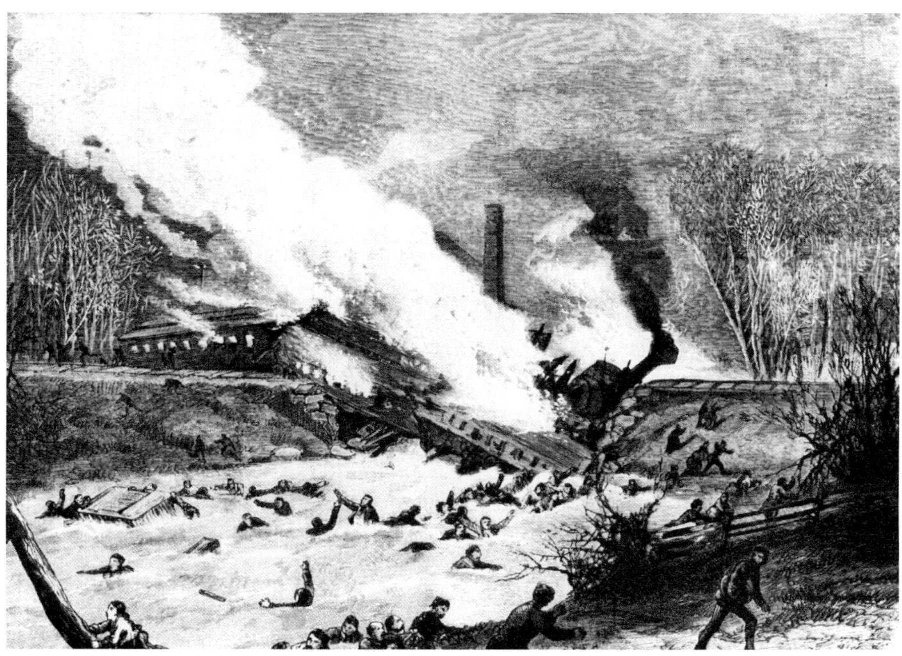

Terrible disaster at Richmond Switch, 1873. *Rhode Island Railroad Museum.*

from the stoves in the cars. Including the engine crew, seven people perished in the conflagration, most suffering severe burns. Fortunately, a mail train was following only ten minutes behind the boat train and was flagged down before it hit the wreckage. It backed up to Westerly, immediately bringing back medical personnel, without whose assistance the death rate would surely have been higher.

Ninety-one years later, in 1964, little Wood River Junction would gain another, more contemporary kind of notoriety. In 1964, the United Nuclear Company built a nuclear fuel reprocessing facility less than half a mile from the location of the wreck at Richmond Switch. On July 24, Robert Peabody, a worker at the plant, was pouring a solution of a uranium compound into a mixer. Evidently, the concentration of uranium was higher than he thought, and he saw a blue flash and was knocked over. Forty-nine hours later, he was dead of radiation poisoning. His was the first and only death due to acute exposure to radiation in a commercial nuclear facility in the United States. This "criticality" accident was similar to two others that resulted in fatalities in government laboratories shortly after World War II.

Why was this apparently jinxed location called first "Richmond Switch" and then "Wood River Junction"? In 1867, a new railroad charter was granted by the Rhode Island legislature to the Wood River Railroad to build a line from Greene—on the Rhode Island–Connecticut border on the Hartford, Providence and Fishkill Railroad—through Hope Valley to Richmond Switch on the Stonington Line. The name "Richmond Switch" antedates the short-line railroad, there having been a passing track, station, water tank and siding for the use of the agricultural community in the town of Richmond. It is not clear what was on the minds of the organizers of the Wood River Railroad, because at that time, there was little industry along the potential route. Possibly they hoped to tap some of the textile traffic from the Pawtuxet Valley mills, but they would have faced formidable competition from both the Stonington Line and the Hartford, Providence and Fishkill Railroad.

In any event, they either couldn't raise the money or had second thoughts, because a new charter was issued in 1872 to the Wood River Branch Railroad to build a line from Hope Valley (then Locustville) to Richmond Switch, or Wood River Junction, as it was known thereafter. The line was capitalized at $250,000, but only $60,000 of stock was issued, of which the Stonington Line purchased $20,000, thus in effect becoming a not-too-silent partner.

The line was completed, and the first train ran in July 1874. There were a half dozen small mills along the route that generated traffic, but perhaps the largest source of income was the Nichols and Langworthy Machine Company at Hope Valley. Nichols and Langworthy was a general machine factory, producing stationary steam boilers, textile machinery and printing presses. Perhaps the most famous "alumni" of Nichols and Langworthy were machinists Stephen Wilcox and George Babcock, who invented the water-tube boiler in 1867. This boiler design permitted much higher boiler pressures to be used than previous configurations. The two inventors established the industrial giant Babcock and Wilcox, which produced the boilers and engines for over half the U.S. Navy's ships built during World War II and pioneered boiler design for the nuclear power plant industry. The Nichols and Langworthy plant was largely leveled by a fire in 1909 and went under completely in 1925.

From the beginning, the Wood River Branch Railroad was a generally unprofitable operation that never paid a dividend in its seventy-odd years of operation. Net annual earnings in the 1880s were typically $2,000 to $3,000. Perhaps this was not surprising, as the passenger fare from Hope Valley to Wood River Junction was $0.25 until 1884, when it was raised to $0.30. The board of directors was aware of Rhode Island economic tradition; however, as the minutes from the annual meeting of 1895 note, the railroad's superintendent was authorized to offer special rates of fare to members of the Rhode Island General Assembly.

The Wood River Branch Railroad had conventional rolling stock in the early days but got funkier as the money started to run out. Its first locomotive was purchased new from the Rhode Island Locomotive Works for $8,500. It was the then-ubiquitous 4-4-0 American type used for both freight and passenger trains. Following the custom of the day, it was named, rather than numbered, in honor of Gardner Nichols, president of Nichols and Langworthy. It was in service until 1906. This was the last new locomotive purchased by the Wood River Branch Railroad. For that matter, it was almost the last *anything* purchased new by the charming but threadbare little line.

The second locomotive, the *Wincheck*, named after a local pond, came to the Wood River Branch Railroad by a more circuitous route. It was built in 1872 as a switch engine for the Boston and Providence Railroad, sold to the Narragansett Pier Railroad, another Rhode Island short line, and then finally sold to the Wood River Branch Railroad in 1883. Photographs exist of the road's "business train," a bizarre construction consisting of two four-wheeled carts fastened together by a steel strap, powered by a gasoline engine and equipped with bench seats. It was called, with no small irony, the *President's Special.*

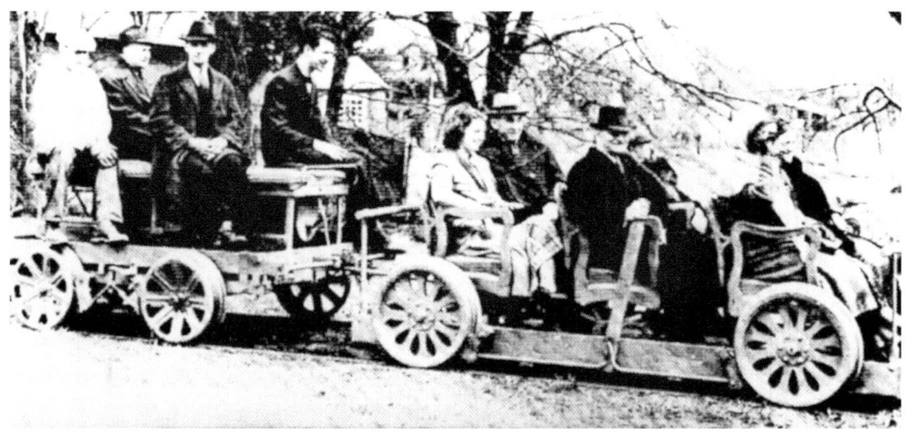

The *President's Special* of the Wood River Branch Railroad. Lucy Rawlings Tootell is the young woman in the third row. It is doubtful that the President's Special would meet many, if any, of the Federal Railroad Administration's safety requirements. *Rhode Island Railroad Museum.*

To give an idea of how close to the economic edge this little line operated, in the company's annual report for 1881, it was reported that there was not a single piece of spare rail on the property. If a rail broke on the line, a section of rail would be "borrowed" from another piece of track—not specified, but hopefully from a siding.

Some idea of the local community's attitude toward the Wood River Branch Railroad is found in a wonderful, albeit unattributed, quote from Merle K. Peirce's excellent online article from the 1897 *Westerly Sun* about the minuscule railroad:

> *Two men start for a trip around the world. One starts from Hope Valley and the other from Wood River Junction. Can the Hope Valley man reach Wood River Junction (by the usual route, of course) by the time the other completes the circuit of the globe and reaches his starting point at the Junction?*

In 1917, Mr. Roy Rawlings established a grain mill at the end of the line in Hope Valley. He was to become one of the major customers of the line, and we will meet him again soon. Mr. Rawlings had been the speaker of the Rhode Island General Assembly, showing that even at this late date, South County's influence was still strong in the state.

The New York, New Haven and Hartford Railroad, having taken over the Stonington Line, also assumed the Wood River Branch's bonded indebtedness. In 1924, a $56,400 first mortgage payment came due, but the larger road did not foreclose. It was having financial difficulties of its own and had no interest in assuming the problems of a six-mile-long headache. Rather, when floods hit the little line in 1927, the New York, New Haven and Hartford Railroad assisted the smaller line in getting back to operation, evidently hoping to preserve the bit of income that the mills along the way provided. However, passenger service ended, and the line's only motive power was a tiny four-wheeled, gas-powered switch engine. By 1937, the New York, New Haven and Hartford Railroad tired of supporting the smaller road and sold the entire railroad—right of way, track, equipment and buildings—to Roy Rawlings, the grain mill owner, for $301.

Rawlings and his two children, Lucy Rawlings Tootell and Rob Roy Rawlings (both of whom went on to become Rhode Island legislators, Lucy a Democrat and Rob Roy a Republican), became members of the board of directors, and in 1941, Lucy was elected vice-president of the road, at the time the only woman in the United States to hold such a position. The road scrabbled on until 1947, when a fire destroyed the grain mill and the line's major reason for existence. It was put up for sale with no takers and quietly passed into history. Much of the documentation of the Wood River Branch Railroad we owe to the efforts of a single person, the remarkable Lucy Rawlings Tootell, who lived to the age of ninety-nine and founded what seemed to be half the historical societies in South County.

The line has been gone too long for Google Earth to find many traces. At Wood River Junction itself, you can see a line of trees curve to the north side of the Amtrak tracks, bend to the north and then follow a straight line past a school bus parking area and then by one side of a small subdivision that must have been laid out by a German developer because the names of the streets are O'Shea Lane, O'Rieley Court, O'Keefe Drive and O'Sullivan Drive. Past this Bit O' Erin, the tree line (and probable right of way) continues northwest until it crosses a turf farm and then becomes indistinct, as the line would have bent to the west near Woodville. The black-and-white Google Earth aerial photograph of March 28, 1995, clearly shows the remains of the bridge abutments where the line crossed the Wood River and the right of way some distance past the bridge. Beyond Woodville, there is a possible right of way through the trees in a northward direction, until it intersects the suspiciously named Old Depot Road, where the Canonchet station would have been, and then continues north until it appears to become Mechanic Street, which goes past the old Nichols and Langworthy mill and then into Hope Valley. Such are the mortal remains of the Wood River Branch Railroad.

NARRAGANSETT PIER RAILROAD

Rowland G. Hazard was not a man to be trifled with. Son of the founder of the textile mill in Peace Dale in South County, Hazard had modernized the mills in the 1840s, becoming rich in the process, and became a promoter of abolitionist and educational causes. He also served in the Rhode Island state legislature during the 1850s and 1860s.

Hazard frequently journeyed to New York on the Stonington Line. To save himself time, he bought batches of tickets in advance from the old West Kingston depot. However, tickets were normally good only on the date they were sold, and the date was stamped on the ticket. On November 3, 1854, Hazard boarded at Kingston and showed the conductor his ticket. The conductor looked at the ticket and told Hazard that his ticket was no good, because it had a prior date stamp on it, and he would have to buy a new one.

Hazard, with some degree of indignation, replied that this had never happened to him before and he had no intention of buying a new ticket; he had already bought one, but if there was a difference in fare between the two dates, he would be happy to pay that. The conductor replied that, no, he would have to buy a new ticket. Hazard then asked the conductor if he knew to whom he was talking. The conductor replied that he didn't give a tinker's damn whom he was talking to and departed to find the president of the Stonington Line, Captain Charles P. Williams of Stonington, who coincidentally was riding in a different car.

Williams returned, Hazard repeated his story and Williams told him that he would have to either pay the full fare or he would be ejected from the train at the next stop. Hazard refused and was unceremoniously deposited on the platform at Westerly, causing him to miss his boat.

At the next available opportunity, Hazard roasted and blasted the railroad before the state legislature, condemning it for its fare policies in Rhode Island (without mentioning the incident that had prompted the diatribe). Hazard argued for much greater regulation of railroads, a concept that brought fear and loathing to the breasts of railroad officials. A few years later, Hazard was involved in the building of his family's very own railroad, the Narragansett Pier Railroad, and was not above using his oratorical skills and influence in determining favorable policies for the new line.

The Hazard family had roots that ran wide and deep in Rhode Island. Established in the 1600s, the Hazards started the family fortune in agriculture in South County, with excursions into naval heroism (Oliver Hazard Perry of "Don't give up the ship!" fame) and, through marriage, connections to some of the other great American fortunes (Belmont, Auchincloss). The South County branch of the family had the odd tradition of alternately naming a male Rowland Hazard and one of his sons Rowland Gibson Hazard and then returning to Rowland Hazard for the next generation. This custom has proven vexatious for historians, because there have been occasions when there were several adult Rowland Hazards attending to family business, and it is not always evident which Rowland was doing what.

The Rowland G. Hazard we are concerned with was born in 1801 and lived until 1894. His father, Rowland Hazard, built a small cotton mill in 1802 on the banks of the Saugatucket River in South County, in a village that would later be called Peace Dale, after Rowland's wife, Mary Peace. The plant soon transitioned to manufacture both cotton and wool fabrics, specializing in inexpensive materials like linsey-woolsey, a linen/wool blend, and "Negro cloth," a rough, unbleached cotton. Both were shipped to southern markets and primarily used to make clothing and blankets for slaves. Rowland G. and his brothers took over the mill in the late 1820s.

Rowland G. became increasingly active in abolitionist activities, making his products less welcome in the South. In 1845, a fire gutted the mill, and the brothers decided to rebuild and also redirect. The product line was shifted to high-quality woolen yarns, which proved to be very popular. Water

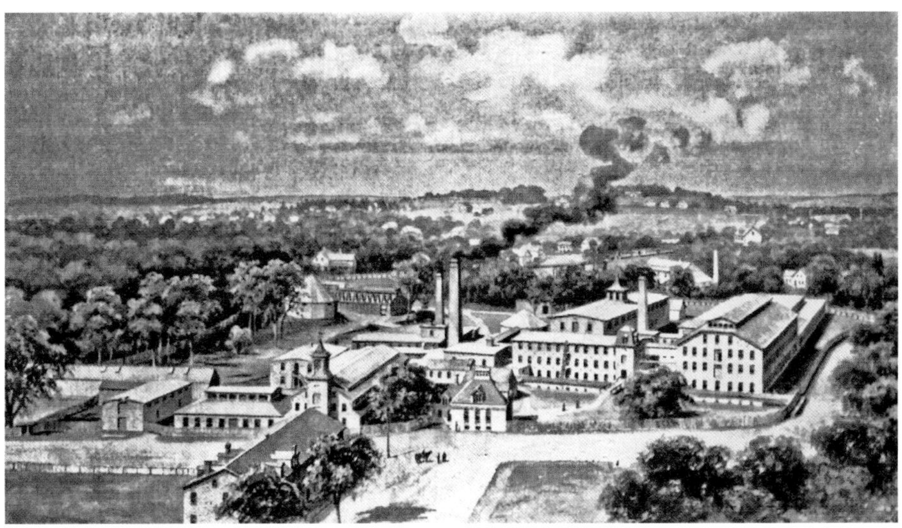

The Peace Dale mills. A Narragansett Pier Railroad train can be seen in the background. *Collection of Edward J. Ozog.*

had been the original source of power for the mill, and although new water wheels were put on line, steam soon became the dominant power source. The boilers were fueled by coal, which at first was brought to a dock in Narragansett Pier by ship and then transloaded to wagons for transport to Peace Dale, a cumbersome and expensive process.

While the mill was expanding and prospering, the village of Narragansett Pier, four miles away on the coast, was developing as a summer resort, more populist in orientation than Newport and having a bit more raffish of a reputation, somewhat like Las Vegas's today. Summer hotels were established in the 1860s, but the eight-mile, hour-long dusty stage ride from Kingston Station inhibited all but the most dedicated "sea bathers."

By 1860, three powerful forces were in play that practically cried for a railroad to be built from the West Kingston stop on the Stonington Line to Narragansett Pier. First, the mill at Peace Dale needed a more economical way to get coal for its power plant from the dock at Narragansett Pier to the powerhouse. Second, the town of Narragansett Pier could not fully develop as a resort until there was easy, fast, comfortable transportation all the way from the major East Coast cities to the Pier, as it came to be known locally. Finally, it would be convenient for the Peace Dale mill to have rail transportation inbound for its raw materials and outbound for its finished products.

In 1868, Rowland G. allied with William Sprague and the A. & W. Sprague Company to build a railroad from West Kingston to Narragansett Pier and obtained a state charter toward that end. The Spragues were another enormously wealthy and politically connected Rhode Island family engaged in the textile industry. William Sprague's brother Amasa was murdered in 1843 in one of Rhode Island's most famous cases. An Irish immigrant, John Gordon, was arrested, tried and convicted of the murder on the flimsiest of evidence. The conviction was largely based on anti-Irish, anti-Catholic sentiment. He was hanged on February 14, 1845. On June 19, 2011, Rhode Island governor Lincoln Chafee posthumously pardoned Gordon.

The Sprague Company was based in Cranston. Neither William Sprague nor the Hazards had any railroad experience. The partnership did not come to fruition. The financial Panic of 1873 largely destroyed the Sprague Company's financial position, and Rowland G. and William Sprague were unlikely bedfellows from the start—Rowland G. was active in the temperance, free library and women's suffrage movements, whereas ex-governor Sprague was a hard-drinking man who was involved in a very messy and public divorce.

Not long after the original charter was obtained, a preliminary survey was made of the route. Like the earlier survey for the Stonington Line, it bypassed Kingston. This plan made commercial interests in Kingston very nervous, as a line going directly from West Kingston to Peace Dale, Wakefield and the Pier would place Kingston in a very disadvantageous economic position.

After the dust from the Panic of 1873 had settled, the surviving potential investors in the railroad were the Hazard family, a few hotel operators in the Pier and a few small-fry businesses in Wakefield. Just before the original charter was to expire in 1875, Rowland G. called a meeting in Peace Dale to reorganize the railroad company without the Sprague interests.

The vexing issue of the route remained to be settled. There were two clear candidates. The first would go up and over Kingston Hill, and the other would skirt to the south of Larkin Pond and Tefft Hill, thence into Peace Dale, Wakefield and then the Pier. The Kingston route would be more expensive to build, but Elisha R. Potter Jr., a rabid Kingston booster, raised $15,000 to cover the additional costs of the route and a station in Kingston proper. What made the ensuing debate more colorful was the fact that Potter and Rowland G. had been at loggerheads over every conceivable issue for almost as long as anyone could remember.

On January 26, 1876, in the centenary year, a meeting of all stockholders was held to vote on the routing of the railroad. The Kingston route was resoundingly defeated. The Potter and Hazard families then launched a feud that lasted many years.

Although the Hazard family was extremely generous to its community and their workers, in business, they pinched the proverbial nickel until the buffalo screamed. In building the railroad, they demanded first-class materials for Walmart prices. Their first locomotive was bought on a low bid from Mason Works in Massachusetts. Rowland G. fired off a series of letters to Mason demanding extras. Finally, Mason responded thusly: "I have never furnished Flag Staves. They are expensive and boyish…One pump is sufficient…You paid $800 less for an engine than I have ever sold before. You should not expect too much in the way of extra furnishing."

The first train rolled on July 17, 1876. Initially, the major profit center was passenger traffic, but with the coming of the automobile and the decrease in allure of Narragansett as a destination in favor of trendier resort areas, passenger traffic lagged, and freight service was insufficient to make up the difference. The daily operation of the Narragansett Pier Railroad became financially onerous to the Hazards, and in 1910, they began discussions with the New York, New Haven and Hartford Railroad, then under the

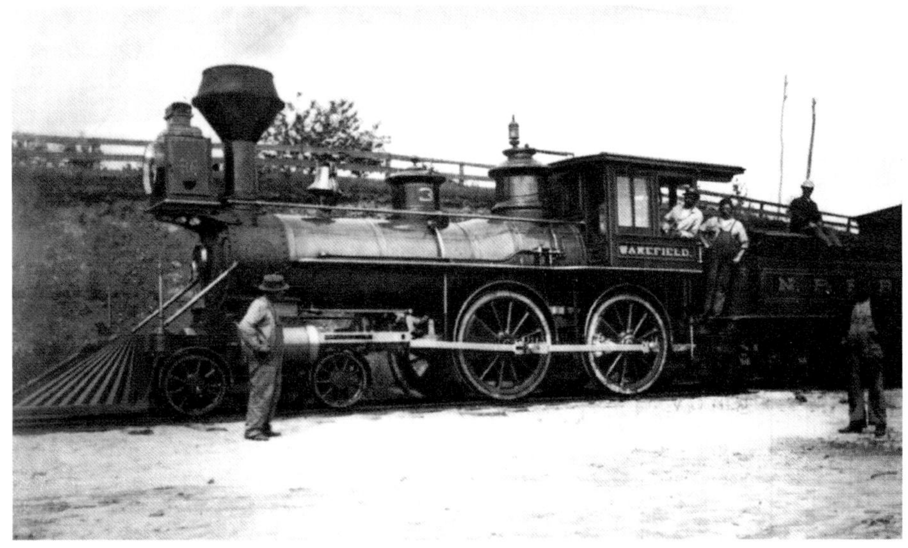

Locomotive No. 3, the *Wakefield*, bought new from Brooks in 1883 and sold six years later. *Collection of Edward J. Ozog.*

control of J.P. Morgan. One might reasonably ask what interest Morgan could possibly have in an eight-mile-long railroad. In 1910, the New York, New Haven and Hartford Railroad was looking at a single potential major competitor that might threaten its New England lines: the Grand Trunk Railroad based in Canada. The Grand Trunk Railroad was making noises about extending lines south through Massachusetts and to Narragansett Bay. One way it might do so would be to acquire the poor little Narragansett Pier Railroad. From the perspective of time, it is difficult to see this as a serious threat to Morgan—where would you put a major port facility at the Pier? But acquiring control of the short line would be cheap insurance, and the Morgan interests took over.

As was typical of railroad dealings of the time, the transaction was not simple. Rather than coming under direct control of the New York, New Haven and Hartford Railroad, the Narragansett Pier Railroad was placed under the aegis of the Rhode Island Company, the Morgan-controlled holding company that owned or managed all the electric streetcar lines in Rhode Island. The Rhode Island Company was already experiencing heavy financial weather, and its management of the short line could best be considered benign neglect. In 1918, all railroads were taken over by the federal government for the duration of World War I. In 1920, the railroads returned to private ownership, but by that time, the Rhode Island Company was bankrupt; the New York, New Haven and Hartford Railroad was more worried about survival than competition; and the Narragansett Pier Railroad was returned to its unhappy original owners.

In the 1920s and '30s, the road began a long, slow decline. Passenger service, one of the reasons for building the road in the first place, was the first to be downgraded. In 1921, the line that had made a good income by hauling the private railroad cars of the ultra-rich replaced all of its passenger trains with rail buses, quaint hybrid vehicles that looked like what they were: buses on railroad wheels. These soon acquired the affectionate local name of "Mickey Dinks" after two of the early motormen. The line's regular passenger cars were not scrapped but kept in reserve for extra summer trains and the ancestors of today's "railfan trips."

The era of steam locomotives ended in 1937 with the purchase of a diminutive four-wheel Plymouth gasoline-powered switch engine. A 1941 photograph shows her fitted charmingly with a smokestack-shaped exhaust pipe, bell and sand dome, giving her a passing resemblance to a steam engine. More gasoline- or diesel-powered locomotives were added over the years, but none gave perfect service.

World War II brought added business but also added expenses and wear and tear on the equipment and buildings of the line. By the end of the war, as had happened in many previous years, the line ran at a deficit.

The Hazard family finally decided that it was time to bail, but potential buyers were scarce. In 1946, however, a group called American Associates bought the line for $25,000, and herein lies a bit of a mystery. American Associates was a family trust headed by a man named Royal Little, who had established a large and profitable textile firm he called Textron in 1944. Little went on to become the inventor of the modern American conglomerate corporation. Starting in 1950, Textron started buying companies that made products that had nothing to do with one another, like helicopters, garment bags and golf carts. Little had a home in Narragansett, and it is not unreasonable to think that he might have been testing his ideas for conglomerates with the purchase of the Narragansett Pier Railroad, which on the face of it had little to do with the manufacture of parachutes, a major component of Textron business at the time.

The American Associates era was not a happy one for the Narragansett Pier Railroad. All passenger service was eliminated in 1952, and the line between Wakefield and the Pier was abandoned not long after. In 1953, the Wakefield Branch Company, a local lumberyard, bought the remains of

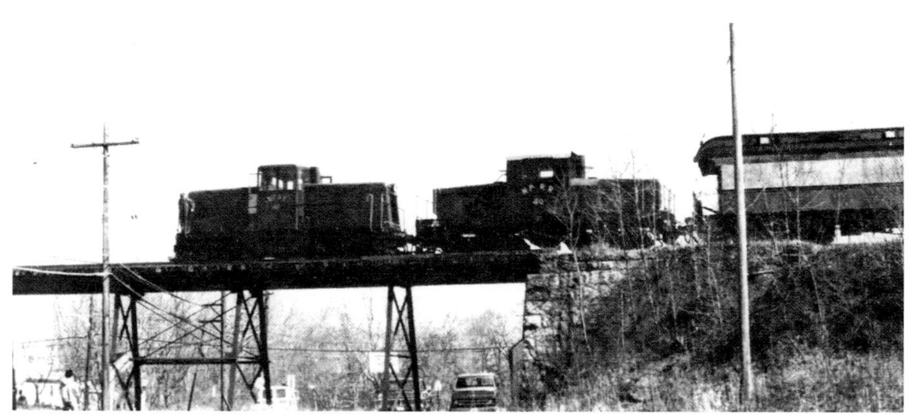

A sad moment—the last train on the Narragansett Pier Railroad. The equipment was being brought to Kingston for shipment to new final destinations. *Rhode Island Railroad Museum.*

the line for $12,000. Some improvements in facilities and equipment were made, and the extraordinary purchase of a brand-new locomotive was made in 1958. However, the demise in 1963 of the largest fish-processing plant in nearby Galilee, which exported tank car loads of liquefied fish guts for fertilizer and accounted for over half the line's business, started the playing of the funeral march. In 1964, the line was sold to a J. Anthony Hanold, an investor who attempted to convert the railroad to a tourist line. From the start, the cards were stacked against him and another railfan who later bought the line from Hanold. There was little of touristic interest at either end of the line, and the vegetation along the right of way had grown so much that the right of way appeared to be like a tunnel through trees. Finally, the line was purchased by the then-current owner of the mill buildings in Peace Dale, Anthony Guarriello, who intended to tear the trestles down in Peace Dale to improve the traffic flow in the village. The line was officially abandoned in its entirety in 1981.

In 1890, the running time for the train between Kingston Station and Narragansett Pier (with three stops) was twenty minutes. Today, on a Friday afternoon in summer, it takes an hour to an hour and a half to drive the same distance. Ah, progress.

Depending on one's point of view, there is a happy ending to the story. After seemingly endless discussions and negotiations with the myriad government agencies involved, the old right of way became the William

O'Neill bike path in the mid-1990s, under the federal Intermodal Surface Transportation Efficiency Act (ISTEA). One can now travel the entire length from Kingston Station to the outskirts of the Pier, with over 95 percent of the path along the original route. Kingston Station survives, as does the Peace Dale station, now a private residence, and the second Pier station, now a laundry and dive shop. A few pieces of Narragansett Pier Railroad rail equipment are still extant, including a caboose at the Valley Railroad in Essex, Connecticut, and a Vulcan sixty-five-ton locomotive, sadly rusting away in Micaville, North Carolina.

NEWPORT AND WICKFORD RAILROAD AND STEAMSHIP COMPANY

By 1870, the Gilded Age had begun with a vengeance in Newport. The first of the elaborate summer "cottages" had been built, and it almost seemed that money was flowing into the town faster than it could be spent. Getting to Newport from New York, however, was *so* tiresome. The sailing yachts the gentlemen used for racing were not really suited for family travel, and the more sedate ones used for cruising still had to deal with the possibility of unpleasantness around Point Judith. The train trip all the way through Providence and Fall River was exhausting, even in one's private railroad car. Clearly, there had to be a better way to Newport from the west.

In the meantime, across the bay, the quaint little colonial village of Wickford was quietly dying. After being bypassed by the Stonington Line in 1837, Wickford had for a while enjoyed a thriving ship- and boat-building trade, but its harbor was too small to build the kinds of boats and ships that were needed as the nineteenth century approached its three-quarters mark. There was only one small mill in Wickford, but there were several in the nearby villages of Hamilton, Lafayette and Belleville, and as their workers tended to live in the immediate vicinity of the mills, Wickford got little trade from them. The quaint houses and charming streets began to exude the early signs of decay.

The situation and time were right for a railroad-steamship combination line to connect the Stonington Line directly to Newport via Wickford without the Providence detour. Such rail-boat operations were common from the 1830s to the 1920s. In 1864, the Newport and Wickford Railroad and Steamship Company was formed, primarily with Newport and New York capital. The early directors were a tony group. The president of the

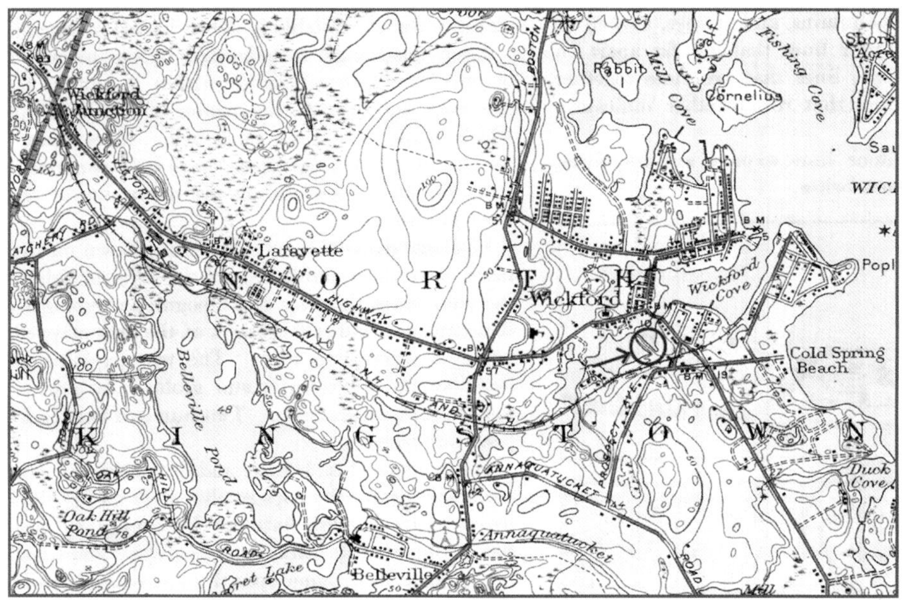

The Newport and Wickford Railroad in its latter days. The final portion to the ferry dock on Steamboat Avenue is gone. *USGS map 1942.*

corporation, Mr. George M. Miller, was noted as being a guest at Mrs. John Carter Brown's "villa" in Newport in 1888, along with Cornelius Vanderbilt II and his brother Frederick. Other directors included Senator George Peabody Wetmore (Skull and Bones '67) and Representative George Gordon King.

Construction of the railroad started in 1870 and was relatively simple and straightforward. From a switch off the Stonington Line main at Wickford Junction, where Ten Rod Road crossed the tracks, the line basically followed a few hundred feet to the south of that road past the Rodman Mill at Lafayette, through Belleville and then to a station just to the south of Wickford. From there, the track continued about six-tenths of a mile along what is today Steamboat Street to the ferry landing (Wickford Landing) at Poplar Point. There could be found a turntable and tracks for storing private cars. There was also a turntable at Wickford Junction. The whole line was only about three and a half miles long. The majority of the line's income in the early days was from passengers, but it also had the mail contract for Newport, and there was freight service to the mills along the line.

It took about ten minutes for the train ride, and the boat journey was about seventy-five minutes in mostly protected waters. The line was not

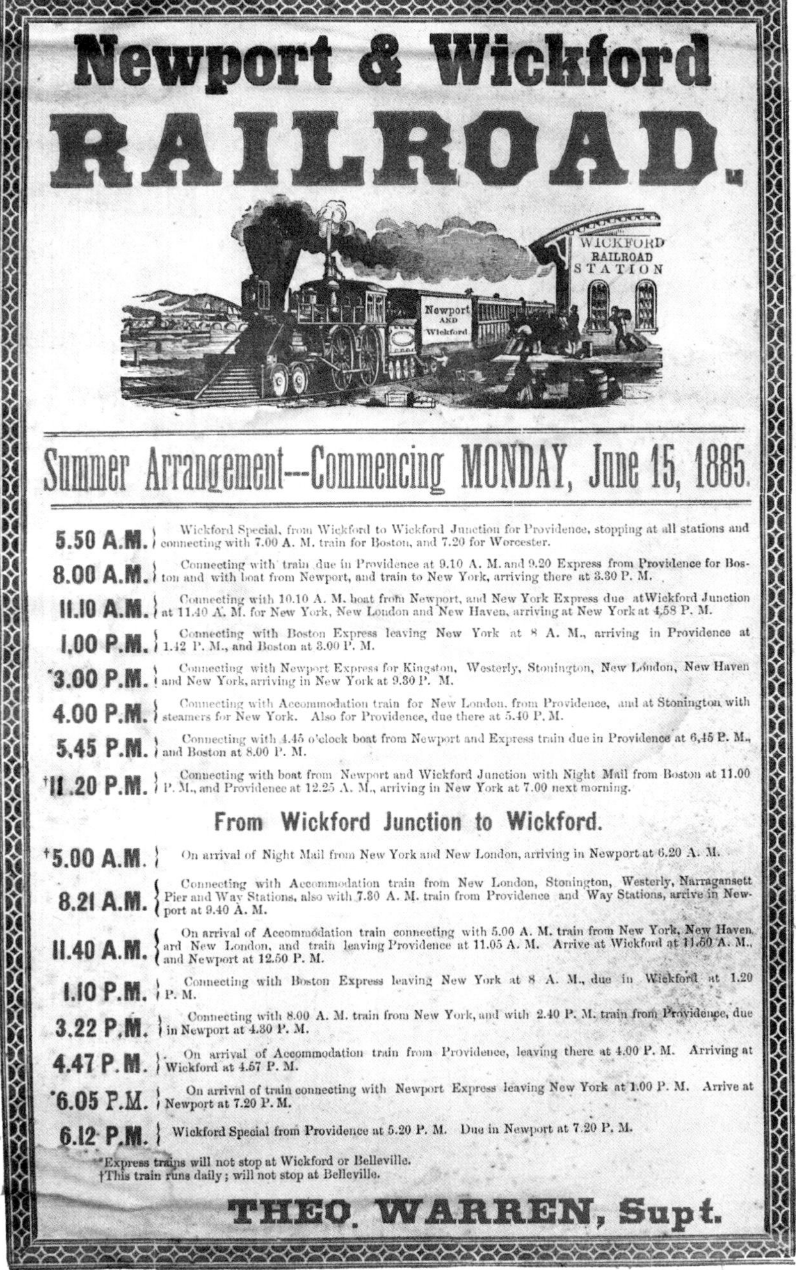

Poster announcing Newport and Wickford Railroad service for the summer of 1885. *Rhode Island Railroad Museum.*

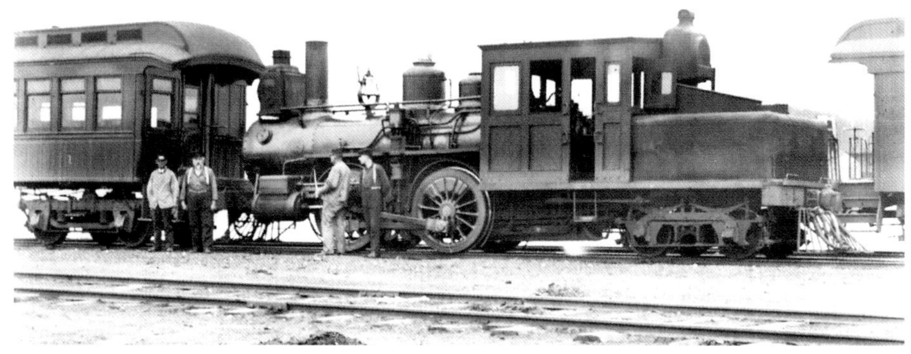

A Forney locomotive on the Newport and Wickford Railroad. These bizarre little engines were originally designed for back-and-forth service on elevated urban railroads. *Collection of Edward J. Ozog.*

heavily endowed with equipment. It only had one locomotive at a time and had one coach and one combination car. The locomotive type the railroad used would surely win a World's Ugliest Locomotive contest. (Note to the reader: One of the reviewers of this chapter was outraged at the author's suggestion that this engine was ugly. He suggested "ungainly" instead. Beauty is in the eyes of the beholder, of course, so the author invites readers to form their own judgment.) It was a double-ended tank locomotive called a Forney and was originally designed to shuttle trains back and forth on urban elevated railroads. That suited the Wickford railroad's operation perfectly, as it avoided the necessity of turning the engine at the end of the line (even though there were turntables available at either end).

The line had a series of small steamships, the first two, the *Eolus* and *Tockwogh*, being side-wheelers. They seemed to be rather accident prone, being involved in a series of fires and collisions until the *Tockwogh* burned to the waterline in April 1893. The third and final vessel, the *General*, was screw powered and lasted until the end of passenger service in October 1925.

The fortunes of the Newport and Wickford Railroad and Steamboat Company paralleled those of the Gilded Age itself. The Panic of 1893 and the election of Theodore Roosevelt to the presidency in 1900 marked the end of the era of ultra-conspicuous consumption practiced by the builders of the Newport mansions. Twenty years of at least break-even operations were followed by losses such that by 1908, the line was entering receivership.

The New York, New Haven and Hartford Railroad immediately began sniffing out the possibility of a takeover—preferably at a bargain basement price. Toward that end, the larger railroad began circulating a story that it intended to build a tunnel under the Providence River that would allow a direct connection between New York and Newport, as reported in the *New York Times* on August 28, 1908. If actually built, such a structure would kill the little line, making it of no value. This was evidently a bargaining chip, because the tunnel was never built, and the Morgan line bought the Newport and Wickford Railroad and Steamboat Company in 1909.

What followed was a pattern that was as depressing as it was common among the Rhode Island short lines. The short segment of line between Wickford Station and Wickford Landing was abandoned in 1938, although it hadn't been used for over a decade. There was a brief resurgence of activity just before and during the early part of World War II. The navy was building a huge naval air station at Quonset Point north of Wickford. Eventually, the navy would have an extensive network of tracks on the base and a connection with the New York, New Haven and Hartford Railroad

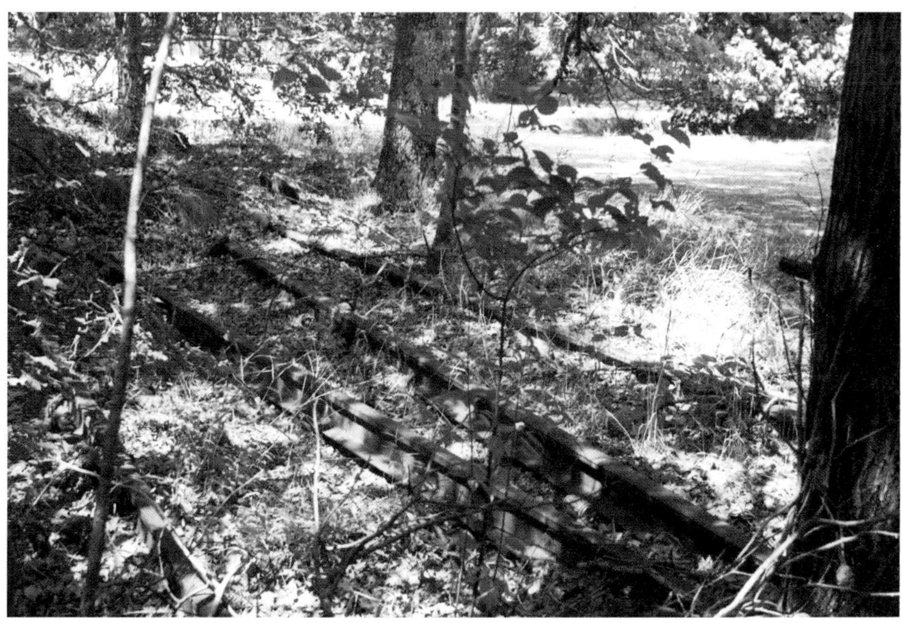

All that remains of the Newport and Wickford Railroad—a few pieces of rail at Wickford Junction. *Photo by Frank Heppner.*

mainline, but in the beginning, the easiest rail access for the base was to switch cars over to the short line from Wickford Junction and unload at Wickford Station. After the war, the line was maintained for local freight service as the Wickford Branch until its final abandonment in 1963.

Google Earth provides a very clear view of the entire old right of way, and there are even a couple of hundred feet of intact track (at the time of writing) at Wickford Junction. The railroad bridge over Ten Rod Road at Wickford Junction shows that it was built for four tracks: the two center tracks for the old Stonington Line main; the north track, which had been a mainline passing track that ran from Kingston to Davisville; and the south track for the Newport and Wickford Railroad and Steamship Company's line that ran for a few hundred feet before it connected to the mainline. The new Wickford Junction commuter rail station (discussed in the final chapter) is under construction on the north side of the tracks. There is one known surviving piece of rolling stock, an Osgood-Bradley combination coach from 1908 that now serves as the snack car at the Connecticut Trolley Museum in East Windsor.

THE WARWICK RAILROAD

The Warwick Railroad has a more complex corporate history than any other railroad in Rhode Island, and on a per-mile basis, it may be the most complicated in the United States. For a time, it was also the shortest standard-gauge, common-carrier, non-harbor-connecting railroad in the country, at slightly less than a mile in length on its mainline.

The Warwick Railroad was chartered in 1873 and first operated in 1875, apparently to provide service from South Auburn, a few miles south of Providence, to a burgeoning real estate development in Oakland Beach and later to a summer religious camp in Buttonwoods, both in Warwick. The line was initially operated by the New York, Providence and Boston Railroad, but in 1876, it was cut loose to operate on its own. It was not very successful as a stand-alone railroad and survived in that guise only until 1879, when it went bankrupt and was sold under protest by some of its bondholders to another bondholder named J. Dull of New Jersey for $31,000 and became the Rhode Island Central Railroad. That line, in turn, was purchased from Mr. Dull by the New York, Providence and Boston Railroad only two years later and was rechristened the Warwick and Oakland Beach Railroad. It operated under the sponsorship of the New York, Providence and Boston

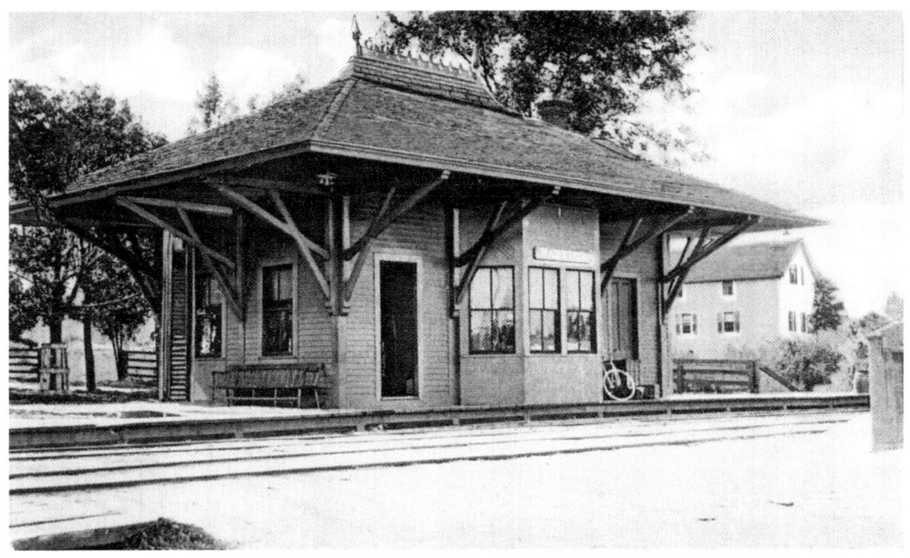

Warwick station on the Rhode Island Central Railroad pre-electrification. *Collection of Edward J. Ozog.*

Railroad until *that* railroad was absorbed by the New York, New Haven and Hartford Railroad in 1892.

In 1899, the New York, New Haven and Hartford Railroad transferred the Warwick and Oakland Beach Railroad (Rhode Island Central Railroad) to a subsidiary, the Rhode Island Suburban Railway. This change was more than nomenclatural because the Rhode Island Suburban Railway operated trolley lines and electrified the little railroad, essentially converting it to a streetcar road. Providence thus had inexpensive, direct access to the playground areas, like Rocky Point, developing around Oakland Beach. In 1921, the United Electric Railway absorbed the Rhode Island Suburban Railway and was the operator when passenger service finally ended in 1935. Freight service using small electric locomotives continued on the two miles of line between Auburn and Lakeside. This service survived after passenger service ended, as several fairly large industrial and distributing companies had developed along the line. United Electric Railway continued to operate until 1949, when the line was sold and reborn under the Warwick Railroad name. Each time the railroad's name changed, it seemed to shrink a bit. The new Warwick Railroad pulled the plug on its electric engines two years later, converting to secondhand diesel switchers and abandoning a mile of track for good measure. In 1960, the line was

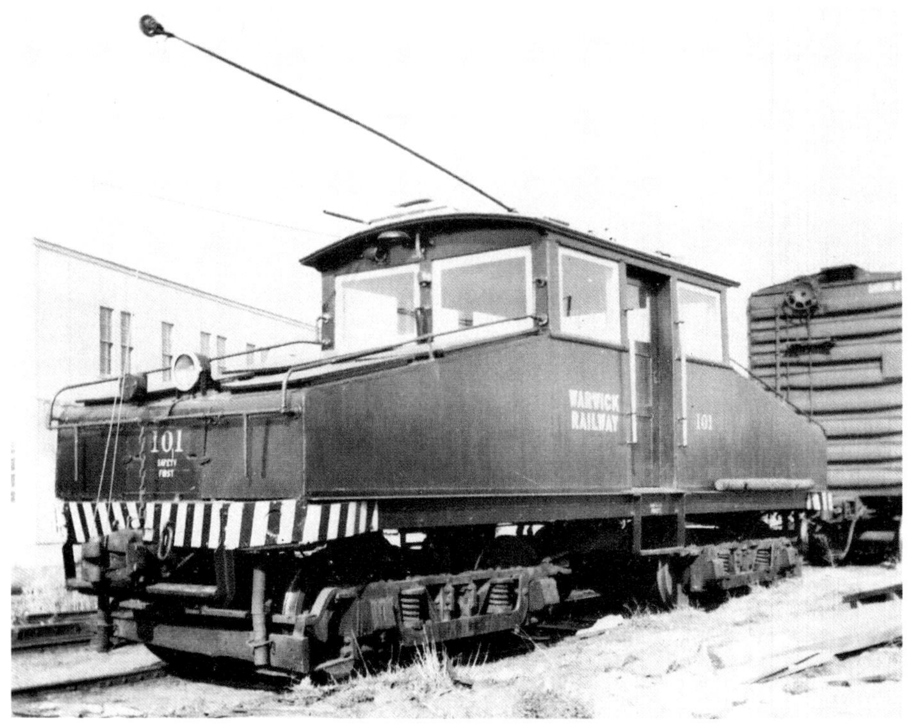

Electric freight locomotive of the Warwick Railway. *Collection of Edward J. Ozog.*

again sold to a man named Oscar Greene, who operated it with his wife and a clerk until 1980, when he retired. One of his engines was sold to the Seaview Transportation Company, which operates the industrial trackage at the Quonset Business Park. It remained there until 2008, when it was scrapped. Greene sold the line in 1982 to the Providence and Worcester Railroad, which kept it active as an industrial spur until 1999, when its last customer stopped shipping goods. The line can still be seen on Google Earth about a third of a mile northeast of the junction of Amtrak with the abandoned Pontiac Branch in Cranston.

MOSHASSUCK VALLEY RAILROAD

It is appropriate that the Littlest State had *two* of the shortest railroads in the United States. The champion was, of course, the reincarnated Warwick Railroad at about a mile, but the runner-up was the Moshassuck Valley

Railroad, which operated as an independent line for over a century with only 1.8 miles (generously) of track. The Moshassuck Valley Railroad was also one of two Rhode Island railroads that had an Indian in its corporate logo, the other being the Narragansett Pier Railroad.

The Moshassuck Valley Railroad was chartered in 1874 to service the huge Sayles Bleachery, an enormous textile mill in Lincoln, just north of Pawtucket. A bleachery is a specialized operation devoted exclusively to bleaching cotton fabrics in preparation for printing. The Sayles Bleachery was established in the mid-1850s by the Sayles brothers, William and Frederick. The success of the bleachery enabled the brothers to buy other textile operations concentrated around the original plant.

By the 1870s, the mill was putting out forty tons of finished materials a day. The mill had been built in the 1850s and was at least a mile from the nearest track of the Providence and Worcester Railroad when that line was built in 1875. Rather than load its products on to horse carts and then transfer them to rail cars on the nearby Providence and Worcester Railroad, the Sayles brothers decided to build their own connector railroad. Construction started in 1876 and was completed in 1877. The line ran from the mill to Woodlawn station on the old New Haven Railroad.

The vast majority of the trade of the line was with the complex of mills around the bleachery, but other businesses gradually developed along the line. One novel business was the sale of used horse stable bedding hay from the nearby Lincoln Downs Race track. The hay, with its…attachments, was sent to a plant in New Jersey that grew mushrooms for Campbell's Soup. Waste not, want not.

There even developed a modest passenger service. From the start, the line had one or two passenger cars and, in 1896, bought a steam "dummy," so called because they were almost silent. A dummy was essentially a passenger car with a boiler and a small steam engine. The boiler reduced the passenger capacity. They were frequently used in applications like the Moshassuck Valley Railroad's frequent bi-directional service on short runs. Passenger service lasted until the 1920s.

The textile operations at Saylesville, as the community was now called, declined with the rest of the industry in New England, and the bleachery was closed in 1960. There was still enough light industry for the railroad to survive, however, and in 1967, the road was sold to a company about which little is known—Standard Transportation. In 1981, the Providence and Worcester Railroad acquired the line and serviced the on-line businesses with its own locomotives. Barker Steel, a rebar manufacturer, is the last active shipper. Today, because there is a wye track at the Lawn (formerly known as Woodlawn) junction, the primary use for the tiny Moshassuck Valley Railroad is reversing the direction of Providence and Worcester and Amtrak trains. Yet the line abides.

What is remarkable about the five short-line railroads described here was their longevity. They averaged ninety-six years in independent existence. They were also testaments to rugged Yankee individualism. Four of the five lines were, at least for some part of their existence, owned by single individuals or families. All the lines, during most of their careers, operated on the financial brink. How to square their undesirability as investments with their long lives? Surely the idea that a railroad exists to serve the community plays some role. At least in some cases, the concept that a short line railroad is the world's largest model railroad set was compelling to the owners. What the Rhode Island short lines lacked in length, they made up in color and interest. Fortunately, most of them (with the exception of the Newport and Wickford Railroad and Steamship Company) are well documented photographically, and thanks to Google Earth, their imprint on the land can still be traced.

Chapter 10

JUICE LINES

Rhode Island Gets Wired

The electric motor would eventually do for urban transportation what the steam engine did for transport between towns and cities. Until the 1830s, most internal transportation in cities was by foot. Few people could afford horses, especially immigrant workers. Average walking speed for a pedestrian in a city is about four to five miles per hour. For the wealthy or commercial enterprises, a single horse and lightweight carriage or a horse and rider could comfortably double that speed. In the 1830s, the first horse-drawn omnibuses began to appear in American cities. These started out as elongated stagecoaches with a rear, rather than a side, entrance. They operated on fixed routes and sometimes fixed schedules. The real novelty of the omnibus was that it did not operate as a taxi does today: a specific hire for a specific journey. Rather, one got on board with others who had destinations along the route and then got off at will. The omnibus was the dominant form of public transportation in Providence, as in most cities, from the late 1830s to the 1860s.

The next technological advance in city transportation came when the omnibuses were placed on tracks. This reduced flexibility but added enormously to efficiency. A brace of horses could pull at least three times more passengers if the bus body was supported by steel wheels on steel rails than it could with wooden wheels bouncing on cobblestoned streets.

The "horsecar" was not greeted with universal acclaim. The early style of street rail was elevated above the street level, causing problems with both carriages and equestrians. Technology came to the rescue with a type of rail that could be buried in the pavement, with only a groove for the flanges on the wheels. This groove still exists in the rails used by modern streetcars and is often why bicyclists oppose the expansion of city streetcar lines, as they perceive the groove to be a safety hazard for them.

The first horsecars appeared in New York City in 1832, but the technology was surprisingly slow to be adopted by other cities, and it wasn't until 1861 that the first horsecar line was proposed in Providence and enabling legislation was passed by the general assembly. Although fundraising and stock-selling proceeded for a number of separate lines, the first company to actually put horsecars on a track was the Providence, Pawtucket and Central Falls Railroad, and the first horsecar clopped out of Market Square in Providence on May 26, 1864, a year and a month before the end of the Civil War.

In the following year, horsecar lines proliferated. By the end of 1864, there were seven separate companies providing horsecar service in and from Providence. Most of the capital for these railroads came from individuals who had commercial interests in localities at the far end of the proposed lines. They correctly perceived that the value of their interests, primarily in real estate, might dramatically increase if there was reliable, inexpensive transportation to the heart of the city.

Even as these separate lines were a'buildin', there was realization that a single system for the whole city and environs would be advantageous not only for the financial community but also for passengers—there could be a single fare, greater likelihood of a through trip from one end of the city to the other without changing cars and so on. William Sprague, the textile tycoon we met in connection with the Narragansett Pier Railroad, took on the challenge of amalgamating the separate horsecar companies and formed the Union Railroad in 1865. This company eventually absorbed all the Providence horsecar lines.

SHE WAS ONLY THE STABLEMAN'S DAUGHTER, BUT ALL THE HORSEMEN KNEW HER

As the horsecar lines proliferated in cities across the United States, there was increasing realization that this technology produced a byproduct that was threatening the very existence of large cities and possibly even the lives of its citizens. That byproduct, indelicately expressed, was horse manure.

The horsecar simply added to the existing problem of horses used to pull carriages and carts. The arithmetic is simple and compelling. The average adult workhorse produces about 35 to 50 pounds of manure a day. In addition, that same horse produces about a quart of urine. Each horsecar required on average eleven horses a day to service it, as the horses usually worked in pairs and in shifts. At the peak of the horsecar era, Providence had about five thousand horses in service for transportation, both for horsecars and drayage. That's at least 175,000 pounds of manure and 1,250 gallons of horse urine a *day*, most of which was deposited in the streets and eventually ended up in Narragansett Bay. Expressed another way, that is 63,875,000 pounds of manure a year. That's a lot of manure, but New York City's horses produced about 2,500,000 pounds of manure a *day*. A certain amount of horse manure has value as fertilizer, but the urban horse produced far more ordure than could be absorbed by the fertilizer market.

The germ theory of disease was beginning to gain acceptance at the peak of the horsecar era, and there was a nagging feeling that the ever-heightening mountains of fly-encrusted dung in horsecar cities might have something to do with, for example, the periodic cholera epidemics that struck American cities, killing thousands of people with each outbreak. It appeared that the horsecar was a Faustian bargain, bringing prosperity and convenience at the cost of the indiscriminate loss of lives (although it must be said that this burden did fall disproportionately on the poor, whose neighborhoods were more crowded and whose state of sanitation was generally lower than might be found in the affluent areas). It appears that the horse was viewed in 1880 as the automobile is today.

MR. SPRAGUE'S GAME-CHANGING INVENTION

In the early 1880s, the commercialization of electricity was about to burst on the American scene. Thomas Edison obtained his first light bulb patent in 1879, and the first experiments on long-distance transmission of electric current were being done by Westinghouse, Tesla, Edison and other rivals all during the decade of the '80s.

Frank J. Sprague (apparently no relationship to the Rhode Island textile and horsecar Spragues), a young ex–naval officer from Connecticut, resigned his commission to work for Thomas Edison in 1883. However, Sprague didn't get along with Edison and soon left to form his own company. A bit earlier, while his ship, the USS *Minnesota*, was docked in Newport, Sprague devised the electrical inverter, a machine that converts alternating to direct current, thus demonstrating the inspirational effect Rhode Island can have on clever people. At about this time, Edison was developing an integrated system of producing electricity by generators, transmitting it by wires and then using that electricity to drive motors, which could be used for any purpose that required rotary motion.

Sprague was fascinated by the problem of motorizing the horsecar (which, without the horse, wouldn't be a horsecar anymore but would henceforth be a *street*car). There were two difficulties: first, existing electric motors were not suited for operation on a streetcar, where the loads were variable; and second, electricity requires two pathways to a motor—this is why an electric plug has two prongs and there are two wires in an electric cord. How could you get the electricity to the moving car without a miles-long extension cord? Like many great ideas, Sprague's solution was both simple and elegant.

Electricity for lighting was being carried all over cities at this time, primarily by means of wires strung on overhead poles. Sprague said, "Why not string one of those wires above the track, make the track itself one of the electric pathways and then have an insulated spring-loaded rod connected to the motor slide along the wire, thus completing the circuit through the motors?" Like most great ideas, the overhead wire and "trolley" pole was developed by several people at almost the same time. A man from Detroit named Charles van Depoele also came up with the idea, but Sprague was more successful in acting on his invention and put into operation the first successful electric-powered street railway in the United States in Richmond, Virginia, in 1888. By 1900, there were more than thirteen thousand miles of electric railway in America, and the horsecar was on its way to becoming a nostalgic curiosity. Sprague had another invention that revolutionized cities: an electric motor–powered elevator. Prior to this, elevators had been powered by steam or hydraulic devices. Sprague's elevators were much faster and could carry heavier loads than either of their predecessors. Frank Sprague was thus truly the father of the modern city.

RHODE ISLAND ENTERS THE TROLLEY AGE

Experiments on electric propulsion for streetcars began not in Providence but in Woonsocket. In 1887, the first electric streetcars in New England hesitantly sparked their way along the streets, but the system was not successful for a variety of reasons, including the fact that one of the early cars caught fire from electrical sparks dropping on the roof. This pioneer electric line died in isolation. In Newport, the Newport Horse Railroad was incorporated in 1885. The name was evidently a ruse; the wealthy "summer people" of Newport adamantly opposed any kind of tracked local transportation, but a horse railroad was seen as less undesirable than one of the newfangled electric lines. The true nature of the operation was revealed in 1889 when the company was renamed the Newport Street Railway.

The opposition of the Newport wealthy to the operation of the trolley line was both fierce and hypocritical. In June 1889, a group of the Newport elect formed the Newport Improvement Association, whose primary initial purpose was to stop the streetcars, even if it required buying the stock of the new company and disbanding the company. The unstated reason for the opposition to streetcars was the fear that if the lines ran close to the exclusive and, at the time, difficult-to-reach Newport beaches, "undesirables" might have access to them. The initial president of Newport Improvement was August Belmont Jr. In 1902, Belmont would finance the construction of the Interborough Rapid Transit System in New York City, the first underground electric railroad in the city. Curiously, the tracks of the IRT ran nowhere near Belmont's New York residence at 550 Park Avenue; thus, he was spared the inconvenience and noise of its construction. An early speaker before the Improvement Association arguing against the establishment of a streetcar system in Newport was Rhode Island senator Nelson W. Aldrich. Aldrich would later own the successor to the Union Railroad in Rhode Island, the United Traction and Electric Company, which operated almost all of Providence's streetcars. However, Senator Aldrich's house, at 110 Benevolent Street in Providence, was not on a streetcar line, so he did not have to put up with noise and uncouth passengers passing before his house. The Newport Improvement Association thus may be the first example of NIMBY applied to transportation. Surprisingly for the era, the plutocrats were unsuccessful, and tracks were laid and operations started later in 1889. The Newport Street Railway not only survived but also expanded and, at the end of the streetcar era, became the Newport Electric Corporation, which was absorbed by the Narragansett Electric Company.

Providence Nibbles At and Then Heartily Endorses the Trolley

The Union Railroad was slow to embrace electric power delivered through overhead wires, but once it did, it did so with a vengeance. After some sluggish experiments with battery power and the ancestor of today's gasoline engine, the Union Railroad started to electrify its horsecar lines in 1891, and the job was essentially finished by 1894. Electric trolley service was inaugurated on January 19, 1892, and the last horse ambled into the barn in 1894.

Like most revolutionary technologies, the electric streetcar brought both anticipated and unanticipated changes. Trolley service was faster, more frequent and more reliable than its predecessor, but it also required a radical change in the nature of the railroad's workforce and its working conditions. Men experienced with horses were suddenly unemployed and unemployable unless they could quickly acquire the skills of a motorman or lineman.

During the decade of the 1890s, the street railroads enjoyed the fruits of the labors of the clever inventors of technical improvements. Unfortunately, there were other "inventions" that did not bode well for the users of these municipal services.

Broadly categorized as "utilities," a remarkable number of utility services we now take for granted went into operation first as novelties and then as necessities. Electric service, gas service, telephone service, street railway service—all had certain things in common. First, they required a hefty up-front capital investment. As the United States had decided many years before, the major sponsor of such enterprises was to be private capital (with some assistance from government subsidy, either visible or invisible). Second, they required permission from the municipality to operate, as they would use public streets or public lands for their rights of way. Also, the municipality expected some payment for the right to operate on municipal property. Third, by their very nature, they tended toward monopoly. This makes a certain amount of sense. One would not want ten different companies' gas lines entering your house, from which you could pick one over the other. Very clever people soon figured out that by taking advantage of these characteristics of utility operation, one could become extremely rich. The same principles still apply in modern utilities like cable or Internet service.

Horsecar systems were expensive to operate. The old investment maxim, "Never invest in anything that eats," was true with a vengeance in the horsecar era. On the other hand, the initial capital investment was relatively small. This meant that these systems would typically raise capital locally and that capital investment could be recaptured rather quickly. Local investors tended to be responsive both to community needs and the requirements of their labor forces. The labor environment in horsecar companies was often stable, working conditions were good for the times and there was little pressure for unionization.

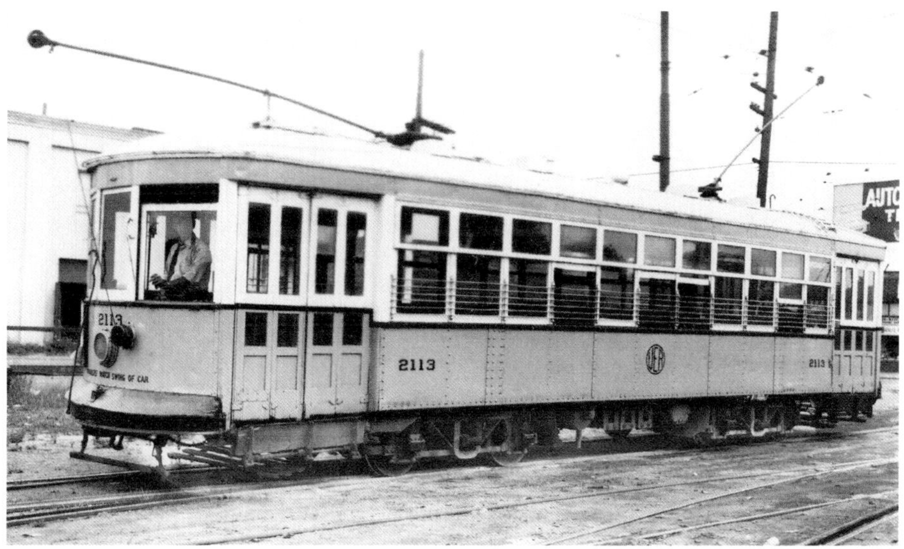

United Electric Railway double-truck trolley from the end of the trolley period. *Collection of Edward J. Ozog*

The streetcar changed all that, starting in the 1890s. The initial capital investment for power plants, wiring and bigger and more expensive cars could easily be ten times as much as for a horsecar line of the same length. As a result, the capital requirements for streetcar companies could not be entirely met locally, and the local sponsors for streetcar lines sought outside sources of capital. Once built, the streetcar companies were under enormous pressure from their investors to economize operation and to recapture capital costs as quickly as possible. This was done in two main areas: reduction of labor costs and favorable financial arrangements from the cities in which they operated.

In Rhode Island, two individuals were largely responsible for both the modernization of the street railway system and its removal from local control. Republican senator Nelson W. Aldrich was once described as the "General Manager of the United States" because of his influence at the intersection of the federal government and large industrial combines. In the early 1890s, he took an interest in street railways and their modernization. With a group of associates from the American sugar industry, whose fortunes he had massively increased through the establishment of high protective tariffs, he formed a syndicate in New Jersey called the New England Street Railway Company. This company bought sufficient shares of Providence's

Union Railroad to gain control and then formed a holding company, the United Traction and Electric Company, to operate Providence's streetcar system. Aldrich, while a sitting United States senator, was named president of United Traction in a stunning and very public display of conflict of interest. Alongside Aldrich on the board of directors was Marsden J. Perry, who had acquired monopoly control of most of the electric companies in Rhode Island. During the transition period of electrification, the folksy Union Railroad morphed into a rapacious monopoly that, through outright bribery and influence peddling, negotiated favorable contracts with the City of Providence and embarked on a period of worker exploitation that resulted in a transit strike in 1902.

Following the establishment of United Traction, there then followed a bewildering series of name and ownership changes for Rhode Island streetcar companies. In 1902, the United Traction and Electric Company morphed into the Rhode Island Company, which was essentially an amalgamation of almost all Rhode Island trolley and electric companies. In 1906, the gray eminence of J.P. Morgan made an appearance in Rhode Island streetcar circles. Fearing potential competition from other railroads coveting access to Narragansett Bay, Morgan's New York, New Haven and Hartford Railroad bought the Rhode Island Company for $15 million, essentially

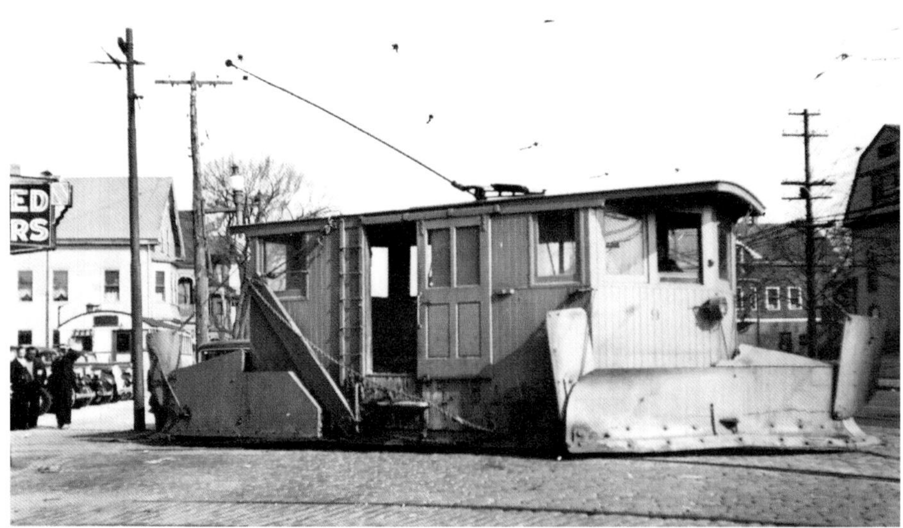

Electric street railroads had the same operating requirements as intercity lines. This undated photograph shows a double-ended trolley snowplow. *Collection of Edward J. Ozog.*

establishing a monopoly on all transportation in the state. However, after all the effort expended to acquire sole control of Rhode Island's streetcars, the Rhode Island Company proved to be a bad investment and was a drain on the New York, New Haven and Hartford Railroad's other operations. Heavily overcommitted in other areas, and prompted by antitrust laws, Morgan unloaded the Rhode Island Company in 1914. After several more reorganizations and a receivership in 1918, the name of the trolley system stabilized as the United Electric Railway during the rest of the trolley era.

Total monopoly of streetcar service was achieved just about the time the Model-T Ford went on the market and just as electrification doomed the horsecar, Henry Ford's invention sounded the death knell for the streetcar. The economy and speed of the streetcar were no match for the "convenience" of the automobile, and the last streetcars ran early in the morning of May 16, 1948. The occasion was marked by a ceremonial Last Run, attended primarily by railroad enthusiasts, and capped with a eulogy at Swan Point Cemetery, which, appropriately, was the last stop on the final operating trolley line in Providence. Very few survivors of the trolley age remain, the most conspicuous perhaps being the twin ex-trolley car tunnels under the East Side, still being used by city buses and *sub rosa* skateboarders.

WHERE LITTLE CABLE CARS CLIMB ALL THE WAY TO THE BARS

Providence was the only New England city to have cable cars, which is somewhat surprising given that a number of medium-sized Yankee cities have hilly terrain, but its construction was as much a matter of opposing the monopoly of the Union Railroad as it was of geography.

The greatest concentration of wealth in Providence was on College, or "Quality," Hill, also known as the East Side. Thayer Street, then and now, was the commercial center of the East Side, where the restaurants and saloons were situated. The east–west streets ascending the hill had grades much too steep for horsecars, and the Union Railroad had built north–south lines that required either a nosebleed-inducing walk up the hillside streets to meet them or very long detours that avoided the steepest part of the hill. One wag noted that he "had to go downtown by way of Warren." Since Andrew Hallidie's first successful cable-drawn transit system, the Clay Street Hill Railroad in San Francisco, was built in 1873, dozens of American cities had installed cable railways for their hills. The Union Railroad was indifferent to the pleas of College Hill residents for cable service, so a group of local residents/investors led by Walter Richmond requested a charter from the Providence City Council to build a cable railroad that would start at the Seekonk River, go over College Hill and then proceed south to Olneyville, using the Union Railroad's right of way.

The Union Railroad fought the charter fiercely, being opposed not so much to the cable car idea as the concept that it might have competition. Eventually, a compromise was reached. The cable car line would only extend from Market Square up and over College Hill via Waterman and Angell Streets. Dedicated trailer cars coming in behind Union Railroad teams coming in to Providence from Olneyville would be transferred over and attached to the cable railroad's grip cars for the hill climb.

Construction started in 1889, and the first revenue run was January 1, 1890. The Providence Cable Tramway, contrary to dire predictions from the Union Railroad, was immediately profitable and, in 1893, carried 3,044,212 passengers. So impressed was the Union Railroad by this performance that it immediately began buying shares in the tramway company's stock. It acquired majority control on October 23, 1890.

With electrification of the Union Railroad, the days of cable operation were numbered, as cable operation was, relatively speaking, much more

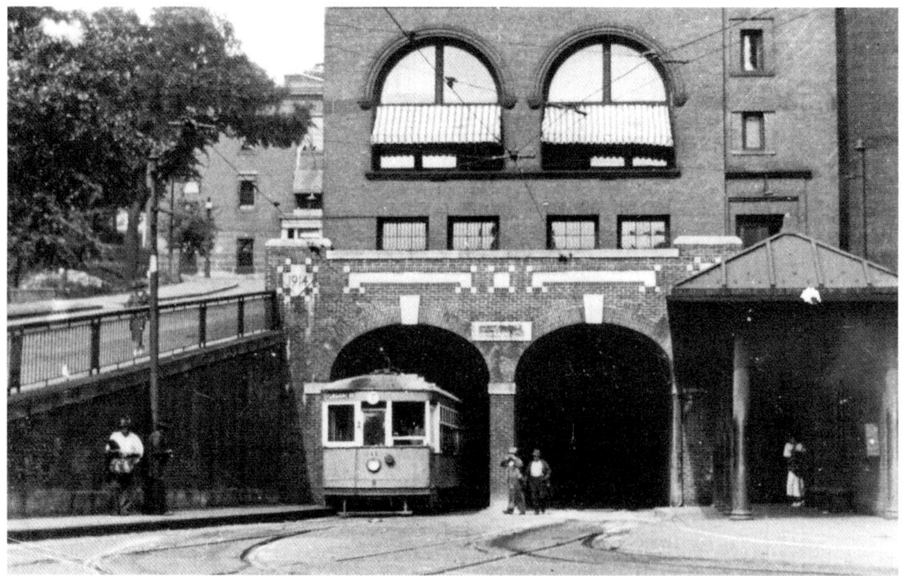

West portal of the trolley tunnel built in 1914. It is still in use today by city buses. *Collection of Edward J. Ozog.*

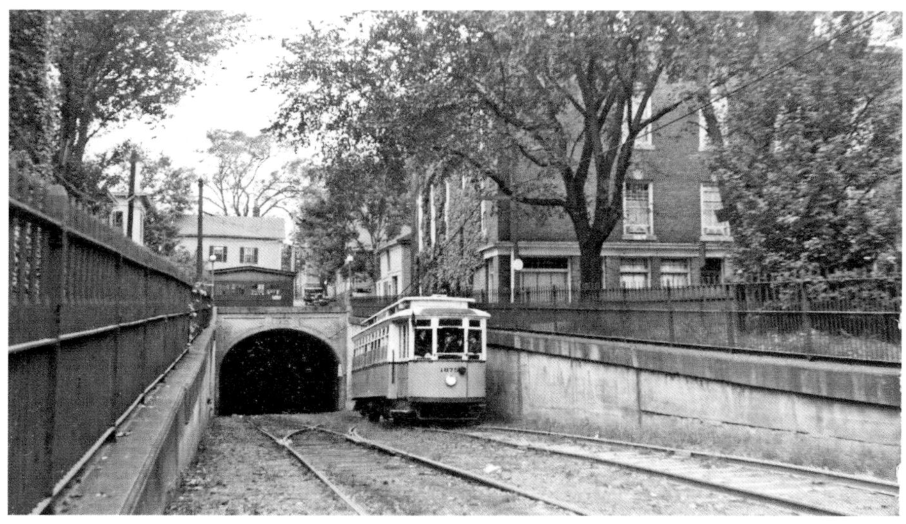

East portal of the trolley tunnel, opening near Thayer Street. *Collection of Edward J. Ozog.*

expensive than electric traction, but College Hill was still too much for the early electric cars. Eventually, the East Side trolley tunnels built in 1914 solved the problem of getting downtown from the East Side. After the cable car system was shut down in 1895, the former cable line was modified so that a counterweight running on rails in a tunnel beneath the tracks was connected to an underground cable, which ran beneath the tracks, over a large pulley at the top of the hill and then down to a car ascending the hill. Electric motors in the car, rather than a motor-driven cable, provided enough power to get the counterweight-balanced car and a trailer car up the hill. Essentially, the system became a funicular, similar to Angel's Flight in Los Angeles or the Peak Tram in Hong Kong. This hybrid system operated until 1914.

Suburban Operations

There were several trolley systems that crossed state borders or were isolated from Providence, but only two had features distinctive enough to be recorded here: the Providence and Danielson Railroad and the Sea View Railroad.

The Providence and Danielson (Street) Railroad opened in June 1901, replacing the last operating stagecoach line in Rhode Island. It had two

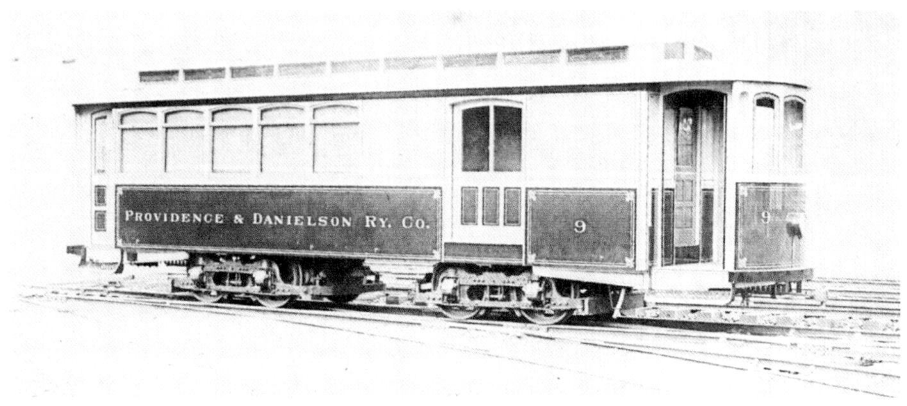

Providence and Danielson Railroad funeral car. *Collection of Edward J. Ozog*

branches, both of which started at Market Square in Providence. One headed northeast and terminated at the village of Chepachet. The other meandered through western Rhode Island, crossed over the border into Connecticut and then ended in Danielson. The two lines combined were thirty-six miles long. There were two unusual aspects of the Providence and Danielson Railroad. First, it primarily operated through a rural rather than suburban area for much of its length, and second, it hauled mostly freight rather than passengers. The freight was of an agricultural nature, with a few textiles from small mills along the way. One unusual car hauled an unusual cargo: occupied caskets. Trolley lines were often built near cemeteries (the land was cheap), and in an era before automotive hearses, a specialized trolley car with seating space for the funeral party and cargo space for the departed was often a feature of trolley lines, including the Providence and Danielson Railroad.

The Providence and Danielson Railroad was absorbed by the Rhode Island Company, but in 1918, when the general assembly was deciding the fate of that failing conglomerate, line by line, it noted that although the little trolley line was not even earning its operating expenses, it did provide a service to Providence and therefore should not be abandoned. Ominously, the assembly report noted that future prospects of the line were dim because in the town of Scituate, through which the trolley line passed, the City of Providence was buying land for its future Scituate Reservoir, which would flood the right of way. Sure enough, in the early 1920s, the reservoir was built, and the line of the Providence and Danielson Railroad today lies in a watery grave.

THE SEA VIEW RAILROAD

Of all the small trolley lines that lay outside Providence, the Sea View Railroad (often alternatively spelled Sea View Rail Road) had the most distinctive local flavor and left the most indelible impact on local culture. All through coastal South County today, one can find Sea View cafés, markets and other mercantile establishments eighty years after the last trolley rattled its way to Narragansett Beach. The industrial railroad serving the Quonset industrial area named itself the Sea View Railroad in honor of the original trolley line.

The Sea View Railroad was born in Westerly in 1887 when three men—a local physician, Dr. Herbert Stillman, one of the ubiquitous Hazards (Isaac) and a member of another old Rhode Island family, Howard Champlin— obtained a charter to build the Sea View Railroad from Watch Hill to Narragansett Pier. Surveys were conducted, but the line was never built—if it had been, it would have had one of the most spectacular routes in Rhode Island, following right along the southern coast. Amendments to the charter were obtained that would have permitted building north to Wickford. Following nearly a decade of inaction, a druggist named William C. Clarke Sr. of Wakefield and Narragansett Pier bought out the original shareholders and secured two additional amendments to the charter. One would permit the building of an electric railroad from Narragansett Pier north to Wickford, East Greenwich and Apponaug to the Cranston city limits, where cars of the Sea View Railroad could connect with Union Railroad equipment. The second would permit the laying of tracks from Narragansett Pier south along Point Judith Road, ending at Sand Hill Cove. This proposed line (which was never built) had a potential impact far beyond the transport of sun worshippers to the beach. The federal government started work in 1905 on a huge breakwater at Point Judith/Galilee, and there was discussion of making the newly protected waters into a major port, something which, for better or worse, never happened. At this time, however, the Sea View Railroad's charter offered a future possibility of a rail connection to a potential large port, an observation that soon drew the attention of some major railroad players from out of state.

After years of languishing, construction was started from Narragansett Pier to the East Greenwich line in 1899, and service began to East Greenwich in September 1900. Trolley railroads today are not generally thought of in a freight context, but freight service was important to the Sea View from the beginning. It had to haul coal to its own steam-operated power plants, which sold off surplus electricity to the community, and it also carried agricultural products through Union Railroad connections to Providence. One of the large stationary steam engines used to power the Sea View Railroad's generators at its Hamilton powerhouse is today preserved and operating at the New England Wireless and Steam Museum in East Greenwich.

The Sea View Railroad and the contiguous Narragansett Pier Railroad had a fractious relationship. They were competitors for the summer visitor trade to Narragansett Beach. Visitors from Providence could get to Narragansett Pier either by taking a Stonington Line train to Kingston and then transferring to the Narragansett Pier Railroad, or they could take a Union Railroad trolley to East Greenwich and then transfer to the Sea View Railroad. In 1904, the Sea View Railroad entered into an agreement with the New York, New Haven and Hartford Railroad so that three trains a day that originated in Providence would stop at the Hunt's River Sea View Railroad station in East Greenwich, where passengers could transfer by walking across a platform. This annoyed the management of the Narragansett Pier Railroad no end, and they soon pressured the steam railroad to discontinue the arrangement. What was especially galling to the Narragansett Pier Railroad was that the Sea View Railroad's terminus in Narragansett was right on the north end of Narragansett Beach, so passengers could get off the cars and walk straight into the ocean, whereas the Narragansett Pier Railroad's terminus was south of the beach and involved an omnibus ride to get to the strand.

Despite mutual distaste, in 1902, the Sea View Railroad signed an agreement with the Narragansett Pier Railroad to electrify its tracks from Sea View Junction (approximately where Narragansett Elementary School is today) through Wakefield and into Peace Dale. This arrangement was successful—too successful, from the point of view of the Narragansett Pier Railroad, and it refused to renew the five-year lease in 1907. With wonderful bravado, the Sea View Railroad said essentially, "Fine. You won't let us play with you, we'll lay our *own* tracks between Narragansett and Wakefield." And it did. Its line went from Sea View Junction and roughly paralleled the Narragansett Pier Railroad about two hundred yards to the north until MacArthur Boulevard, where the old 108 House restaurant used to be. (Another Swamp Yankee characteristic. We tend to give references in terms of something that doesn't exist anymore. "Ayup, go nawth 'bout a mile, then turn right where Malcolm used to pahk his old Ford truck.") From MacArthur Boulevard in Wakefield, the line cut diagonally northwest until it met today's Dale Carlia Corner and then headed west on Main Street. It was the Sea View Railroad's intention to continue southwest and eventually go to Westerly, but it would first have to cross the Narragansett Pier Railroad's track near Robinson Street. The Narragansett Pier Railroad adamantly refused permission, and the Sea View Railroad's expansion plans died there.

The Sea View Railroad was absorbed by the Rhode Island Company in 1906. The Rhode Island Company was controlled by J.P. Morgan's New York, New Haven and Hartford Railroad, which was building and attempting to maintain a monopoly on transportation in Rhode Island. However, sometime between 1906 and 1912, the Sea View Railroad was approached by representatives of Canada's Grand Trunk Railroad, which was audaciously planning to invade Morgan's turf by building a new, heavy-duty railroad from Palmer, Massachusetts, to Providence, with a possible extension south to the potential new port at Point Judith. The Grand Trunk Railroad offered to build the Point Judith extension for the Sea View Railroad, in exchange for trackage rights, but Morgan's minions were able to successfully block the offer. The Grand Trunk Railroad began its new line, the Southern New England Railroad, and did some impressive engineering work in Massachusetts, but aside from building a few bridge abutments in Providence, it didn't make it to Rhode Island.

Fate was not kind to the Sea View Railroad during the Rhode Island Company's regency, and when the line was returned to its original stockholders in 1918, the equipment was in a shambled state, and most of the passengers had departed for their Model-Ts. The line was sold for scrap and was gone by 1920. The author once owned an old house near the Hamilton powerhouse of the Sea View Railroad and, during its restoration in the 1970s, discovered a rail from the Sea View Railroad, which had evidently been "liberated" sometime in the '20s to shore up the first floor.

Google Earth reveals many traces of the Sea View Railroad. From West Main Street in Wickford, the old right of way generally follows the existing National Grid power line north to East Greenwich. Crossing West Main Street to the south, the power line crosses Academy Cove and then leaves Wickford and roughly follows Boston Neck Road through Hamilton (where the original car barn still stands, although heavily modified). South of Saunderstown, the line departs from the road but can easily be followed along the power line right of way. A few pilings are left where the line crossed the Narrow River on a causeway. After crossing the river, the original line went southeast to the beach, while the branch to a connection

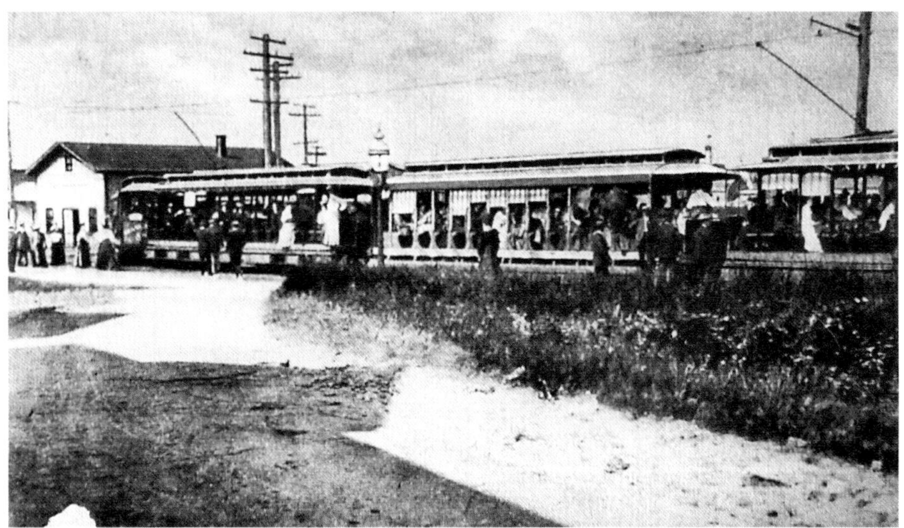

End of the Sea View Railroad line at Narragansett Beach. *Collection of Edward J. Ozog.*

with the Narragansett Pier Railroad and the Sea View Railroad's own right of way to Wakefield skirted Pettaquamscutt Cove to today's Narragansett Elementary School.

The electric railroads were enormously important in the development of today's Rhode Island, establishing the geography of a central city surrounded by suburbs. The electric railroads were long dead when the freeway system was developed in the 1950s, but freeways essentially re-created the idea of narrow, high-density transportation corridors between the suburbs and the city, albeit in an environmentally corrosive, economically less efficient and slower way. Only now, with discussion of restoring streetcars and light rail systems, are we gaining an idea of what we threw away for the convenience of the automobile and how expensive it will be to try to go back.

Chapter 11

THE STRUGGLE FOR KINGSTON STATION

The Reverend John Hall was frustrated and angry. A lover of New England architecture and native of Newport, the Episcopal chaplain of the University of Rhode Island (URI) had recently teamed up with Barbara Dirlam, wife of a URI economics professor, to see if something could be done about the deplorable state of Kingston Railroad Station. In 1972, the station was at a nadir. Years of neglect had left the exterior and interior in a shambles. The building owner, the Penn Central Railroad, was in bankruptcy. The operator of the trains serving the station, Amtrak, was hanging over the edge of a financial precipice by its fingernails. The town of South Kingstown showed a profound disinterest in anything associated with the station except the back taxes it was owed by the railroad. Time to call in the irregulars, so Hall and Dirlam formed a volunteer group that would be called the Friends of the Kingston Railroad Station (called "Friends" from henceforth).

Hall and Dirlam quickly discovered, as has every other volunteer individual or group associated with the station, that almost nothing about restoring, preserving or maintaining it has been or is simple. A look at the current situation will suggest why. The building is owned by the Rhode Island Department of Transportation but falls under the aegis of two divisions within that agency: Intermodal Planning and Property Management. Half of the building is leased to Amtrak and the other half to the Friends. Rhode Island Public Transport Authority buses stop at the station and have to be coordinated with the Amtrak trains. The Town of South Kingstown Police shares policing duties with Amtrak Police and Rhode Island State Police (it took several years to work out an arrangement whereby town police can give parking tickets on state property, something that normally never happens). The Town of South Kingstown administers the bike path that terminates at the station, and bike riders use the bathrooms in the state-owned building on the Amtrak-leased side of the station. The town pays nothing to Amtrak for the maintenance of the bathrooms, which is done by the Amtrak station agents, who are annoyed when exhausted bicyclists take sponge baths in the facilities. The opportunities for friction and non-cooperation are almost endless.

Innocently enough, Hall and Dirlam thought that if no "official" entity was either interested in or had the capacity to do a building restoration, even a minimal paint job, why, the good-hearted citizens of the area could just pitch in and do it as a volunteer project. Ah, not so fast! No industry is more heavily unionized than a railroad. When the small group that Hall and Dirlam founded first approached the Penn Central Railroad in 1972 and offered to rehab the station for free, they were immediately told that it would be impossible. If there was any work to be done around the station that fell within the job description of any furloughed railroad union member, that work would have to be done by a union member. However, if the group wanted to hold fundraisers to raise money to *pay* union members their accustomed union wages with benefits, that could probably be arranged. As Rhode Island was moving toward the bicentennial year of 1976 in a deep recession engendered by the sudden loss of tens of thousands of defense jobs in '73–74, this was not an attractive prospect. On the other hand, the railroad generously offered to sell the decrepit station to Hall and Dirlam for the "asking price" of only $65,000. Perhaps Amtrak might then be persuaded to rent the station from the hapless pair. This was the first hint that actually chipping paint and wielding brushes would be the easiest part of the job.

Undaunted, the Friends decided that there *had* to be a way to allow a civic group to help restore a privately owned building that had historic and cultural significance and began what seemed to be an endless series of meetings, site visits and jawbonings on the phone. Early on, the Friends made a conscious decision to avoid, if at all possible, an adversarial relationship with any of the involved parties, tempting as that might be when frustrations mounted.

The local press took an early and very conspicuous interest in the developing story of a citizen restoration of the station, and the visibility

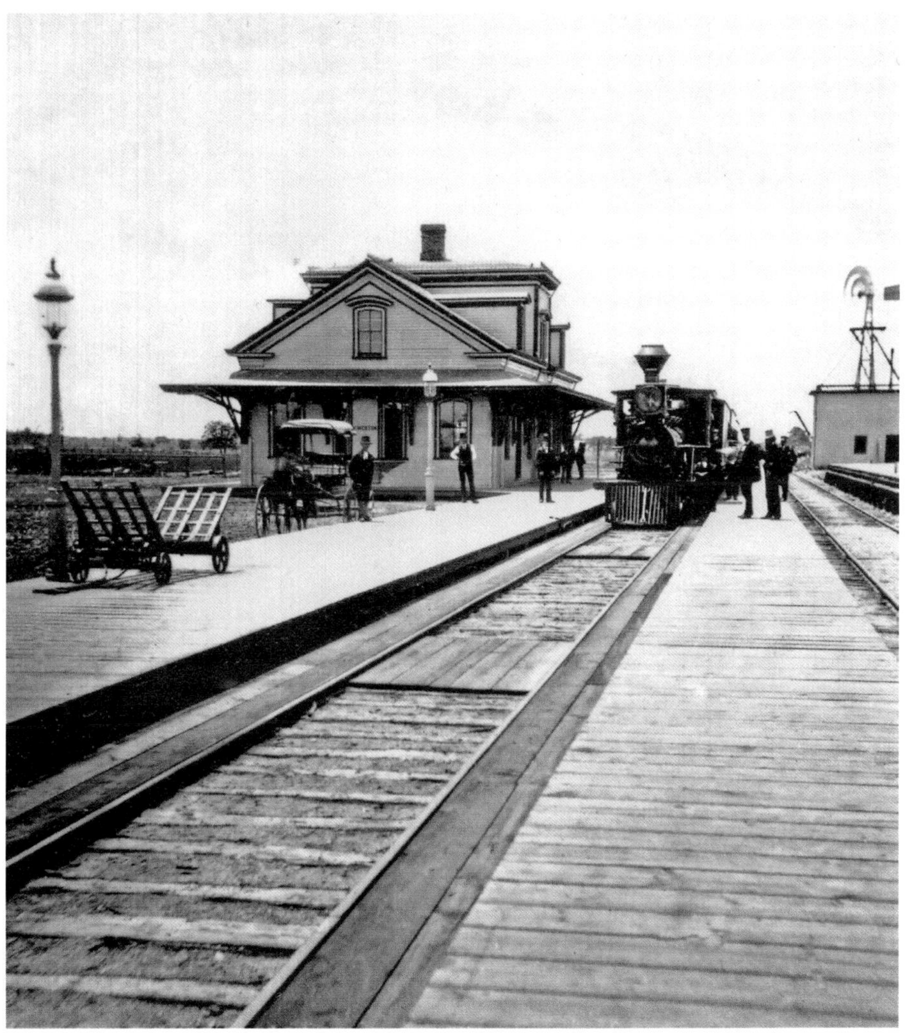

Kingston Station, circa 1875, the year it was built. *Rhode Island Railroad Museum.*

this attention engendered undoubtedly helped persuade the heavily bureaucratized groups the Friends had to deal with that cooperation was more in their best interest than strict adherence to "the rules." Eventually, Amtrak, the Penn Central Railroad, the State of Rhode Island and the appropriate unions all got on board the restoration effort.

Once permission to work on the station had been secured, perhaps the most divisive question was, "What color shall it be?" The railroad enthusiasts argued that it should be painted in one of the traditional New York, New Haven and Hartford Railroad colors. The railroad had several paint schemes for its buildings over the years. In the railroad's declining days, the color seemed to be whatever could be purchased in bulk and was cheap. The architectural connoisseurs argued, with some merit, that these paint schemes were drab and ugly. The argument went back and forth, and the final scheme approved by Amtrak, as it had agreed to supply the paint, was a ground color of Newport Blue, with black and white trim. It was not historically correct for the station, but (almost) everyone agreed it was beautiful once the job was finished.

The final restoration project was a massive and complex effort (at least for the small community of Kingston). It was decided that direct citizen labor would do most of the exterior scraping and painting, and given the size of the station, that meant a lot of citizens. Over 180 local folks clambered over the station during the June 3–7, 1974 work period. Amtrak bought all the paint and supplies and rented the exterior scaffolds. It also sent down from Boston a young man named Paul Carey, who turned out to be a species of Superman. He sometimes slept overnight in the station so he could get an early start and was in charge of work on the interior. Amtrak and Penn Central crews did most of the interior work and refinished the beautiful old benches. Frank Keefe was the Penn Central representative. He was originally

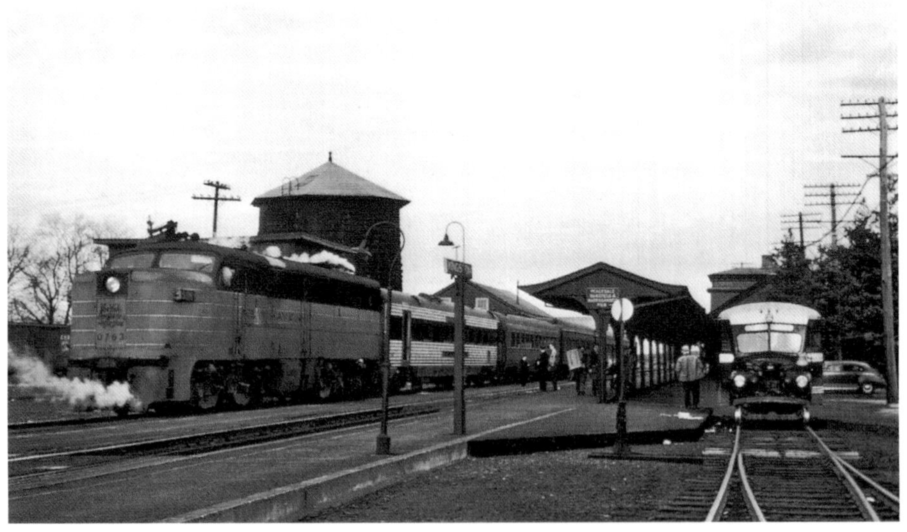

Kingston Station in the early 1950s. On the left is a New York, New Haven and Hartford Railroad local train, powered by an ALCO PA locomotive. On the right is one of the Narragansett Pier Railroad's ultra-cute little rail buses, called Mickey-Dinks by the locals. Rhode Island Railroad Museum.

sent to make sure that the well-meaning volunteers didn't end up destroying the station, but he caught the fever and stayed for the whole week, scraping and painting. The union issue was resolved by the Friends' agreement to hire a United Transportation Union flagman to protect folks working on the track side of the station while trains went through. Everyone agreed that this was a reasonable arrangement.

The whole community pitched in. Local fire and highway departments sent in ladder and lift trucks. State highway crews came to knock down brush and tend to lawns that had been neglected for years. The garden clubs and the elementary schoolchildren raked, planted and installed window boxes. Local markets and restaurants contributed food and drink.

It is difficult to realize, in this litigious and regulatory age, how simple life often was just a generation ago. The Friends had modest liability insurance requirements because people tended to be careful rather than depending on lawsuits for compensation. The station was covered with lead paint, which the Friends cheerfully scraped off without masks. Curiously, many of the people who had this exposure are now in their seventies and eighties.

On June 13, 1974, the executive committee of the Friends sent a "thank-you letter" to the *Narragansett Times*. It concluded, "At the end of our project, we shared a bottle of champagne, and somebody put on a recording of the Hallelujah chorus. Then we hung around in the darkness, because nobody wanted it to end."

The First of Many Celebrations

Something about Kingston Railroad Station puts people in a celebratory mood. Just a month after the restoration week started, a public celebration was staged at the station to mark the completion of the job. Almost as much time was spent organizing the celebration as the job itself. Naturally, trains were involved. One train, on the Narragansett Pier Railroad, started in Peace Dale. It consisted of a tiny switch engine, an 1885 coach and a 1912 caboose. Its passengers included about sixty Amtrak officials and ladies dressed in colonial clothing, presumably psyching themselves up for the upcoming bicentennial. As drinks were served on board and the five-mile trip took nearly an hour, the passengers can be presumed to have been in a mellow mood on their arrival in Kingston. The other train originated in Providence and bore politicians, including Governor Phil Noel and Senator Claiborne Pell, a longtime railroad supporter. Kingston Railroad Station has been a

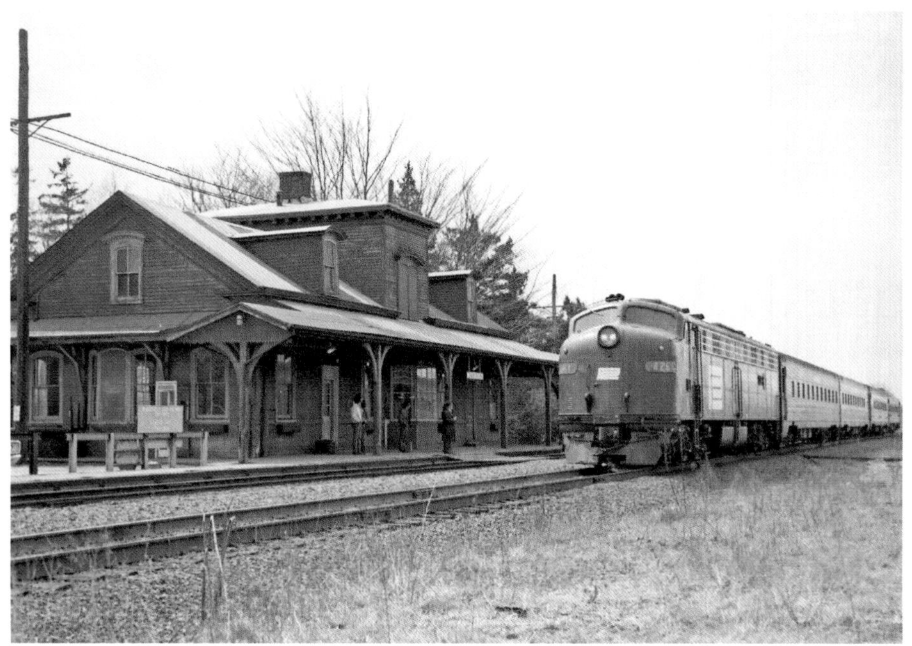

A Penn Central train powered by a single Electro-Motive Diesel "E" locomotive pauses at Kingston. The train appears to be on the "wrong" track. Normally, trains headed in an eastbound direction would be on the other track. No explanation is evident from the picture. *Rhode Island Railroad Museum.*

magnet for politicians since the restoration because it provides a wonderful photo-op background. Governor Noel issued a proclamation declaring July 2 "Friends of Kingston Railroad Station Day," the Narragansett Bay Chorus sang "I've Been Working on the Railroad" and the author, who was by then chairman of the Friends, gave a speech extolling the virtues of rail transportation and, in comparing trains with planes, evoked the late railroad author Lucius Beebe's description of airliners as "hellbound aluminum cartridges of death." Beebe was never known for understatement.

THE KEY TO THE STATION'S SALVATION

After the excitement of the restoration was over, the Friends decided that they needed to perform one more task to try to ensure the station's future. Placement of a building on the National Register of Historic Places gives a structure a certain amount of legal protection if it were to be threatened with demolition. The application process was time consuming, but the building was listed on the National Register in 1977 and officially posted on April 26, 1978. Their mission deemed completed, the Friends then voted themselves out of existence.

THE INTERREGNUM

After the restoration, the station began a long, slow decline. Ownership was transferred to Amtrak, but Amtrak had little money for upkeep on an old, high-maintenance wooden station. The years began to take their toll.

In the meantime, some of the members of the Friends who were more interested in trains than historic preservation kept in touch and, after the station restoration, adopted another forlorn, threatened institution—Train #508. The 508 was the last commuter train in Rhode Island. Formerly operated by the New York, New Haven and Hartford Railroad and then by the Penn Central Railroad, its financing was subsidized in the 1970s by the State of Rhode Island.

The 508 started running in 1893 and was threatened with abandonment many times, starting in 1949. However, its passengers were loyal (Mr. George A. White rode the 508 from 1909 to 1964), and politically connected (Governor and later Senator John H. Chafee had been a regular). Although the losses incurred by the 508 were undeniable, "public necessity" was the trump card when the railroad petitioned the state's public utilities commission for abandonment.

However, the general improvement in roads and completion of a five-mile segment of RI 4, a four-lane divided highway in South County, changed the picture in 1972. The opportunity for South County commuters to share fellowship with fellow drivers from the north in the endless morning traffic jams on I-95 in Cranston, experience thrill-ride excitement as the speeding eighteen-wheeler in the fast lane on the Thurber's Avenue curve begins to tip over on top of one's Volkswagen and enjoy the blood sport of competing for the last parking spot in the only lot within blocks of one's workplace in Providence was simply too good to pass up for many former 508 riders, and patronage began to plummet. Regular ridership dropped to one hundred passengers, and there were mutterings of abandonment in the Department of Transportation.

A subgroup of the Friends, now calling themselves the Friends of the South County Special, decided that a good old-fashioned publicity stunt was needed to call drivers' attention to the fact that, creaky and wheezing as it was, the 508 was still faster from Kingston to Providence downtown than a car. So they decided to stage a race from Kingston to Providence between a 508 commuter and a racecar driver piloting a street-legal racecar on the public streets.

Joe Knight, the owner of Knight's Datsun (Nissan), was persuaded to be the driver, and he contributed the use of his race-prepped Datsun 260Z. The Rhode Island Department of Transportation sent planner Carl Passarelli to shadow Knight in a state car to be sure that he didn't break any rules—the event was beginning to look more like NASCAR all the time. Regular 508 commuter Sheila Forman volunteered to represent the train, and she wore running shoes instead of her regular pumps, because she and Knight would have to sprint á la Le Mans from the starting line to their respective vehicles.

The race started on January 15, 1975, at 7:42 a.m., the regular arrival time in Kingston of the 508. Mrs. Forman was pulled on board the train just as Knight peeled out of the parking lot, burning off about a quarter-inch of

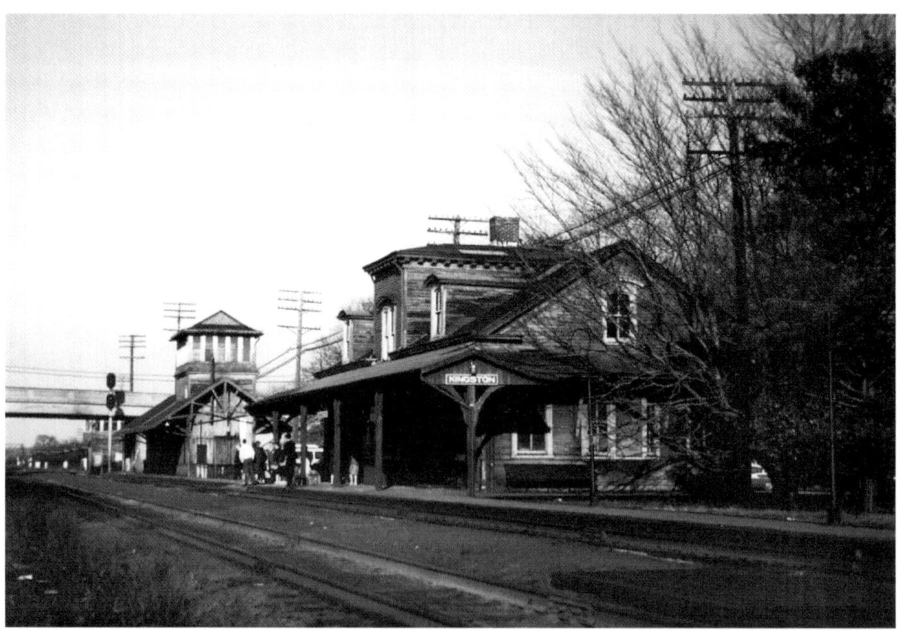

Kingston Station and the Kingston Signal Tower sometime in the '50s or '60s. The tower was torn down by the end of the '60s, and barely visible in the back of the station is what may be a '56 Chevy. This period was pretty much rock bottom for the station. *Rhode Island Railroad Museum.*

rubber. As anticipated, even though Knight fudged a bit on the speed limit, he got stalled in I-95 traffic. The train arrived in Providence at 8:16 a.m., beating Knight by a comfortable three minutes. At the finish line, pom-pom bearers greeted Mrs. Forman, and John Hall, one of the original founders of the Friends, presented Mrs. Forman with the Webster F. Street Memorial Trophy. When asked, Reverend Hall explained that Webster F. Street was the first man to starve to death in a traffic jam. Now, a generation later, it can finally be revealed that Webster F. Street was *not* the first casualty of a traffic jam. Rather, the Webster F. Street Layaway Plan was in fact the favorite fictional cocktail of the "Doc" character in John Steinbeck's *Sweet Thursday* and was named after one of Steinbeck's college mates. It was alleged to contain raw opium and rattlesnake venom.

As a publicity stunt, the race was a stunning success. It was an above-the-fold front-page lead story in the January 15, 1975 *Providence Evening Bulletin*, sharing the lead with "Ford Details Tax Cuts to Aid Economy." Alas, it was for naught. The automobile retained its seductive power, and after a few more years, the 508 remained only in the memories of those who loved it.

Near Disaster

The morning of December 12, 1988, dawned bitter cold in Kingston. Temperatures hovered just above zero degrees, and ice glazed the platforms. The overnight train from Washington, the Night Owl, had stopped at 6:47 a.m., and the southbound from Boston, the Flying Yankee, had just pulled out of the station at about 7:30 a.m. Stationmaster George Steiner whiffed an odor of smoke in the waiting room and fetched a fire extinguisher just in time to see flames start to creep up the corner of the south and east walls. He gave the fire a blast with the extinguisher, but it was moving too quickly through the tinder-dry wood. A 911 call brought in forty South Kingstown Union Fire District volunteers, who, under very difficult conditions, were able to limit the damage to the waiting room. However, the damage to that side of the station was devastating. The roof was burned clear through in places, and the interior walls were completely charred. The cause of the fire was never definitively determined.

Amtrak immediately sent engineering personnel up to the station to assess the damage and consider options for keeping the Kingston stop operating. There had been a small amount of capital funds that Amtrak had earmarked to address long-standing station deficiencies, and this fund was redirected to construct a temporary plywood structure inside the unused south part of the station. This took about a month to complete, but this project consumed all the available funds, and Amtrak freed its local employees to make contacts in the community to see if there might be revenue possibilities there. Now-retired Kingston station agent Jack McCabe, a Friend, called the author on January 9, 1989, and suggested that now would be a good time to revive the Friends of the Kingston Station.

This was quickly done, and the re-formed Friends rose from limbo as a coalition organization composed of the original Friends, the Pettaquamscutt Historical Society, the Rhode Island Railroad Foundation, the West Kingston Civic Association and the Old Colony and Newport Railway (the tourist line in Newport). Early on, it was realized that restoring the station this time would not be a matter of scraping and painting but of convincing financial heavy hitters to part with some significant sums of money.

Meetings were held with Amtrak, and the Friends were told that the building had been insured. This observation soon morphed into the revised idea that Amtrak was self-insured. As it developed, there appeared to be no internal self-insurance fund that could automatically cover major losses like those involved with Kingston Station and that sources other than Amtrak would be needed to rebuild the station.

There then followed one of the most frustrating periods in the Friends' history. Although operations at Kingston were never interrupted, the repairs to the station did nothing for aesthetics, and from the outside, the station looked like a burned-out hulk. Finally, Amtrak prepared a cost estimate for a bare-bones restoration that would restore the station to functionality but would not address the historic nature of the station. The Friends prepared their own estimate, and it was remarkably close: about $200,000. Amtrak offered to put up $100,000 if the state, community and Friends would put up the difference. They did not suggest how much of this sum each entity should contribute—a recipe for squabbling.

At about this time, a bond issue appeared on the state ballot. It was for historic preservation of important buildings, and volunteer groups could apply for grants if the issue passed. It seemed sent from heaven. The bond issue passed, the grant program was established and the Friends applied for, and received, a $100,000 grant. It looked like the station would be saved, if not completely restored.

Then, in an only-in-Rhode-Island twist, it was discovered that some nameless functionary in the bowels of the secretary of state's office had made an error in writing up the bond proposal submitted to the voters. It stated that the bond issue would be secured by revenue bonds rather than general obligation bonds, which was not the case. The matter went to court, and the bond issue was thrown out (along with all the commitments the grants implied). For the Friends, it was an annoyance and a frustration. Other preservation groups, however, had already started work on their projects because their buildings were close to falling down, and they had borrowed money using the grants as collateral. In some cases, they had to pay these loans off out of personal pockets. This had an enormously chilling effect on relationships between nonprofit groups and the state for many years. None of the volunteer groups so affected ever got their money back from the state.

During most of this period, the Friends worked with the office of Senator Claiborne Pell. Senator Pell was a charming and eccentric man. A rich man who had wealth through his own family and through marriage, he drove a beater Chrysler LeBaron convertible whose top was patched with duct tape and was reputed to have twelve suits—all identical. He was very interested in psychic phenomena, but he was also chair of the Senate Foreign Relations Committee, thus one of the most powerful men in Washington. In addition, he sponsored the Pell grants, which have carried millions of students through college. He was also an ardent and proactive enthusiast for railroad transportation. He sponsored the 1967 High Speed Ground Transportation Act, which paved the way for nearly all the improvements in rail service to Kingston.

Senator Pell became impatient with Amtrak's inaction and put pressure on Amtrak to "do something" about Kingston Station. Their response was to send examiners up to the station to determine the most economical way to address the Kingston issue. Their conclusion appeared to be to have the building condemned and torn down and put up some sort of shelter, as had been done at other locations. Upon hearing this, then-agent Jack McCabe retrieved the bronze plaque showing that the building was on the National Register of Historic Places and showed it to them. That ended demolition talk, but not long after, a For Sale sign appeared on the building, to which there were no takers. It appeared that a stalemate had developed.

The Rescue

Senator Pell's office had been most cooperative, but he was not on any Senate committees that distributed funds that might be used for station restoration. However, Rhode Island's other senator at the time, John F.

Chafee, was. Senator Chafee was chairman of the Senate's Environment and Public Works Committee, which was an incubator for what sometimes are derisively called "pork barrel" projects. Of course, one man's pork is another man's ham dinner, and many transportation projects that paid for themselves many times over, like the restoration of Kingston Station, came out of this committee.

In 1991, President George Bush signed an omnibus bill called the Intermodal Surface Transportation Act (ISTEA) sponsored by Representative Norman Mineta (D) of California. The key word in this bill was "intermodal," a new political buzzword that referred to any intersection between several modes of transportation. A train station is almost by definition an intermodal facility because typically cars, buses, transit and trains all connect in one place. ISTEA was one of the largest suppliers of public works funding for transportation since the building of the interstate highway system in the '50s and was one of the first programs in many years to direct money to anything but highways or aviation. Public works funds were routed through Senator Chafee's committee.

One of Senator Chafee's staffers was aware of the plight of Kingston Station and suggested that the station not only be restored but also become the first national demonstration project of an "intermodal facility." Out of ISTEA, $2 million was allocated, and the State of Rhode Island agreed to pony up $500,000 to finish the project if Amtrak would turn over ownership of the station to the state, in exchange for a low/no-cost lease for space in the station. Ironically, the federal administrator of the funds and the project—the Federal Highway Administration—had nothing to do with railroads.

The Friends were dumbfounded. After years of exploring bake sales to buy a few cans of paint, seemingly overnight the station was to be showered with cash, in sums that contained two commas. It appeared that the long drought was over. It took some mental adjustment to move out of poverty mode, but the Friends soon became an active member of the Project Advisory Committee and were involved with most of the decisions made in the restoration. During this period, Dave Whelan was president of the Friends and spent endless hours on site looking out for the interests of the station.

The project was huge in relationship to earlier restoration plans. It included a new parking lot, rerouting the roads around the station, physically moving the station away from the tracks, building new canopies and platforms and a complete and accurate exterior and interior historic restoration, departing from the original design only to comply with Americans with

Disabilities Act requirements and to incorporate modern utilities, like electricity and indoor plumbing. There still was wrangling over exterior paint color. For this restoration, a spectrographic analysis of the paint, which was a quarter of an inch thick in places, demonstrated that the station was painted originally in three shades of brown. Samples were prepared and painted on the walls, and delegates from all the affected groups were invited for a "reveal." The colors were unveiled, and everyone was horrified. The colors were *really ugly* by consensus of those present. The Rhode Island Historical Preservation & Heritage Commission came to the rescue by ruling that the station could be painted in "the colors that were present on the building for the longest period of its service," which happened to be those of an early New York, New Haven and Hartford Railroad scheme. The project was done in two stages. Renaissance man Steve Devine from the Rhode Island Department of Transportation's Intermodal Planning Division was the de facto coordinator of this very complex project. In 1993–94, the fire damage was repaired and the building stabilized for its move (the station had to be physically moved away from the tracks in preparation for high-speed operations). Preliminary work was done on the grounds, and the site was prepared for the new foundation. There was a pause in the work while

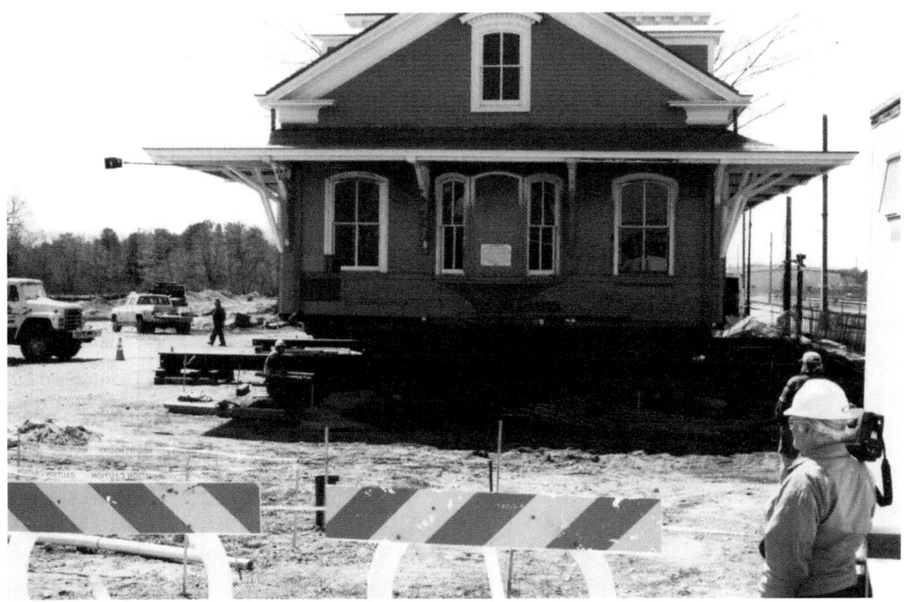

Moving the station during the restoration in the mid-'90s. *Rhode Island Railroad Museum.*

one of Rhode Island's periodic financial crises raised storm clouds, and then the work continued in 1996 and was completed in early 1998. At the same time, work was being done to convert the old Narragansett Pier Railroad right of way into a bike path ending at the station; this enabled the station to be considered "intermodal" under a new definition of the term. Finally, the hammers and saws were put away, the paint brushes were cleaned and the contractors moved to their new jobs. But the Friends were not yet done with Kingston Station.

THE GRAND CELEBRATION

Some of the Friends had been involved with this old building for almost fifteen years. Children who were babes in arms at the original restoration celebration were now high school sophomores. Collectively, tens of thousands of hours had been donated by people with very expensive talents—architects, lawyers, engineers. With the completion of the restoration, everyone was exhausted, and it was time for a party. Not just a party, but a *party*—one that would be remembered for at least another generation.

The theme of the party jumped out right away: "Where the Old Meets the New." Kingston Station looked like Mark Twain would be comfortable catching a train from its platform, but it was wired for computers, had an ultra-modern fire detection and suppression system and would soon have trains whizzing by at 150 miles an hour.

History did not record exactly who came up with the key idea, but it was stunning in its simplicity: "Unh, why don't we just get a steam engine and have it touch noses with Amtrak's newest locomotive in front of the station, just like that old 1869 photo of the engines meeting at the completion of the transcontinental railroad?"

That simple idea required a year to execute, and it involved, among other things, persuading Amtrak to allow an eighty-year-old steam locomotive to operate on the Northeast Corridor under its own power during the busiest time of the day.

The Friends' plans for the celebration were, if nothing else, ambitious. The navy's Blue Angels were contacted to see if a flyover was possible, but the weekend was already booked. The governor and Rhode Island's entire congressional delegation were invited to participate, and all came. Politicians who had nothing to do with the project requested invitations, which were cheerfully extended. You never know who might be helpful in the future.

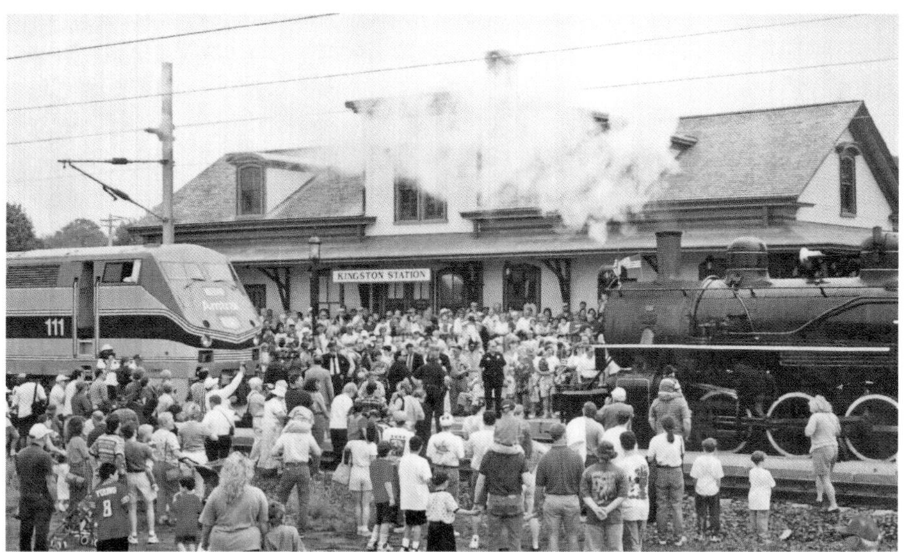

The Grand Celebration of 1998. *Rhode Island Railroad Museum.*

The steam engine was the biggest challenge. The last time a steam engine had passed through Kingston was in 1976, when the American Freedom Train chugged through. The Valley Railroad in Essex, Connecticut, was contacted and agreed to lease an engine and crew to the Friends for the sum of $8,000 a day (fuel included). Miraculously, this sum appeared through a donation from the APC Corporation. Amtrak was still the reluctant party. What would such an antique chugger do to the tracks?

After endless negotiations, a contingent of Amtrak civil and mechanical engineers agreed to meet with their counterparts at the Valley Railroad. All the parties gathered around a conference table in the Valley Railroad's business car in Essex, Connecticut. The Friends moderated the meeting. The Valley Railroad's master mechanic for steam was the first to speak. He said, in a pronounced Yankee accent, "Well, ah'm not so sure I want to trust my locomotive to yo'ah tracks. You got some spots theah, they're like the Cyclone at Coney Island." It was the perfect way to begin the conversation. The outraged Amtrak folks began to defend their tracks, saying of course they were suitable for a steam engine. After about ten minutes of discussion, all the Amtrak guys were trying to nail a ride in the cab of the steamer when the day came.

On May 31, 1998, a special train was cleared to operate between Old Saybrook, Connecticut, and Kingston. It consisted of Valley Railroad

#40, a brand-new Amtrak Genesis locomotive, two other Amtrak diesels from different historical periods, a brand-new Amtrak sleeping car that would be open for display and a coach to hold all the Amtrak officials who wanted to ride the Special. The steamer periodically stopped along the way for fire engines to replace the water in its tank. At Kingston, the Genesis was detached from the rest of the train and ran up to Quonset, where there was a wye track where it could be reversed and then burbled back to Kingston. In front of three thousand visitors and dozens of VIPs, the New slowly advanced to meet the Old. The Wakefield Civic Band played nineteenth-century songs; the South Kingstown High School Jazz Band responded with contemporary pieces; the Genesis gave a long blast on its K5LA air horn; #40 responded with a nostalgic wail of its Crosby three-chime steam whistle; Jack McCabe of the Friends introduced the speakers, who included Senators Pell and Chafee, Congressman Jack Reed, Governor Lincoln Almond and Amtrak general manager William Duggan; and when all the excitement was over, the Friends who had been organizing the affair for almost a year went home and slept for several days.

Post-Celebration

The station restoration had a transformational effect on South County. Just before the restoration, Kingston Station had about 66,000 passengers a year. Now it has close to 175,000 passengers annually, and it has the problems of success. In the summer, there's no place to park. On heavy travel weekends, the trains are sold out. On a busy day, it is not uncommon for 140 passengers (25 percent of the capacity of the train) to board each westbound train at Kingston. Van services carry people to the Block Island and Martha's Vineyard ferries, and rich folks once more travel from Manhattan to the playgrounds of Rhode Island by train. Kingston Station has become the gateway to South County.

The station itself has become a social center and economic engine for South County. Fifteen hundred people came to a Railroad Picnic Day in 2002 (ironically, this would no longer be possible because the parking lot is always full of passengers' cars). There is a small railroad museum in the station run by the Friends, and politicians have discovered that Kingston Station is a bully place to make political announcements. A $4 million overpass provides safe passage to the normally westbound track, and plans were recently announced to build high-level platforms and a passing track at Kingston (at a cost approximately ten times as much as the '90s restoration). Much of this money will remain in the community.

Why has Kingston Station engendered such a seemingly endless series of happy endings over the past thirty-five years? The easy and largely correct answer is the Friends. But why have the Friends had so much success when other restoration efforts in other places have had very different fates? Continuity certainly has something to do with it. Many of the original Friends were young faculty members at URI in the 1970s and are still active. Willingness to be mediators or brokers rather than bosses certainly played a part. But mostly it is the station itself.

Kingston Station looks like a place you call home. It's a place where you really can see young lovers running toward each other on the platform. Parents waving to their kids going off to college, standing in the train vestibules like '40s movie stars. Tears of joy and tears of sadness. Greetings and farewells. It is a place to love—and to preserve.

Chapter 12

THE RAILROADS OF RHODE ISLAND TODAY

Ever since the first train made its way from Boston to Providence in 1835, the operation of railroads has been about communication and information processing at the fastest speed possible. Dispatchers have to be in touch with trains hundreds of miles away to keep them separated when they are on the same track. Someone has to know the destination and contents of every car in a freight train to get them expeditiously to their recipients. As trains became faster, their communication and data processing needs increased also.

Most electrical means of communication developed in tandem with the railroads. The first electrical communication system, the telegraph, was developed by Samuel F.B. Morse. The first telegraph lines were strung along the Baltimore and Ohio Railroad's right of way between Baltimore and Washington, D.C., and the world's first telegraph message, "What hath God wrought?" was sent over that line on May 24, 1844. The telegraph system was first used to dispatch trains in 1851, and its use became almost universal within a few years. Alexander Graham Bell was awarded the first patent for the telephone in 1876, and in only three years, the Boston, Revere Beach and Lowell Railroad was dispatching its trains by telephone—a very early adoption of a new technology. The first railroad use of two-way portable radios in the United States was by the Santa Fe Railroad in 1944. Ironically, the use of radio by the railroads was slowed by the very efficiency of wired communications. Airplanes had no choice but to use radio for communications, but most of a railroad's communication needs could be met by wired means. However, the development of the walkie-talkie mobile two-way radio during World War II speeded adoption of radios by train crews to communicate with one another across the mile-long length of a freight train.

Modern communications technologies were also pioneered by railroads. The first cellphone network in the United States was developed for use by the Metroliners of the Penn Central Railroad in 1969. There were pay phones on the train that communicated with the early antecedents of cellphone towers. President Richard M. Nixon made one of the first cellphone calls in the world when he rode a Metroliner from Washington, D.C., to Philadelphia on January 24, 1970. What he said was not recorded. Both microwave and fiberoptic technologies were pioneered by a subsidiary of the Southern Pacific Railroad, Southern Pacific Communications, which developed these technologies for the railroad's internal communications needs in the '70s. Both the microwave towers and fiberoptic pathways were built along the railroad's right of way, a commonplace situation for major communications companies today. When Southern Pacific Communications won the right to sell phone service to the general public, the company had an internal contest to come up with a new name. It was finalized as Southern Pacific Railroad Intelligent Network of Telecommunication—Sprint for short.

The railroads have been a lead industry for commercial computer and information technology development. The Union Pacific Railroad for many years was one of the largest industrial users of mainframe computers. The first engineering model of the Digital Equipment Company's first "minicomputer," the PDP-1, was delivered as a gift to a railroad. A very small railroad. The recipient, MIT's Tech Model Railroad Club, used the PDP-1 to develop the world's first two-player computer game, *Spacewar!*, in addition to operating its miniature railroad. Minicomputers had the advantage of interactivity, a critical quality in railroad management. In the late 1960s, railroads first used an ancestor of today's barcodes called KarTrak to keep track of freight cars.

These stories are by way of preface to suggest that railroads are and have been a technologically dynamic enterprise, and that dynamism has been reflected in modern developments of railroads in Rhode Island.

TODAY'S RAILROADS

At present, the "live" railroads in Rhode Island are Amtrak; the MBTA; the Providence and Worcester Railroad; the Seaview Transportation Company, which operates the freight trackage at Quonset; the Newport Dinner Train; and the Old Colony and Newport Railway, which operates the tourist train in Newport. The MBTA's trains are operated under contract by a private firm, the Massachusetts Bay Commuter Railroad Company (MBCR), whose contract expires in 2013. Collectively, Rhode Island's railroads have fewer than one hundred miles of mainline track. The lead government agency that both promotes and coordinates rail transportation in the state is the Rhode Island Department of Transportation (RIDOT). Recent directors of RIDOT have been very proactive for rail, and the physical impact of that activity can be seen all over the state.

Tying together everything but the lines on Aquidneck Island are the tracks of the Northeast Corridor, which follow the 1847 realignment of the Boston and Providence Railroad from Attleboro through Pawtucket to Providence, and the New York, Providence and Boston Railroad (Stonington Line) from Providence to Westerly and then across the border to Connecticut. These tracks in Rhode Island are primarily owned by Amtrak but in a few places are owned jointly with the Providence and Worcester Railroad. The Providence and Worcester Railroad itself has its own single-track line from Providence to Worcester, where it connects with east–west carriers, in addition to industrial tracks in Providence and freight rights over the Northeast Corridor. These rights are primarily used for alcohol trains for "gasohol" and for automobile carriers and carloads of plastic pellets at the connection with the Seaview Transportation Company's fourteen miles of track in the Quonset Business Park.

The Shore Line has never been considered a genuine "high-speed" route. There are too many curves, and they are too sharp for real high speeds. Today, the Acela express trains travel the 228 miles between New York City and Boston at an average speed of 63.7 miles per hour (including stops). By contrast, in 1935, the steam-powered Twin Cities Hiawatha traveled the relatively straight 410 miles between Chicago and Minneapolis at an average speed of 62.1 miles per hour (including stops). After the tracks between Manhattan and New Haven were electrified in 1914, a further impediment to rapid service was imposed by the necessity of stopping all trains at New Haven long enough to change from electric engines to steam (and then diesel engines after they replaced the steamers) for the continuing trip. This added ten to fifteen minutes to the trip, and one of the goals for all comprehensive improvement programs for the Northeast Corridor in New England has been to electrify the line all the way to Boston, eliminating the changeover in New Haven.

The piece of federal legislation that initiated modernization of the Northeast Corridor in New England was the Northeast Corridor Improvement Project of 1976. It had as its goal no less than the complete modernization and electrification of the Northeast Corridor, along with improvements in its locomotives to permit higher speeds. At the time of passage, truly high-speed trains like the Acela Expresses were not contemplated.

Work started on the roadbed and track in 1977 at Kingston Station. The objective was to replace the old wooden-tie, short-rail track with concrete ties and welded rail, which was made in lengths of up to a mile, instead of the thirty-nine feet of the old bolt-together rail. Instead of armies of John Henrys slinging sixteen-pound sledgehammers, the modern rail-laying crew consists of a few technicians and a mind-boggling quarter-mile-long machine that simultaneously pulls up the old track, lays the new track and then redeposits track ballast as it slowly crawls along the right of way.

The start of electrification of the New Haven–Boston leg of the corridor was delayed until 1996 due to lack of funding and was not completed until 2000. While electrification work was being done through Connecticut, Rhode Island and Massachusetts, modern electric locomotives were introduced in the southern part of the route, which had been electrified for many years. The Electro-Motive Division of General Motors produced the AEM-7 electric locomotive for Amtrak, and the first deliveries were made in 1979. The AEM-7 is not a particularly handsome locomotive, and its nicknames support that observation. To railfans, it is a Toaster because it is electric and, frankly, bears more than a casual visual relationship to that homey kitchen appliance. To Amtrak employees, it is a Meatball, a sobriquet that has no apparent visual basis. The name derives from the fact that the demonstrator locomotives were made in Sweden and, when they were brought over here for testing, were immediately nicknamed "Swedish meatballs." Over time, the "Swedish" was lost, leaving the puzzling appellation. Despite their appearance and unflattering nicknames, the Meatballs have proven to be generally good and reliable locomotives and routinely pull their regional trains at 120 miles per hour through the faster portions of the line in Rhode Island. Although their external appearance has changed but little over the years,

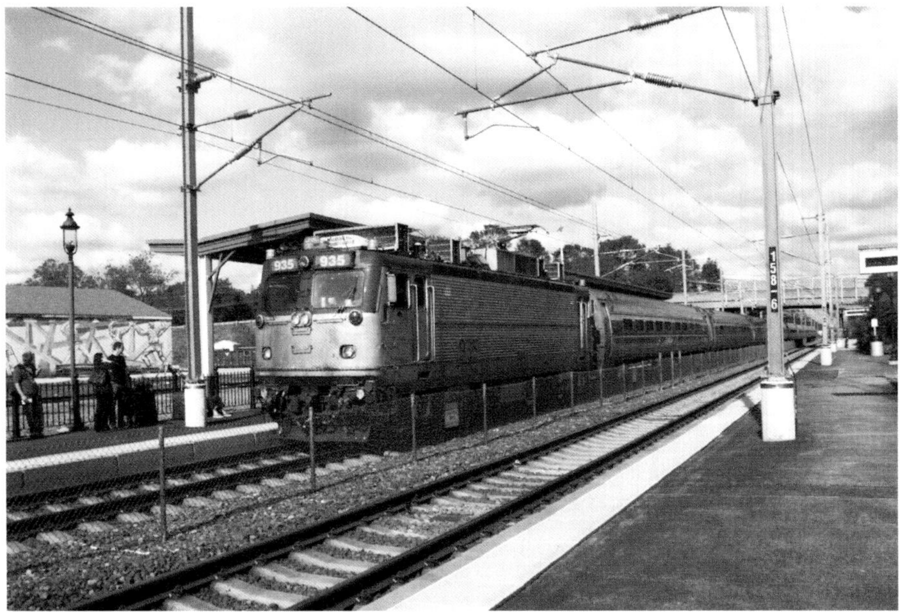

A Toaster (AEM-7) pulling a regional train at Kingston. *Photo by Frank Heppner.*

their "guts" have been constantly updated. Electric train service through Rhode Island started January 31, 2000.

At about the same time work was started on the installation of the electric wires and their support systems on the Northeast Corridor, Amtrak began discussions with several manufacturers for a new generation of passenger trains for the refurbished tracks. There were several design considerations from the beginning. The new trains would be electric powered from overhead wires and would be built as a "trainset" rather than conventional cars with a locomotive. A trainset is symmetrical and bidirectional; the train doesn't have to be turned around to begin its return trip. Also, in a trainset, the cars are permanently coupled together, and there is a "power unit" rather than a locomotive at each end. There would need to be some engineering feature that would let the trainset go around curves at a higher speed than a conventional train without causing passenger discomfort. There was some sensitivity to this issue because an earlier attempt at a high-speed train on the northern part of the corridor, United Aircraft's TurboTrain from the 1960s, used a primitive tilting mechanism to go around curves faster than it might otherwise. Unfortunately, the mechanism was undamped, so after leaving the curve, the cars would continue to rock back and forth like a pendulum, leading to motion sickness in even the hardiest seafaring passengers if they sat in the dome at either end of the train.

From the beginning, a number of controversies plagued the new trains. There were cost overruns and delays from the manufacturer, Bombardier/ GEC Alsthom. The new train had a tilting mechanism like the earlier TurboTrain, but it was damped and computer controlled, so mal de rail was no longer a problem. Unfortunately, if the train zipped around a curve too enthusiastically, the bottom would swing out so far that there was a perception there was some danger of swiping a train on an adjoining track, so speed limitations were placed on some curves.

The name for the new train equipment caused confusion. Amtrak decided to "rebrand" all of its Northeast Corridor service, so it came up with a neologism, Acela, to describe *all* of its trains. The new trains would be Acela Expresses, the conventional trains would be Acela Regionals and Amtrak commuter trains would be Acela Commuters. This caused endless confusion, so finally the moniker Acela was only used for the high-speed trains.

The new trains were put in service on December 11, 2000, and were an immediate hit. In Rhode Island, they make a single stop in Providence.

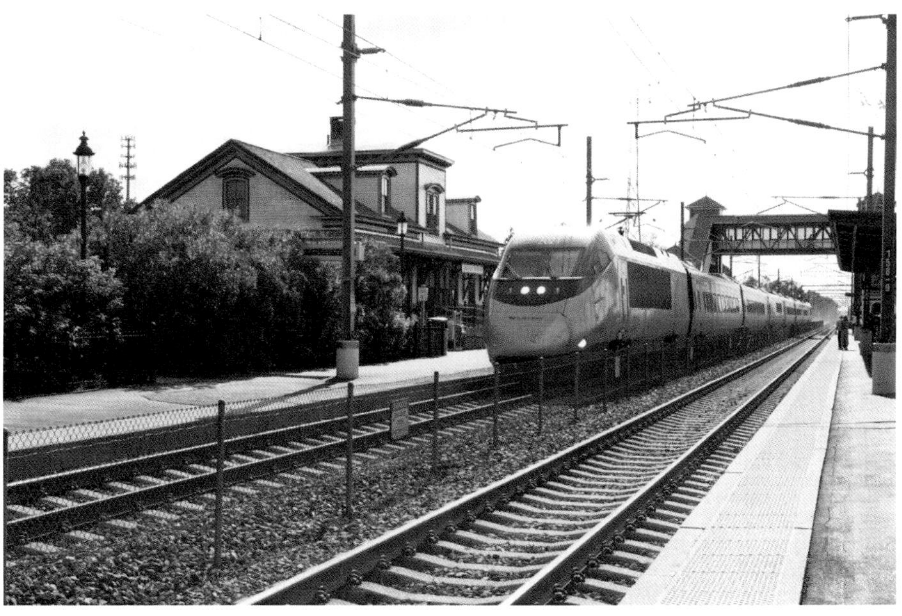

An Acela passing through Kingston at 250 kilometers per hour (this sounds a lot faster than 150 miles per hour, the same speed expressed in English units). *Photo by Frank Heppner.*

Given the volume of traffic generated by Kingston, people often ask why the Acelas don't also stop at Kingston. Convenient as this would be, the main reason the Acelas have shorter travel times than the regional trains is not their peak high speeds but the fact that they make many fewer stops. If Kingston were a stop, there would soon be other communities clamoring for stops, and that would be the end of high-speed service.

Overall, the Acelas are a successful design. They *look* fast, and an Acela trainset zipping through Kingston at 150 miles per hour is an impressive sight. Like a number of Amtrak designs over the years, the Acela's paint scheme has raised a few eyebrows, with its randomly placed Alexander Calder–ish ovals of paint. However, compared to the porpoise-faced new Spanish high-speed trains or the platypus-visaged latest generation of Japanese Shinkansen trains, the Acela is positively handsome. Although nothing is certain in today's economy, there are plans to refurbish and add more cars to the existing trainsets and purchase new ones. To someone who watched the old New York, New Haven and Hartford Railroad's wheezers gasp into Providence in the late '60s, the idea that fast, modern and comfortable trains would be serving Rhode Island in the new century would have been unfathomable.

FREIGHT IMPROVEMENTS

What goes around comes around. From the beginning of the twentieth century into the 1940s, there was so much traffic, both passenger and freight, along the New York, New Haven and Hartford Railroad's tracks through South County and up into Providence that there were long stretches of multiple track—three and sometimes four parallel tracks. North of Providence to the state line, the railroad had four tracks, just like the Pennsylvania Railroad south of Manhattan or the New York Central Railroad north of Grand Central Station. Big-time railroading. Google Earth reveals that the existing Amtrak right of way north of Kingston at one time accommodated three tracks, and the old Kingston switch control panel display in the Rhode Island Railroad Museum in Kingston Station clearly shows the multiple main tracks of a major railroad.

Over the years, with the decline of the New York, New Haven and Hartford Railroad's fortunes, the extra tracks were removed because they had high maintenance costs and were increasingly redundant with the reduction in number of trains. However, with the surprising success of Amtrak and the resurgence of rail freight business from the port area of

Providence and the Quonset Industrial Park, the presence of only two tracks on the mainline became a bottleneck in Rhode Island. The introduction of the Acela trainsets dramatically worsened the situation.

The Acela and Regional trains travel at different average speeds. To avoid delays, the Acelas have to periodically switch over to the other track of a two-track mainline to pass the Regionals. Unfortunately, that means that all the trains on the other track, going in the opposite direction, have to be held well in front of the meeting place to avoid head-on collisions. There is then a cascade effect where one train makes the second late, which in turn makes a third train late and so on. The presence of a still-slower freight train makes the situation even worse. More "crossover tracks" to permit more locations where one train could overtake and pass another on the second track would be a help, but the only real solution is to restore the ancient and long-removed third track at "choke points" where many trains tend to meet.

Also, in another example where progress creates problems, the introduction of overhead wires over the tracks in electrified zones limits the height of freight cars. The newest generation of freight cars is called double-stack cars because they can contain pairs of the ubiquitous freight containers seen behind eighteen-wheelers on every interstate. A typical double-stack car is a shade fewer than twenty feet tall above the rails, which is cutting it very close to the overhead wires on electrified lines. As both shippers and railroads *love* double-stack cars, the electrification of the corridor improved the quality of passenger service greatly but also inhibited the development of modern freight shipping in Rhode Island. Also, the new generation of auto carrier rail cars stacks the autos three high, with the total height again approaching twenty feet. Much of the traffic coming from the Quonset Business Park consists of auto stack cars. What to do? Now comes FRIP to the rescue.

The FRIP (Freight Rail Improvement Project), whose primary Rhode Island sponsor was Senator Jack Reed, was a $200 million project, of which only a quarter was direct federal funding. The balance came from state funds and federal highway funds allocated to Rhode Island. This project took about ten years of securing funds and four years of construction in Rhode Island. It consists primarily of a new third track (in many places replacing the long-removed *old* third track) from Davisville to the outskirts of Providence. This new track does not have overhead wires, so there are no height restrictions due to electrification. From a point just north of Davisville to south of T.F. Green Airport, there is not a third track but a five-mile, two-track section where the old roadbed was actually lowered to

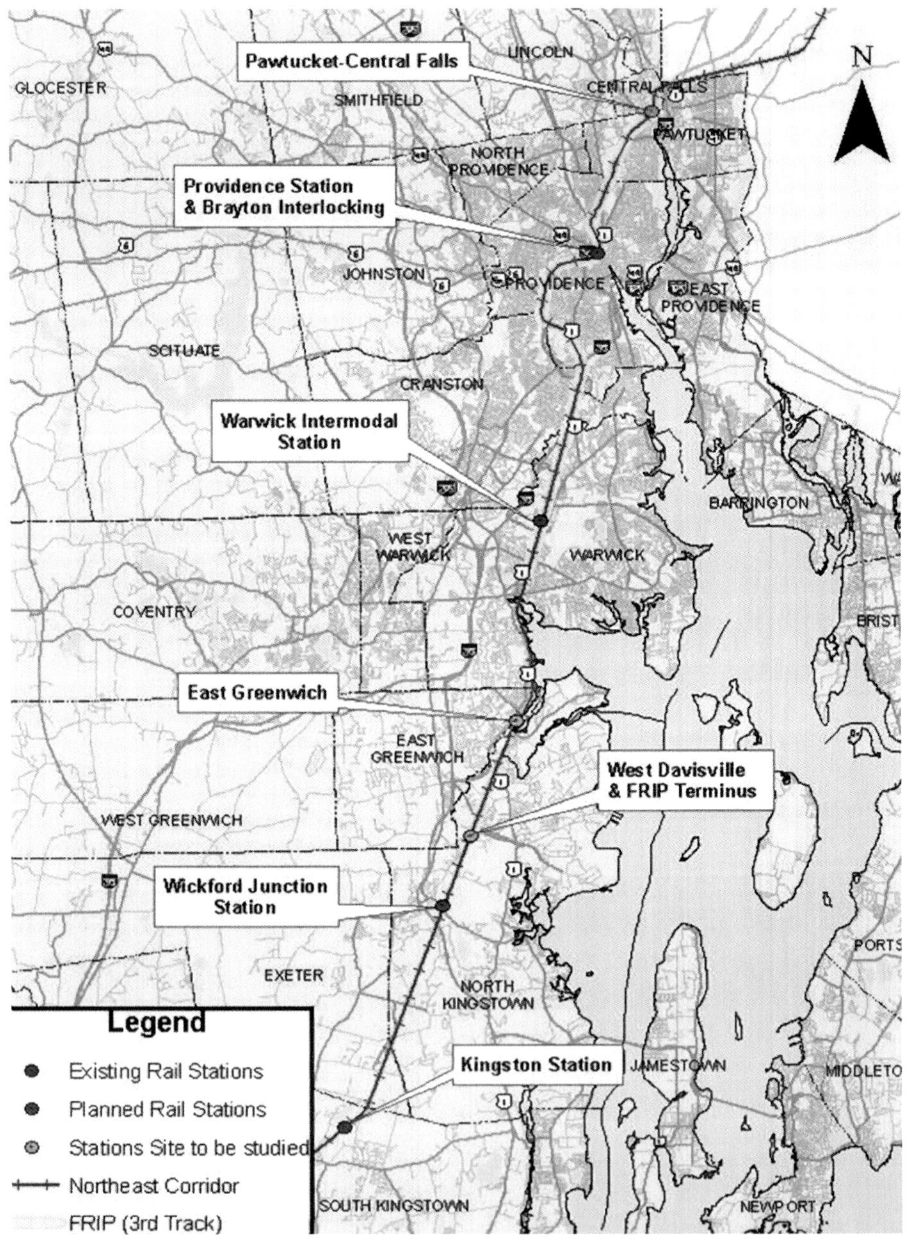

Map showing FRIP track. *Rhode Island Department of Transportation.*

permit sufficient clearance under the wires for stacked freight cars. Highway bridges over the tracks also had to be raised; this was neither a trivial nor an inexpensive project, and it reflected Rhode Island's appreciation of the future importance of rail freight to the general economy.

Today, extra-size freight cars can move directly from Davisville to Providence, thence to Worcester over the Providence and Worcester Railroad's newly refurbished line, which now has adequate clearance under overpasses for the extra-height cars. The idea of developing Quonset into a full-fledged container port has been a political football since the idea was first broached many years ago, but the objection that the containers would have nowhere to go but the already overcrowded highways has now been removed.

New Life for the Commuter

When the Penn Central Railroad folded, the MBTA bought the segment of the old Boston and Providence Railroad between Boston and the state line in 1973. It is now known as the Providence/Stoughton Line. It continued to provide rail commuter service between Boston and Providence until 1981, when funding from the Rhode Island government dried up. Some commuters continued to use Amtrak between Providence and Boston after commuter service stopped. Although the fare was much higher than that of the old MBTA, the running time was much less and the trains more comfortable. However, as Amtrak trains started to fill up for medium-

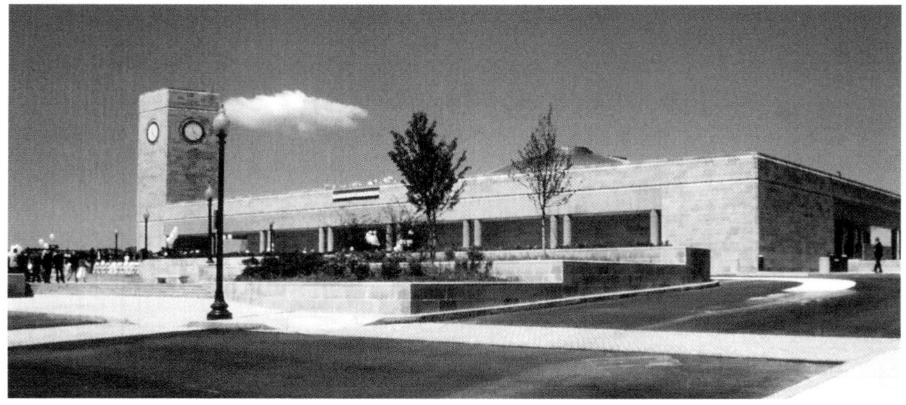

Current Providence station, served by Amtrak and MBTA. *Photograph by Edward A. Ozog.*

long-distance runs, fares for short distances increased disproportionately. In an almost-full train, a Providence-Boston passenger might prevent a New York–Boston passenger from being able to get a ticket, so in recent years, Amtrak has discouraged short-distance travel in its trains along the Northeast Corridor.

In 1988, after an agreement between the Rhode Island Department of Transportation and MBTA was signed, limited commuter service was restored on the MBTA from Boston to Providence, and in 2006, full seven-days-a-week service resumed. Initially, there were only five round trips a day, and now there are fifteen. Providence is now the second-busiest station on the MBTA system. It appeared that the once moribund commuter train had a new life.

South County Commuter Service

A massive study on the possibility/desirability of restoring South County commuter service was prepared for RIDOT in 2001. It examined the options that existed at the time: 1) a stand-alone, Rhode Island–financed train service like the old 508; 2) an extension from the south by Connecticut's commuter rail service; and 3) an extension to the south by the Boston-based MBTA. The latter was chosen as having the most advantages. The most practical locations for new stations in Phase 1 of what RIDOT called South County Commuter Service were in Warwick, at the location of the T.F. Green Airport, and Wickford Junction, where there was a nexus of highways converging on the junction that would provide road access to the station. Technically, Warwick is not in South County, so perhaps the service might more accurately be described as "Going Toward South County Commuter Service."

Formidable obstacles—economic, logistic and political—stood in the way. The tracks over which the new service would operate belonged to Amtrak, which proved to be a very reluctant fiancé. With the introduction of Acela service and the relatively small number of crossover tracks that permit passing, Amtrak's perception was that every non-Amtrak train operating on its tracks increased the probability of delays to its own trains. As "on-time" record was to be a selling point for the Acelas, new commuter trains clogging its tracks was not an exciting prospect. Also, the lawyers had to insert their two cents' worth, and every person on an Amtrak station platform who was a commuter, not an Amtrak passenger, increased liability for Amtrak, as would a commuter train disaster if it occurred in or near a commuter station. Resolving these issues took much negotiation and large quantities of financial solace, in advance, to assuage Amtrak's fears.

There were also practical considerations. MBTA trains are currently powered by diesel locomotives and thus don't require overhead wires. Additional tracks for the commuter trains would have to be built at Warwick and Wickford Junction, and their cost would be considerably reduced if they weren't built with overhead wires—but then Amtrak trains couldn't use them. This would prove to be an issue when the question was raised whether Amtrak trains might not also stop at Warwick or Wickford Junction, as they now stop at Route 128 near Boston. For now and the foreseeable future, Amtrak trains will not be stopping at the new stations. Perhaps the most challenging technical consideration to putting new tracks in operation at the new stations was including them in the "interlocking" system. This is a technically obsolescent term that describes the mechanism used to signal trains when it is safe to move forward and which routes trains to different tracks. "Interlocking" referred to the fact that even human error could not send one train into the path of another. Nowadays, the interlocking function is handled at a central location on the Northeast Corridor and operates somewhat like the air traffic control system. However, this system is incredibly complex and is not designed to be easily changed, as changes in railroad track alignments are rare. Changes in interlocking are expensive and time-consuming to make because there can be no errors in the system. Solutions exist for these technical problems, but the eight-hundred-pound gorilla sitting on the tracks was, who was going to pay for all this?

The answer, of course, is that you are, through public funding. The United States thus appears to be joining the rest of the industrialized world, where railroads are viewed as a necessary component of a contemporary society, which, because of its intensive capital costs, cannot be expected to pay for its own way if fares are kept low enough for it to be mass transportation. Belatedly, the trains of the Northeast Corridor are joining their winged airline companions in enjoying generous federal and state support. (The airline industry has been very successful over the years in disguising its subsidies, which are in the billions of dollars, by simply avoiding the word "subsidy.")

The Warwick station, dubbed the "InterLink," connects the tracks to the airport via a 1,200-foot-long enclosed motorized walkway. It went into service in late 2010 with a limited number of Providence- and Boston-bound commuter trains because the incomplete interlocking system would

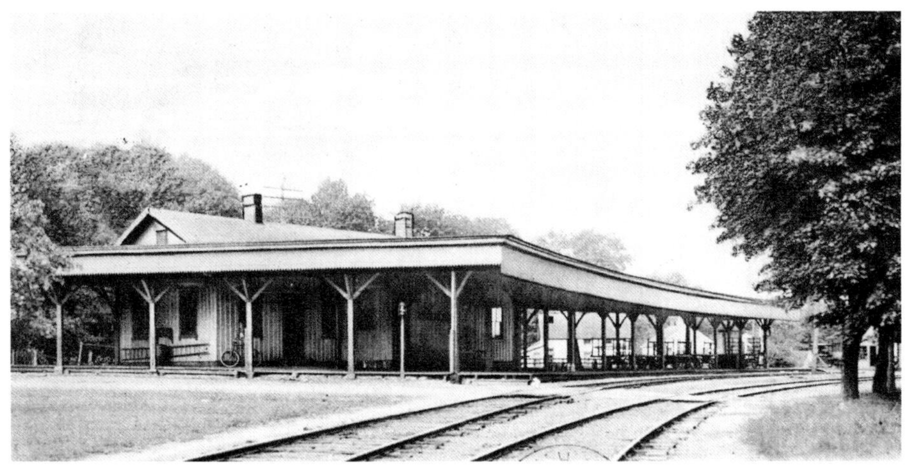

Original Wickford Junction station, built in 1871. The pair of tracks leading to the foreground belongs to the Newport and Wickford Railroad, and the main Stonington Line tracks run in back of the station. *Collection of Edward J. Ozog.*

not permit more trains to be run. It also serves as a rental car garage. Currently, it faces a kind of chicken-and-egg dilemma. There are not enough trains at present to Boston and Providence to make the service particularly attractive to commuters, but there aren't enough current rail commuters to make additional trains an economically attractive proposition at the moment. This was the case when commuter service was restored to Providence; the trains were empty at first, but when a "critical number" of daily trains was reached, patronage skyrocketed. More trains are scheduled to be added to the South County service in 2012, ultimately reaching twenty-four stops a day. The Wickford Junction station is in some ways a more promising commuter project than Warwick. It lies near three large suburban shopping centers, with their typical complements of Walmart, Home Depot, Super Stop and Shop and other consumer palaces. There are reasonably attractive suburban residential areas nearby, and the auto commute to Providence, let alone Boston, is horrendous; thus, there is a real chance for rail commuting to both Boston and Providence to become a viable proposition without much additional non-rail infrastructure improvement.

RIDOT is currently conducting studies for extensions to passenger rail service, with possible stops in Pawtucket, Cranston, East Greenwich, Kingston and Westerly. There are major issues with some of these locations, and the irony is inescapable. At one time, all these sites had rail commuter service, and the cost of restoring it now will be staggering. We are now starting to realize just how costly our love affair with the "convenience" of the automobile has been, both in dollars and lifestyle.

Kingston is scheduled to have some improvements, financed by stimulus funds, over the next few years that will increase its attractiveness as a candidate for commuter service. Full-length, high-level platforms will be built, supplementing the existing short, handicapped-access platforms on both tracks. In addition, the long-abandoned and torn-up third track will be restored as a passing track for Acelas. Both of these improvements should have a significant effect on existing Amtrak train operations, reducing loading and unloading times for the twenty-plus regional trains that stop in Kingston and presenting greater operational flexibility for the Acelas.

END OF THE LINE, FOLKS; EVERYBODY OFF, PLEASE

As the Boston-bound first-class Acela passenger on #2164 gently dabs the last crumbs of his lobster salad off his lips and enjoys a final sip of his Chivas (neat, of course), if he briefly glances out the window as his train glides at 150 miles per hour past Hundred Acre Pond near Kingston, he will be viewing essentially the same scene his ancestor on the New York, Providence and Boston Railroad's train from Stonington to Providence saw 176 years ago. He will, of course, be traveling in considerably more comfort and won't have to worry about his hair catching fire from flying cinders emerging from the smokestack of the gasping little engine of the primeval train.

The railroad industry in Rhode Island, like the state itself, has been an enterprise of wildly swinging cycles. In the late 1960s, when the author came to Little Rhody, the surviving mainline operation, the New York, New Haven and Hartford Railroad, was sounding the death rattle. The trolley lines were all dead, rail commuter service was on its way out, freight traffic was moribund and the passenger stations hadn't received maintenance for years. Today, forty years later, there is a new passenger station in Providence, two new stations in Warwick and Wickford Junction are finished or nearly so and the old stations at Kingston and Westerly have been completely refurbished. The mainline track has been completely rebuilt and electrified, and there are half again as many passenger trains stopping at Providence as there were in 1969.

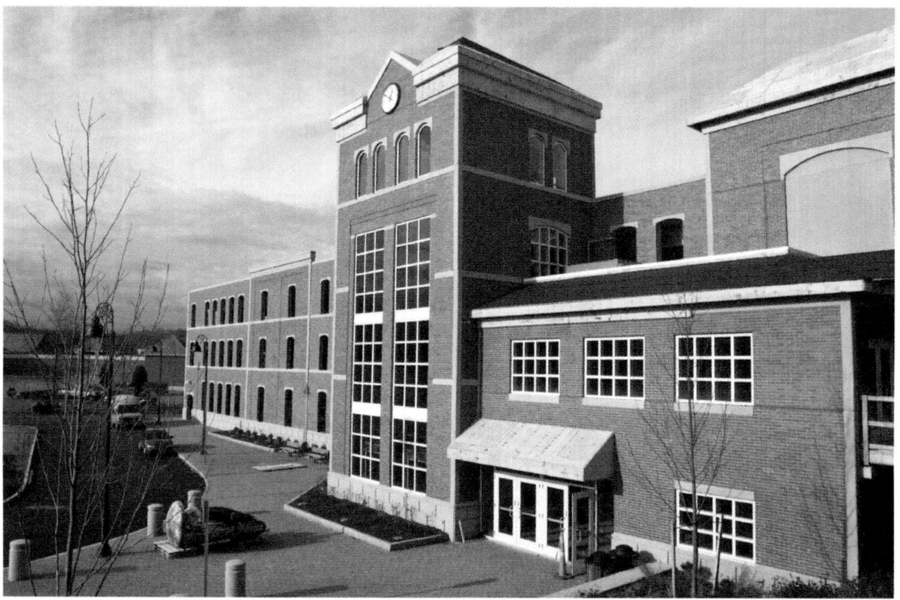

The new Wickford Junction commuter station under construction in 2011. The new station will cost approximately 6,500 times as much as the old station, but of course, the old station didn't have a one-thousand-car garage and commercial space attached. *Photo by Frank Heppner.*

The present railroad scene in the state would be unimaginable and probably dumbfounding to Rhode Island's railroad pioneers—McNeill, Whistler, Mason, Fisher, Hazard, Aldrich and Clarke. In fact, it would even be astounding to the good citizens of Kingston who happily scraped lead paint off Kingston Station just three decades ago.

Where do the tracks lead from here? If a genuinely high-speed rail line like the TGV routes in France is built between Boston and New York, it will almost certainly bypass Rhode Island (or possibly graze it at Woonsocket) and go from Boston to Hartford and then down to the Big Apple. This line, due to real estate costs, will be staggeringly expensive, and its cost will have to be balanced against the benefits received from a less dramatic but far less expensive upgrading of the Shore Line. The advantage of upgrades to this line will not be so much an increase in top speed but the ability to handle more frequent and comfortable trains with much better on-time records.

The state has recently invested hundreds of millions of dollars in new commuter train facilities. However, stations, fares and trains alone will not persuade hardcore auto commuters to make the transition to rail. One's choice of transportation mode is as much emotional as logical or economic, and some careful thought will be needed to convince drivers to make the move to the rails. If a driving commute is expensive, stressful, dangerous and inconvenient, why do people still persist in their ritual twice-a-day auto commute even when other alternatives are offered?

History might provide an answer. In the late 1960s, a group of students in the Davis Railroad Club, in association with student government at the University of California at Davis, decided to start a bus line at the heavily bicycle-oriented campus. On nice days, the bike paths were jam-packed, but on the frequent rainy days during winter and spring, students abandoned their bikes and drove in to campus, filling the parking lots to overflowing. Buses appeared to be a solution to this problem.

The Railroad Club leased a couple of school buses and established inexpensive bus routes parallel to the bike paths. They were a disaster. You could play a game of basketball inside the empty buses. What the founders had failed to consider was that the last type of vehicle college students wanted to ride in was a school bus. A *yellow* school bus.

Regrouping, a now-forgotten genius in the club had an idea. They turned in the school buses and borrowed money to buy a couple of London double-decker buses. Instant success. London buses were the Beatles. The Stones. Swinging. Rebellion. In other words, everything that a cool college student wanted to be associated with in the '60s. The bus system, now called Unitrans, survives today with fifteen routes (reflecting the founders' orientation, the original routes were named after San Francisco trolley car lines) and dozens of buses (it still operates some double-deckers), carries three million passengers a year and most of its employees are students.

So what does a car, despite its disadvantages, offer the harried Providence or Boston commuter that a bus or train can't? Privacy. Forty-five minutes of freedom from annoying bosses or employees and problems at home. Control. The driver, not the engineer, decides where the vehicle will go and when. How can public transportation compete with that?

The new age of wireless connected Internet service offers some hope. Increasingly, people (especially business commuters) are texting rather than talking, but as is abundantly clear, texting or any other Internet use and driving are not compatible and may be fatal. You can literally talk yourself to death. However, if there were free, fast, secure Internet service available on trains, the commuter could get on the train at Wickford, hook up and be in his own little private universe for the duration of the commute. He or she could do business, play Angry Birds, engage in social networking and *never be offline*, as is necessarily the case with driving. Inexpensive narrow angle-of-view filters are available for computer screens so a nosy seatmate wouldn't be able to invade the rail commuter's privacy. Perhaps they could be given away with the purchase of a monthly commuter pass. So, if the new rail services are to be successful, physical facilities are not enough. There needs to be a reasonably sophisticated and intense marketing campaign, maybe with free-trial offers, to get the recalcitrant driver out of his or her car and get him addicted to the train. Perhaps it might also be pointed out to stubborn drivers that although they are in control of when they *leave* for work, due to traffic, weather and other unforeseeables, they have little control over when they *arrive*. A boss doesn't care when you leave but is very interested in when you arrive. Well-run commuter trains are much better than cars at producing predictable arrival times. If this approach is to be used in marketing, however, the on-time record of the trains needs to be outstanding.

In just twenty-four years, the railroad will mark its 200th year in Rhode Island. A fitting way to commemorate the occasion would not be a plaque or monument but a set of performance benchmarks, to wit:

- A regional train stopping every hour at each Rhode Island station during the week.
- An Acela train stopping at Providence every two hours during the week. (The Japanese Shinkansen high-speed trains operate at five-minute intervals—on a two-track mainline.)
- Commuter trains every fifteen minutes during commuter times, every hour during non-peak hours.
- At least one commuter train departing southbound from Boston after 10:00 p.m. six days a week for concerts, sports and dinner.
- An on-time record of 97 percent for Acela, 95 percent for regional and 93 percent for commuter trains, where "on-time" means the Swiss definition—within six minutes of the schedule (The Shinkansen trains average twelve *seconds* late during the course of a year.)
- No coaches used that have not been rebuilt within the last fifteen years. (Southwest Airlines' fleet of 737s is 11.7 years old.)

These benchmarks will not be easy to achieve (that is the point, after all), nor can they be achieved solely through effort in Rhode Island. However, by establishing these landmarks, Rhode Island would be making a powerful statement that the railroad, far from being a quaintly antique mode of transportation, is the lynchpin of the modern information- and technology-oriented society that Rhode Island aspires to be.

Late at night, in some of the homes around Hundred Acre Pond adjacent to the Shore Line, children are sometimes wakened by the far-off horn of the weekly Providence and Worcester Railroad freight train passing through Kingston. This romantic sound, promising distant places and infinite possibilities, is as compelling today as the little tin whistle of the first Stonington Line locomotive was to the first swamp Yankee who heard it almost two centuries ago. Railroads have been integral to the development of Rhode Island and will continue to be so for the years to come, and just as Rhode Island is charmingly eccentric, so, too, are its abbreviated railroads.

BIBLIOGRAPHY

Books, Newspapers, Journal Articles, Reports

Adams, Charles F., Jr. *Chapters of Erie and Other Essays*. Boston: Osgood, 1871.

Adams, Virginia H., and Matthew A. Kierstead. "India Point Railroad Bridge." *Historic American Engineering Record*, RI-54, www.loc.gov/pictures/item/RI0449.

Bentley, Joyce S. *Providence and Worcester: The Railroad That Can*. Worcester, MA: Providence and Worcester Railroad, 1985.

Brown, Charles A. "The Providence, Warren, and Bristol Electrification." *Shoreliner* 24 (1993): 4–35.

———. "Wood River Branch Railroad." *Shoreliner* 19 (1988): 30–39.

Carpenter, Richard C. *A Railroad Atlas of the United States in 1946: Vol. 2, New York and New England*. Baltimore, MD: Johns Hopkins University Press, 2005.

Cavanaugh, Maureen. "Kingston Railroad Station." *Historic American Building Survey*, RI-400, 1994.

Cole, J.R. *History of Washington and Kent Counties, Rhode Island*. New York: W.W. Preston & Co., 1889.

Davis, Paul. "Buying and Selling the Human Species: Newport and the Slave Trade." *Providence Journal*, March 12, 2006.

Dubiel, Frank P. *Union Station: Providence, RI*. Fall River, MA: privately published by Frank P. Dubiel, 1974.

Fisher, Charles E. *A Little Story of the Boston and Providence Railroad Co.* N.p.: privately printed, 1917.

———. *The Story of the Old Colony Railroad (revised and enlarged by Frank P. Dubiel).* Fall River, MA: privately published by Frank P. Dubiel, 1974.

Galvin, Edward D. *A History of Canton Junction.* Brunswick, ME: Sculpin Publications, 1987.

Hale, Stuart O. "Narragansett Bay: A Friend's Perspective." Marine Advisory Service, University of Rhode Island, *Marine Bulletin* 42 (1980).

Hall, John. "You Could Get Arrested for a Thing Like That…" *Yankee Magazine* (September 1973): 124–31.

Harlow, Alvin F. *Steelways of New England.* New York: Creative Age Press, 1946.

Hayes, Derek. *Historical Atlas of North American Railroads.* Berkeley: University of California Press, 2010.

Henwood, James N.J. *A Short Haul to the Bay.* Brattleboro, VT: Stephen Greene Press, 1969.

Hilton, George W. *The Cable Car in America.* Berkeley, CA: Howell-North Books, 1971.

Hinckley, Anita W. *Wickford Memories.* Boston: Brandon Press, 1972.

Ignasher, Jim. *Rhode Island Disasters.* Charleston, SC: The History Press, 2010.

Karr, Ronald D. *Lost Railroads of New England.* 3rd ed. Pepperell, MA: Branch Line Press, 2010.

———. *The Rail Lines of Southern New England.* Pepperell, MA: Branch Line Press, 1995.

Kellner, George H., and J. Stanley Lemons. *Rhode Island: The Ocean State.* Sun Valley, ID: American Historical Press, 2004.

Kirkland, Edward C. *Men, Cities and Transportation: A Study in New England History 1820–1900.* Vol. 1. New York: Russell & Russell, 1948.

Klein, Maury. *SK 1890: Letters from the Past.* N.p.: South Kingstown Planning Department, 1978.

Lamb, J. Parker. *Perfecting the American Steam Locomotive.* Bloomington: Indiana University Press, 2003.

Lewis, Edward A. *The Blackstone Valley Line: The Story of the Blackstone Canal and the Providence and Worcester Railroad.* Seekonk, MA: Baggage Car Press, 1973.

Lowenthal, Larry. "The Southern New England—'The Old Grand Trunk.'" *Shoreliner* 21 (1990): 6–11.

———. *Titanic Railroad: The Southern New England.* Brimfield, MA: Marker Press, 1998.

Lynch, Peter E. *New Haven Railroad.* St. Paul, MN: MBL Publishing, 2003.

Massachusetts Bay Railroad Enthusiasts. *A Railfan's Guide to Eastern Massachusetts and Rhode Island.* Boston: Massachusetts Bay Railroad Enthusiasts, 1986.

McBurney, Christian M. *A History of Kingston, RI. 1700–1900.* Kingston, RI: Pettaquamscutt Historical Society, 2004.

McCabe, Martha. *The Kingston Train Station: A History.* West Kingston, RI: Kingston Prints, 2000.

Miner, Craig. *A Most Magnificent Machine: America Adopts the Railroad.* Lawrence: University of Kansas Press, 2010.

Molloy, Scott. *All Aboard: The History of Mass Transportation in Rhode Island.* Charleston, SC: Arcadia Publishing, 1988.

———. *Trolley Wars: Streetcar Workers on the Line.* Washington, D.C.: Smithsonian Institution Press, 1996.

Musen, Steve. "Wickford Junction Station." *All Aboard* 25 (2011): 1–2.

Ozog, Edward J. "Another Way to Boston: The New York and New England in Northern Rhode Island." *Shoreliner* 21, no. 3 (1990): 28–37.

———. "Another Way to Boston: The New York and New England in Northern Rhode Island, Part 2." *Shoreliner* 21, no. 4 (1990): 6–13.

Palmer, Henry R. *Stonington by the Sea.* 2nd ed. Originally published 1913 by Henry R. Palmer. Stonington, CT: Palmer Press, 1957.

Prentice, G. Edward. "New Haven Has Contract with Sea View Railroad." *Shoreliner* 15 (1984): 36–37.

———. *Through the Woods and Across the Fields to Narragansett Pier.* N.p.: privately printed, 1983.

Public Archaeology Laboratory. *Amtrak's High Speed Rail Program: New Haven to Boston.* N.p.: Amtrak, 2001.

Renzulli, Mercedes. "The Fate of the Old 508." *Yankee Magazine* (March 1964): 62–63.

Rhode Island Department of Transportation. Kingston Station Intermodal Transportation Facility, Federal Aid Project DPi-0141 (001), Section f(f) Statement. Frederick R. Harris, Inc., 1994.

Rhode Island General Assembly. *Charters Granted by the General Assembly of the State of Rhode Island to the Railroad Companies Having Tracks in the City of Providence.* N.p., 1887.

———. *Railroad Commissioner's Report to the Rhode Island General Assembly.* N.p., 1854.

———. *Report of the Committee of South Kingstown.* Providence, RI: A. Crawford Greene, 1854.

————. *Report of the Joint Special Committee on Railroad Terminal Facilities (28 Sept 1881)*. N.p., 1891.

————. *Report of the Railroad Commissioners Made to the General Assembly of the State of Rhode Island at the January Session*. N.p., 1887.

————. *Report of the Special Commission for the Investigation of the Affairs of the Rhode Island Company*. N.p., 1918.

Roffo, Paolo. "Rails to the Hub." *Railfan and Railroad* (December 2010): 42–51.

Rowsome, Frank, Jr. *Trolley Car Treasury*. New York: Bonanza Books, 1956.

Schneider, Stewart A. "Railroad Development in Rhode Island During the Nineteenth Century." *Rhode Island History* 61 (2003): 37–48.

Schwieterman, Joseph P. *When the Railroad Leaves Town: Eastern United States*. Kirksville, MO: Truman State University Press, 2001.

Stein, Mark. *How the States Got Their Shapes*. New York: HarperCollins, 2008.

Tarr, Joel, and Clay McShane. "The Centrality of the Horse to the Nineteenth-Century American City." In *The Making of Urban America*, edited by Raymond Mohl. New York: SR Publishers, 1997.

Taylor, William L. *A Productive Monopoly: The Effect of Railroad Control on New England Coastal Steamship Lines, 1870–1916*. Providence, RI: Brown University Press, 1970.

Turner, Gregg M., and Melancthon W. Jacobus. *Connecticut Railroads: An Illustrated History*. Hartford: Connecticut Historical Society Press, 1989.

Westinghouse Electric and Manufacturing Company. *New York, New Haven, and Hartford Railroad Electrification*. Special Publication 1698, 1924.

White, John H., Jr. *American Locomotives: An Engineering History 1830–1880*. Baltimore, MD: Johns Hopkins University Press, 1968.

White, Richard. *Railroaded: The Transcontinentals and the Making of Modern America*. New York: W.W. Norton, 2011.

Wood, W. Edward. "The 508 Beats the Car." *Providence Evening Bulletin* 113 (1975): 1–2.

WEB REFERENCES

No citations have been included for Wikipedia articles that the reader can find with a simple word search.

Cranston, Tim. "The View from Swamptown, Vol. III and IV." www.nklibrary.org/sites/default/files/pdf/nklibrary/swamptown/swamptownBook2.pdf.

Granite Railway Company. "The First Railroad in America, 1826–1926." thomascranelibrary.org/legacy/gran.htm.

Howe, Mark. "Hoosac Tunnel History." www.hoosactunnel.net/history.php.

Molloy, Scott. "Mass Transit in Rhode Island, Part 7." quahog.org/factsfolklore/index.php?id+97.

My Home Town on the Web. "Woonsocket's Railroads." www.woonsocket.org/railroads.html.

O'Hanley, Donald M., and George L. Kenson. "History of the Newport RI. Railroad Line." www.ocnrr.com/history1.htm.

Ozog, Edward. "Rhode Island Railroads." sites.google.com/site/rhodeislandrailroads. [This is, bar none, the best site for Rhode Island railroads.]

Peirce, Merle K. "The Wood River Branch Railroad Company." archiver.rootsweb.ancestry.com/th/read/RIGENWEB/2001-02/0981208620.

Rhode Island Department of Transportation. "South County Commuter Rail Service: Environmental Impact 2003." www.dot.state.ri.us/documents/intermodal/socountyrail.pdf.

Rhode Island Department of Transportation. "South County Commuter Rail Service: Operation Plan 2001." www.dot.state.ri.us/documents/intermodal/OperationsPlanMaster2.pdf.

Tarrow, Susan, trans. "The Written Record of the Voyage of 1524 of Giovanni da Verrazano as recorded in a letter to Francis I, King of France, July 8th, 1524." bc.barnard.columbia.edu/~lgordis/earlyAC/documents/verrazan.htm.

INDEX

U

V

W

ABOUT THE AUTHOR

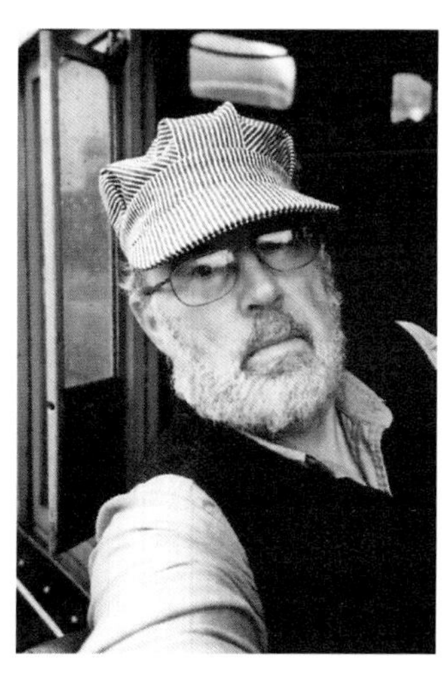

Frank Heppner was born to a railroad family. His father was a doctor for the Southern Pacific Railroad in San Francisco, he had his first train ride when he was three and he made his first scratch-built HO railroad car when he was thirteen (he still has it). He's ridden over 500,000 miles by rail in twenty-three different countries. As a graduate student, he talked his way into cab rides on the Shasta Daylight in California and the Super Chief through Raton Pass. Between train rides, he picked up a PhD in zoology from the University of California at Davis and taught first-year biology to over twenty-five thousand students at the University of Rhode Island. He retired from this "day job" in 2010 after writing more than sixty scientific papers.

He was a founding member of the Friends of the Kingston Station and is today its chairman. He is also active in the Rhode Island Association of Railroad Passengers and is a member of the Little Rhody Division of the National Model Railroad Association.